# CAMBRIDGE LIBRARY COLLECTION

*Books of enduring scholarly value*

## History

The books reissued in this series include accounts of historical events and movements by eye-witnesses and contemporaries, as well as landmark studies that assembled significant source materials or developed new historiographical methods. The series includes work in social, political and military history on a wide range of periods and regions, giving modern scholars ready access to influential publications of the past.

## Paris in Peril

Henry Vizetelly (1820–94), whose two-volume *Glances Back through Seventy Years* is also reissued in this collection, was an English journalist based in Paris during the Franco-Prussian War, which concluded with the downfall of Napoleon III and the end of the second French Empire. First published in 1882, this is the first in a two-volume collection of his writings during this turbulent period. He vividly recounts his experiences of the Germans' devastating siege of Paris, setting it within a military, political and economic context. He argues that the outcome would have been less severe had the French army been better prepared, and shows how attempts to provision the capital ahead of the Prussian advance were thwarted by malnourished cattle and blocked transport links, resulting in near-starvation among the besieged. Providing a judicious narrative of a significant period in France's history, Vizetelly's eye-witness account remains of great interest.

# Paris in Peril

## VOLUME 1

HENRY VIZETELLY

CAMBRIDGE
UNIVERSITY PRESS

CAMBRIDGE UNIVERSITY PRESS

Cambridge, New York, Melbourne, Madrid, Cape Town,
Singapore, São Paolo, Delhi, Tokyo, Mexico City

Published in the United States of America by Cambridge University Press, New York

www.cambridge.org
Information on this title: www.cambridge.org/9781108035378

© in this compilation Cambridge University Press 2011

This edition first published 1882
This digitally printed version 2011

ISBN 978-1-108-03537-8 Paperback

# PARIS IN PERIL.

*Ballantyne Press*
BALLANTYNE, HANSON AND CO., EDINBURGH
CHANDOS STREET, LONDON

*Frontispiece, vol. i.*     OUTSIDE A BUTCHER'S SHOP: PEOPLE WAITING THEIR TURN TO BE SERVED.

# PARIS IN PERIL.

EDITED BY

## HENRY VIZETELLY,

AUTHOR OF

"THE STORY OF THE DIAMOND NECKLACE," "BERLIN UNDER THE NEW EMPIRE,"
"A HISTORY OF CHAMPAGNE," ETC.

With Sixteen Illustrations.

IN TWO VOLUMES.

VOL. I.

LONDON:

TINSLEY BROTHERS, 8, CATHERINE STREET, STRAND.

1882.

# CONTENTS

OF

# THE FIRST VOLUME.

————

|  | PAGE |
|---|---|
| **I. THE GERMAN MARCH ON PARIS.** | |
| I. PARIS IN A STATE OF SIEGE | 1 |
| II. THE DISASTER OF SEDAN | 9 |
| III. THE REVOLUTION | 18 |
| IV. THE GOVERNMENT OF NATIONAL DEFENCE | 23 |
| V. PARIS EXPECTANT | 35 |
| VI. THE GERMANS ARRIVE | 46 |
| **II. THE DEFENCES.** | |
| I. FIRE, AXE, PICK, SPADE, AND TROWEL | 55 |
| II. THE ENCEINTE AND THE DETACHED FORTS | 62 |
| III. THE ARMAMENT | 76 |
| **III. THE GARRISON.** | |
| I. REGULAR TROOPS | 91 |
| II. THE GARDE MOBILE | 98 |
| III. THE NATIONAL GUARD | 105 |
| IV. THE VOLUNTEER CORPS | 109 |
| **IV. THE PROVISIONING.** | |
| I. HOW PARIS WAS ACCUSTOMED TO BE FED | 115 |
| II. HOW PARIS WAS INTENDED TO BE FED | 143 |
| **V. THE INVESTMENT.** | |
| I. THE LAST DAY OF LIBERTY | 159 |
| II. THE AFFAIR OF CHATILLON | 175 |

PAGE

III. PARIS BLOCKADED . . . . . . . . . . . 183

IV. THE MORROW OF THE INVESTMENT . . . . . . 199

V. PEACE NEGOTIATIONS . . . . . . . . . . 213

VI. ATTEMPTS TO PASS THE GERMAN LINES . . . . . 219

## VI. THE COMMUNICATIONS.

I. THE FIRST COURIERS AND BALLOON ASCENTS . . . . 231

II. BALLOON FACTORIES AND DOVECOTES : . . . . . 240

III. GOVERNMENT BY BALLOON . . . . . . . 246

IV. MILITARY BALLOONS . . . . . . . . . . 253

V. "ON ATTEND UNE RÉPONSE" . . . . . . . 257

VI. NEWS FROM OUTSIDE . . . . . . 261

---

# ILLUSTRATIONS TO VOL. I.

OUTSIDE A BUTCHER'S SHOP : PEOPLE WAITING THEIR TURN
TO BE SERVED . . . . . *Frontispiece*

CARICATURES OF THE PERIOD . . . . . 6
"Here, open the Door to your Master !"
"I've a Word to say to You."
War Trophies.
The Harvest of 1870.

REFUGEES FROM OUTSIDE PARIS AT A CANTINE . . . . 42

NATIONAL GUARDS IN THEIR QUARTERS ON THE RAMPARTS . . 106

PREPARING FOR A BALLOON ASCENT . . . . . 238

# PARIS IN PERIL.

## I.

### THE GERMAN MARCH ON PARIS.

#### I. PARIS IN A STATE OF SIEGE.

To-DAY with the spectacle before one of Paris in all
her pride again, as gay, as animated, and as prosperous
under the rule of a Republic as she ever was in
Monarchical or Imperial times, the fact can scarcely be
realized that merely a few years since her very existence
as a city was seriously imperilled. No longer ago than
the 26th of August, 1870, the last Minister of the Interior that the Second Empire called to office mounted
the tribune of the Corps Législatif and announced
that a German army, commanded by the Crown Prince
of Prussia was marching upon the capital of France—
upon the city where César Postiche had held sway
for so many years, which moralists had christened
the Modern Babylon, and which Haussmann and
Alphand had beautified; the city of Cora Pearl and
of Marguerite Bellanger, of the *Biche au Bois*, and
the *Dame aux Camélias;* whose favourite musician was
Offenbach, and whose leading journalist was De Villemessant, whose chief pamphleteer was Rochefort, and
whose greatest criminal was Troppmann; where Hor-
tense Schneider and Thérèsa sang, and where Father
Hyacinthe preached; the scene of Mirès' speculations,

and of De Gramont-Caderousse's follies—in a word, the favoured spot whither, according to a Transatlantic writer, "Good Americans go when they die."

The Emperor Napoleon III. had, mainly from dynastic motives, embarked upon an aggressive war directed ostensibly against Prussia alone, but in which he found himself confronted by all the forces of united Germany. The battles of Wörth, Gravelotte and St. Privat had been fought and lost by the French. Bazaine was shut up under Metz. Macmahon was executing various mysterious strategic movements. Paris had been proclaimed in a state of siege. The Germans were swiftly advancing through the departments of the Aube and the Marne ; and flippant Emile Ollivier—who had declared that he engaged in this calamitous war with " a light heart "—was no longer Prime Minister of France. To the administration over which he presided, another had succeeded, the titular head of which was General Count de Palikao, originally a dashing Algerian cavalry officer and notorious for having looted the Summer Palace, at Pekin, during the Chinese Expedition of 1860.

" If you abandon Bazaine," telegraphed the Count to the Emperor on the morrow of the formal announcement of the German march on the capital, " the Revolution is in Paris, and you yourself will be attacked by all the enemy's forces. Paris will protect herself against external assault. The fortifications are completed." And yet at that moment, as the mendacious Minister of War was perfectly well aware, not only was there not a single gun in position in any one of the ninety-five bastions of the enceinte, but even the armament of the exterior forts had barely commenced. For not the smallest thought had been taken of the defences of the capital until the 9th of the same month, on full tidings of the disaster that had overtaken the French arms at the battle of Wörth reaching Paris. Indeed, had the Crown Prince, instead of turning aside to engage Macmahon, "marched resolutely on Paris," as it was announced he was doing two days previously from Berlin, it would have been impossible to have arrested his progress, and the "metropolis of the world," the "capital of civilization," as the French term their handsome city, though it must have submitted to the humiliation of foreign occupation, would have been spared the hardships and horrors of a siege.

If the new Ministry, over which Count de Palikao presided, did but little towards repelling the advance of the victorious German legions, it cannot be accused of having been unmindful of the danger to which Paris was exposed; for although for good and sufficient reasons it refused the reiterated demand of the Opposition for the arming of the citizens, it made at any rate a show of placing the capital in a defensive state. One of its first acts was to constitute a Committee of Defence, charged with putting those fortifications—which the Parisians had long since made up their minds had been originally constructed to operate rather against themselves than a foreign enemy—in a state of efficiency. Three engineers in chief were appointed, and many thousand pairs of hands were set to work, not merely to carry the fosse across the sixty-nine roads conducting to the city, and so completely encircle it, and to throw up lunettes in front of the various drawbridges, but to construct a series of stone redoubts on certain heights in advance of the exterior forts, or at points where anything like an important break existed in the chain. Ships' guns were transported from Brest, Cherbourg, and other

1—2

military ports, and sailors and marine artillerymen were summoned up to serve them. Gunboats of light draught, to be armed with huge cannon and mitrailleuses, originally intended to operate on the Rhine, but now destined for the protection of the Seine and Marne, were ordered up from Toulon. The Gardes Mobiles were called out, corps of Francs-tireurs were enrolled, and a considerable number of Custom-house officers and Sapeurs-pompiers, in their brilliant brass helmets, arrived in Paris from the provinces, to act, however, it was shrewdly suspected, against the Parisians— should occasion arise—instead of the enemy. Scientific men, moreover, were invited to co-operate with the Government in applying the latest discoveries in physical and chemical science to the defence of the capital. Immense droves of sheep and oxen were collected in the environs and inside the walls, and vast supplies of corn and flour, with fodder of all descriptions, were amassed in the public magazines ; farmers, too, were invited to deposit their stores in the municipal warehouses free of all charge, and were, moreover, warned that if they did not get in their crops and store them within the enceinte, they would be burnt on the approach of the investing armies, to prevent them from falling into their hands.

In the Corps Législatif a war credit of forty millions sterling was voted, a forced currency was given to the notes of the Bank of France, to stop the drain of coin which had been going on for the past fortnight, and the payment of all commercial drafts was temporarily postponed. The members of the Left vainly strove to get a certain number of their party added to the Committee of Defence; but M. Jules Simon, regarding a siege as inevitable, having proposed that all " superfluous mouths " should be

banished from the capital, M. Clement Duvernois, a
Parisian journalist, who had sold his brilliant though
mercenary pen to the Emperor, and been promoted,
only a fortnight before, to the Ministry of Commerce,
made a semblance of catching at the suggestion with
the view of propitiating the Opposition, promising
that it should be acted upon in the event of a siege
becoming imminent.  In deference to public opinion,
General Trochu, an Orleanist, one of the few military
men of note who had been proof against the blandish-
ments of the Empire, and had had the courage to point
out the disorganized condition of the Imperial legions,
was appointed Commander-in-Chief of all the forces in
Paris.

The arrogant conceit which most Parisians evinced
at the outset of the war had moderated considerably,
consequent upon a succession of reverses.  Newspaper
correspondents with the French army no longer headed
their letters " From Paris to Berlin."  Pushing tradesmen no longer offered to subscribe their hundred francs
per day for patriotic purposes until the French troops
made their triumphant entry into the Prussian capital.
No police improvised processions headed by tricolor
flags, no noisy mobs shouting the " Marseillaise," no
excited crowds criticising the campaign, no extravagant
felicitations on fantastic feats of French valour, no
premature demonstrations in honour of fictitious victories impeded the circulation of the boulevards.  Even
the spirit of the caricatures, with which Paris had been
inundated since the outbreak of the war, became suddenly changed.  No longer did the familiar Zouave
knock at King Wilhelm's door demanding immediate
admittance; nor did Bismarck quake and tremble at
the sight of an animated French cannon which called
him aside for a little private talk.  The new composi-

tions depicted a gravedigger pondering beside a corpse-
strewn battlefield, with the title " This year's harvest,"
or else a Mobile and a Landwehrmann, already provided
with crutches and wooden legs—all they were likely to
gain by a prolongation of the war.   Paris, from being
vain, boastful, and demonstrative, had become silent,
grave and stern.   People unable to keep within doors
after business hours, from very excitement sallied forth
to the centre of attraction, the boulevards—which are
the heart of Paris, as Paris is the heart of France—to
while away the time and listen to the latest news.
Occasionally, some regiment of the Line, the last remnant perhaps of the Roman contingent, would march
along to the railway station.   The crowd, which usually
assailed any isolated companies they chanced to meet
with petulant shouts of "à la frontière," saw them
depart silently, as though all hope on their part had
fled ; at most, some few would raise their hats, a mark
of courtesy which the officers acknowledged by saluting
with their swords.   The volunteer corps, on marching
to join the army, awakened rather more enthusiasm,
and the first battalion of Francs-tireurs that left for the
front was warmly greeted as it passed along the
boulevards.   On the night of Sunday, the 21st of
August, a spectacle of another kind attracted the
astonished gaze of the Parisians, when the wreck of
various regiments engaged at Wörth and Weissenbourg defiled past in their soiled uniforms and battered accoutrements, on their way from the Northern
or Eastern railway station.   A considerable proportion of the men were on foot; some limped painfully
along ; a few had their arms in slings, while others
led their wounded horses by the bridle.   It was as
well, at this period of general despondency, that this
mournful cavalcade made its entry into Paris under

"HERE, OPEN THE DOOR TO YOUR MASTER!"

"I'VE A WORD TO SAY TO YOU."

WAR TROPHIES.

THE HARVEST OF 1870.

i. 6.

CARICATURES OF THE PERIOD.

cover of the night, at a moment when the boulevards
had become comparatively deserted.

After the Minister of the Interior's declaration in.
the Corps Législatif, the entire population of the
capital appeared for the first time to realize the extent
of the danger that menaced them. The belief that
the Government had been studiously suppressing news
for several days previously, caused every one to feel
convinced that the peril was nearer at hand than it
really was. People saw the Prussians in imagination
already under the walls, and prepared for a hurried
flight, or else set about laying in stores of provisions,
in case Paris should be invested by the enemy, whose
advent, or at any rate, the arrival of the advance guard,
composed of the conventional four Uhlans, by way of
the Route d'Allemagne, at Pantin, was predicted for
the ensuing Monday morning. Thousands of people
congregated daily at the Préfecture of Police, where
they had to wait for many hours to get their passports
viséd—a formality necessary to be gone through before
they were permitted to leave Paris. The number of
persons, however, who quitted the capital of their own
accord, and those who were sent out of it by reason of
their nationalities, or on the plea of ridding Paris of
its "superfluous mouths," amounted only to a percentage of those who sought refuge within the
walls against the hordes of advancing Prussians.
The two streams flowed on in opposite directions, with
more or less impetuosity, for the next three weeks.
For miles round, long strings of carts and vans,
crowded with immigrants or crammed with furniture,
and waggons laden with corn and flour and agricultural
produce of all kinds, might be seen converging towards
Paris. Such Parisians as were still in pleasant
summer quarters in the environs, hurried back to the

capital *en masse.* One would have thought the
Uhlans were at their heels. Every one possessed of
a cart found it requisitioned by people whose im-
patience would not allow of their thinking about
prices, and several hundred francs were paid for the
hire of a pair-horse tilted vehicle, which, piled up
with furniture and provisions, instantly took the
road to Paris. Every kind of vehicle was in request
—furniture-vans, waggons, market gardeners' and
washerwomens' carts, carriages, omnibuses, cabs,
and trucks. Even the corbillard, or hearse, was had
recourse to, for rich and poor were alike impatient to
place their property under the protection of the
cannon of the ramparts. At the barriers it was a
perfect pell mell, the laundress's cart hustled the
*calèche à huit ressorts,* and the farmer's waggon
jostled the break. The collectors of the *octroi* appeared to have lost their heads, as well they might,
for vehicles kept arriving by thousands every day.
It was no unusual thing for scores of them to have to
pass the night outside the gates of Paris waiting for
the morning, to renew the struggle to cross the rude,
temporary wooden platforms thrown over the moat,
and effect an entrance through the narrow opening of
the fortifications destined for the score or so drawbridges which, when raised, were to shut out Paris
from the rest of the world—who at that time should
say for how long ?

A few days subsequent to M. Chevreau's declaration, it was announced that the Crown Prince's
advance was only a feint to deceive Marshal
Macmahon; still, the inhabitants of the environs
continued to flock into Paris, accompanied this time
not merely by waggons piled up with sacks of corn
and flour, but by seemingly endless droves of sheep and

cattle, which were installed on their arrival in the Bois de Boulogne and other open spaces, in the sheds of the Villette cattle market, and in the unoccupied stables of the various cavalry barracks. A fleet of Seine barges, sailing and rowing boats, moreover, sought shelter within the enceinte.

For days, nay, for weeks, there was a continuous block at all the principal entrances to Paris; a perfect panic had evidently set in, and people outside the walls, even while crediting—as the French are prone to give credence to any absurdity that tickles the national vanity—the extravagant fictions with which the Count de Palikao fooled the Chamber, as, for instance, the utter annihilation of Count Bismarck's regiment of white cuirassiers, and the overthrow of three German corps d'armée in the Jaumont quarries at one fell swoop, showed a marked preference for the doubtful security which the ramparts of Paris might be able to afford them.

## II. THE DISASTER OF SEDAN.

Paris had been virtually left unprotected since the 21st of August, when Marshal Macmahon had precipitately broken up his camp at Châlons, burned his tents, and marched to Rheims, allowing it to be supposed that it was his intention to retreat upon Soissons, there to rest and reconstitute his army. Instead of which, urged by the Council of Ministers and commanded by the Emperor, he consented, against the dictates of his own judgment, to sweep round in an easterly direction to the assistance of Bazaine, in the event of the Mexican Marshal succeeding in cutting his way out to the north of Metz. Believing, however, when he reached Le Chesne Populeux, by way of Rethel, Vouziers, and the hilly wooded

district of the Argonne, that the Crown Prince of
Prussia had by that time arrived at Châlons, and
intended to direct his army on the Ardennes, he
reasoned that should he attempt to reach Bazaine he
would inevitably not only expose himself to be attacked
in front by portions of the first and second German
armies, but to having his line of retreat cut off
by the Crown Prince, and he decided, therefore, upon
at once retreating to Mézières, and thence westward
according to circumstances, leaving Bazaine to his fate.

It was the receipt of this intelligence which induced
Count de Palikao to telegraph to the Emperor, urging
him not to abandon the army of Metz. " Every one
in Paris," he remarked, "has felt the necessity of
extricating Bazaine, and the anxiety with which you
are followed is intense." Macmahon found himself,
however, compelled to move on Sedan, and justified
this step by announcing to the Minister of War that
up to the 31st of August the Emperor still exercised
the supreme command—an announcement which
brought back a rejoinder by telegraph a few hours
afterwards, requiring him, in the name of the Council
of Ministers and the Privy Council, to succour Bazaine.
While these communications were going forward, the
Minister of the Interior was assuring the people of
Paris that the march of the enemy upon the capital
appeared to be checked, and that Marshal Macmahon
was prosecuting his movement to effect a junction
with Marshal Bazaine without experiencing any
serious opposition. The strategists of the boulevards
were great at this particular moment. Each had
his " plan " for crushing, or cutting a way through
the Prussians, and effecting the desired junction;
and people grew nervously impatient at the delay.
With one exception the Paris papers of the 31st

united in saying there was no fresh news from the
seat of war; the mendacious *Figaro*, however, had
learnt from a certain source that the whole of Prince
Frederick Charles's cavalry had been annihilated by
a portion of Bazaine's army : and with the view of still
further raising the spirits of the Parisians, and restoring to them a sense of security, it announced on
the authority of a private letter from the Prince of
Meiningen to his wife, that all the German soldiers
were troubled with sore feet.

From this moment Paris was a prey to extravagant
rumours. It was surmised that the hostile forces
must by this time have come into collision, and as no
official report of the result was forthcoming, imagination sought to supply the place of facts. It was of
the first necessity that the news should be pleasant,
the Parisians, according to one of themselves, re-
sembling the ostrich, which hides its head in the sand
to avoid the hunter, not having the courage to look
disagreeable results fairly in the face. A crop of good
news consequently made its appearance. One paper
asserted that the Mayor of Nangis had received a
letter from his relative, Marshal Macmahon, saying
that all was going well, and all would go better than
it was possible for people in Paris to imagine. The
Emperor's paper, the *Peuple Français*, said that Bazaine
was pushing the Prussians opposed to him towards the
camp of Sedan, while Macmahon had the enemy penned
in the angle between the ramparts of Sedan and the
heights dominating the Meuse. *La Patrie* proclaimed
that Macmahon had effected the passage of the Meuse
in a most brilliant manner, and had compelled the
Prussians to take refuge in Luxembourg, where they
had been disarmed and made prisoners. The *National*
assured its readers that a number of the enemy's corps

d'armée had been overthrown, but that both the French marshals recommended the most complete silence until a decisive success had been achieved. The *Electeur Libre,* more prudent, contented itself by announcing that it had heard on the authority of a despatch received by the Minister of War, that Macmahon, after being thrown back, had assumed the offensive, and forced the enemy to retreat. Count de Palikao, however, preserved a discreet silence in the Chamber on the subject of this despatch. The fact of having had a bullet lodging in his chest for twenty years, which affected his voice, furnished him with a standing excuse for reticence ; in addition to which, he was ever ready with the canting official plea—that it was requisite, in the interests of the public service, for information to be held back. On this occasion, however, he got rid of disagreeable inquiries by mysteriously hinting that if Paris only knew what he knew, it would illuminate that evening !

Even when the truth began to ooze out in the telegrams published by the English and Belgian journals, the newspapers in many instances still continued their deceptions on the public. The *Patrie,* after declaring the King of Prussia's telegrams announcing a victory to be pure inventions, maintained that the Germans had been repulsed before Sedan, and that it was Macmahon who was really victorious. "These despatches," it went on to say, "in no way disquiet us. We have men, Prussia has none left. We have money, Prussia cannot find any anywhere. Prussia is already at the end, while we are at the beginning." The *Opinion Nationale*—an authority on military topics—had heard that a report was current at the Corps Législatif of a great victory gained by Bazaine, but contented itself with ambiguously asserting that affairs were improving, and that the news from the army was really good.

It was left, however, to the *Paris Journal*, the *Gaulois*, and the *Figaro* to endeavour to outstrip each other in mendacious invention. The first of these papers recounted that the Crown Prince's army, attacked in front and flank by Macmahon and Wimpffen, had been utterly routed, leaving upon the field of battle no less than 80,000 killed and wounded. The *Gaulois* quoted a telegraphic despatch, professedly from one of its war correspondents, likewise describing that 80,000 of the enemy had been put *hors de combat*, their corpses, it went on to say, being piled up one above the other, many of them standing bolt upright like sentinels watching over the dead. Another correspondent asserted that the Prussians had been driven *en masse* into the woods and lakes, where, after being mitrailleused, 25,000 had been burnt and drowned. As to the pet journal of the boulevards, this had learnt from most excellent sources that on the 1st of September, Marshal Macmahon, having been reinforced by General Vinoy, had attacked and completely defeated the Prussian army, taking forty guns and many prisoners; a battery of four mitrailleuses had destroyed an entire detachment of the enemy; in fact, "massacre," it said, would not be too exaggerated a term to apply to the fate of the German army.

After being fed for days with reports of victories like the foregoing, it may be conceived how excited the Parisians became when the magnitude of the new reverse sustained by the Army of the Rhine began to unfold itself in all its bitter truth. As regards Bazaine, the fact was he was penned in, as it were, under the walls of Metz, having twice attempted to break out—once on the 26th, and again on the 31st, both times unsuccessfully. As for Macmahon, from the instant the German exploring light cavalry learnt that he had abandoned Châlons, he had been chased by the army of the Crown Prince of Prussia, without knowing it, until he reached Le Chesne Populeux, where he received, as already mentioned, positive injunctions from Paris to relieve Bazaine at all hazards at the very moment, when on finding the danger his own army was in, he had determined upon a rapid retreat to Mézières. The Crown Prince had struck northwards at Ligny, and, proceeding by Bar-le-Duc and Suippes,‑penetrated the Argonne, emerging on its skirts north of Buzancy, and effecting a junction with the army of the Crown Prince of Saxony—which had marched along the valley of the Meuse from Verdun—near Stenay, thereby intercepting Macmahon's march to Montmédy, and forcing him to proceed by Beaumont and Raucourt, near Mouzon, where, with the two German armies in fatal proximity, he proposed to cross the river. On the 29th of August the main body of Macmahon's army had taken up positions at Vaux, between Mouzon and Carignan, whilst General de Failly, with his corps of 30,000 men, was encamped between Beaumont and Stenne.

As usual the French had neglected to reconnoitre the neighbouring woods, and on the following morning, when a portion of his troops had already crossed the Meuse, De Failly found himself suddenly pounced upon at Beaumont by a Bavarian corps of the Crown Prince of Prussia's army, which was massed between Buzancy and Beaumont, occupying the hills and forests on the skirts of the Argonne. The Germans speedily overpowered the French, and drove them back across the river, the routed corps retreating in disorder upon the main body advancing to cross the Meuse, and throwing them into complete confusion. The Marshal, however, succeeded in returning to Vaux, where he rallied his discomfited troops, while the Germans chased De Failly's corps across the river, pressing on to Moulins and Vaux, where some desperate fighting ensued, victory ultimately declaring for the Germans, who drove the French still farther back in the direction of Sedan. They rallied, however, at nightfall, beyond the Chiers, alike dispirited and demoralized, while the Emperor and his attendants, on hearing of the defeat, hastily quitted Carignan, and sought shelter within the walls of the old fortified city of Sedan, trusting that on the morrow the tide of victory might turn.

It was a vain hope, however. On the following day, the 31st, Macmahon's army, composed of some 100,000 men, was attacked in its positions on the plain of Douzy by the armies of the Crown Princes of Prussia and Saxony, numbering in all some 240,000 men, and, pressed by superior forces, was compelled gradually to retreat towards Sedan. As it drew off, the Germans, by skilful manœuvres, succeeded in extending their right wing as far as Francheval, towards the Belgian frontier, whilst their left wing, marching northwards from Chéhery, took up its position at Fremoy, on the western side of Sedan, immediately opposite Donchéry.

The first operation of the Germans, on the 1st of September, was to perfect the circle round Sedan which they had commenced the day before. The Crown Prince of Prussia, supported by the Bavarians under General Von der Tann, succeeded, after twelve hours' hard fighting—during which the French made a most gallant resistance—in completing the investment by crossing the Meuse at Donchéry, occupying Javonne and La Chapelle, and ultimately effecting a

junction between his left wing, and the Crown Prince
of Saxony's right wing, at Francheval. When the
ring was complete, the capture of Sedan, of Macmahon's army, and of the Emperor himself, became
a necessary consequence. In vain the French attempted to break through the circle of fire in which
Von Moltke had enclosed them; every effort they
made was successfully repulsed, and eventually the
hardly pressed and disordered troops were driven to
take shelter under the walls of the old fortified city,
unable to reply to the fearful cannonade launched
against them from all sides. By five o'clock in the
afternoon the situation had become insufferable; the
white flag was hoisted, the struggle was at an end;
and Napoleon, "not having been able to die in the
midst of his troops," placed his sword in the hands of
his "good brother," the King of Prussia, and with
80,000 men surrendered as prisoners of war.

The most contradictory rumours being afloat, people
searched the journals in vain for any telegrams which
might enable them to solve the enigma; the *Journal
Officiel* curtly remarked: "No official despatch has
reached the Ministry of War to-day." The real truth
was, of course, only allowed to ooze out by driblets.
On the afternoon of Saturday, September 3, Count
de Palikao shadowed forth the crowning disaster of
Sedan in a statement to the Corps Législatif, announcing that Marshal Bazaine, after a vigorous
sally, had been obliged to retire again under the
walls of Metz, and that Macmahon, after a series of
combats, attended by reverses and successes—having
at the outset driven a part of the enemy's army into
the Meuse—had been compelled to retreat to Sedan and
Mézières, a portion of his army having taken refuge
in Belgium. The junction of the two armies had
therefore not been made. The situation was serious,

calmly observed the Minister of War, but not hopeless.

Not hopeless! when the truth was that one army was blockaded and the other prisoner, and that there were no reserves. On what was France to rely—on that favourite panacea, a levée en masse? The Government had set the "Marseillaise" free, but the fiery republican strains sung by operatic favourites in the guise of Goddesses of France, volunteers of 1792, and cantinières of the present epoch, had none of their ancient power. French generals of the first Republic used to write, " Send me a reinforcement of 10,000 men, or an edition of the ' Marseillaise ;'" " Without the ' Marseillaise ' I attacked the enemy when he was two to one—with it I attack him when he is four to one ;" or "I have gained a battle; the ' Marseillaise' commanded with me." But other times, other manners.

At a midnight sitting, Count de Palikao, still determined to conceal a portion of the truth, intimated that part of Marshal Macmahon's army had been driven back into Sedan, that the remainder had capitulated, and that the Emperor had been made prisoner. M. Jules Favre met this announcement of fresh disasters by a motion, declaring the Emperor and his dynasty to have forfeited all rights conferred by the Constitution, demanding the appointment of a Parliamentary Committee invested with the governing power, and having for its special mission the expulsion of the enemy from French territory, and further maintaining General Trochu in his post as Governor of Paris. The Chamber then adjourned till the morrow.

But Paris had touched one of those crises when, as Pascal says, a grain of sand will give a turn to history and change the life of nations, and the morrow brought with it the downfall of the Ministry, of the dynasty, of the Empire, and of that bizarre constitutional edifice which had been kept waiting so long for its complemental crown. " The Revolution," so accurately foreboded by Count de Palikao a week previously, "was in Paris;" Napoleon, " by grace the of God and the national will," had ceased to reign ; the young prince, to secure whose succession the war had been embarked in, on the Emperor finding himself overtaken by premature decrepitude, and whose display of courage during his baptism of fire had brought tears we were told to the eyes of admiring veterans, was thrust aside from the vacant throne, and even the Empire itself fell with the defeat and surrender of the vaunted army of the Rhine.

The *Charivari* summed up the nineteen years' rule of the last of the Bonapartes in a caricature representing France bound hand and foot between the mouths of two cannons, one inscribed " Paris, 1851," the other, "Sedan, 1870,"—the Alpha and Omega of Napoleon the Third.

### III. THE REVOLUTION.

The Parisians, remembering Lafayette's dictum that "insurrection is the most sacred of all duties," have made so many Revolutions that they are enabled to reduce the mode of proceeding to a formula, and the overturning of a throne has become with them like any well rehearsed scene in a play ; the opportunity given, it is only necessary for the sovereign people to invade the Chambers, and for the more daring deputies, backed by their presence, to declare a dynasty overthrown, and hurrying off to the Hôtel de Ville, constitute themselves a Government. Within an hour or two afterwards, by the simple display of a few bayonets, possession is secured of the various Ministries, the prefecture of police, the telegraphs, and the printing machines of the *Journal Officiel*; and, heigh, presto! an Empire is transformed into a Republic.

It had been intimated that the Corps Législatif would reassemble at noon, before which time numerous groups collected on the Place de la Concorde, and eventually swelled to a considerable crowd. The bridge leading to the Palais Bourbon was guarded by a detachment of mounted gendarmes, and numerous sergents-de-ville. At about one o'clock two battalions of National Guards, with fixed bayonets, headed by a drummer and preceded by some sixty individuals also belonging to the Guard, but not in uniform, defiled along the boulevards, and, descending the Rue Royale, crossed the Place de la Concorde, amid cries of " Déchéance !" " Vive la France !" " Vive la République !" On arriving at the foot of the bridge they demanded to be allowed to pass, but were refused by the gendarmes, who prepared to oppose their passage. A considerable group assembled on the steps of the Palais Bourbon, on the opposite side of the river, signalled to them to cross the bridge; still the gendarmes barred the way. Fresh battalions of National Guards having, however, arrived, the gendarmes, after flourishing their swords, opened their ranks and allowed them to pass, followed by a considerable portion of the crowd, shouting " Vive la République !" and singing the " Chant du Départ."

The iron gates of the Palais Bourbon having been opened to admit a deputation of National Guards, the crowd precipitated itself forward, and in a few minutes the steps and courtyard were alike invaded. Cries of " Vive la Garde Nationale !" " Vive la Ligne !"

"Vive la République!" resounded on all sides, and the soldiers who occupied the court of the Palais Bourbon, after making a show of resistance, ended by hoisting the butt ends of their rifles in the air in sign of sympathy, joining at the same time in the shouts of the crowd, while the latter, encountering no further opposition, proceeded to invade the passages of the Chamber, at the moment Count de Kératry was attacking the Ministry for surrounding the Corps Légis-latif with troops and sergents-de-ville, contrary to the orders of General Trochu. Count de Palikao, having explained the relative positions of the Governor of Paris and the Minister of War, introduced a bill instituting a Council of Government and National Defence, composed of five members elected by the Legislative Body, the Ministers to be appointed with the approval of the members of this Council, and he, Count de Palikao, to occupy the post of Lieutenant-General. M. Jules Favre having claimed priority for the motion which he had introduced the day before, M. Thiers, pleading the necessity for union, next moved that:—"In view of existing circumstances, the Chamber appoints a Commission of Government and National Defence. A Constituent Assembly will be convoked as soon as circumstances permit."

The Chamber having declared in favour of their urgency, these several propositions were eventually referred to the Bureau, and the sitting was suspended. It was during this period that the crowd penetrated into the Salles des Quatre Colonnes and de la Paix, in the latter of which M. Jules Ferry, mounting on a bench, amid cries of "Vive la République!" informed the multitude that he had given Count de Palikao his word that the people would not enter the actual hall where the deputies of the Corps Législatif deliberate, and which ought, he said, to remain sacred. The speaker having called upon the National Guard to defend the entry, the soldiers on duty retired, and the crowd continued to call for the dethronement, urging that it ought to be immediately proclaimed. Other members of the Left begged them to wait patiently the decision of the deputies, which could not but be favourable to the unanimous demand of the people.

The crowd, however, would not resign their idea of penetrating into the Salle des Séances. They also discussed which members should form a Provisional Government, and a paper inscribed with the names of seven deputies of the Left was affixed to the statue of Minerva. The pillars and walls were also covered with inscriptions demanding the dethronement of the Emperor and the proclamation of the Republic— demands which were re-echoed by the incessant clamours of the multitude.

At half-past two, when the sitting was resumed, the galleries were crowded and very noisy. The members of the Left only were in their places. It was in vain the President attempted to obtain silence, in vain the solemn huissiers commanded it. MM. Gambetta and Crémieux appeared together at the tribune, and the former begged of the people to remain quiet. For a minute something like silence was obtained; but the populace arriving by the various passages, and finding no room in the already overcrowded tribunes, invaded the Chamber from behind. Several deputies of the Left succeeded in keeping them at bay for a time, while the President seconded the exhortations of M. Gambetta in energetic though ineffectual terms.

A partial silence having been secured, Count de Palikao, followed by a few members of the majority,

entered the Chamber, but did not essay to speak, the
bullet in his chest no doubt troubling him more than
ever. A minute or two afterwards, the clamour arose
again, and a noisy multitude commenced invading the
floor of the hall. "Silence, Messieurs!" from force
of habit cried the huissiers in presence of this raging
sea of human beings, but silence ensued not at their
call. Nothing was left to the President but to put on
his hat and retire, which he did, together with Count
de Palikao and the members by whom the latter had
been accompanied. By this time the Chamber was
completely invaded by National and Mobile Guards,
in company with an excited crowd, whose advance it
was in vain now to attempt to repel. M. Jules Favre,
having mounted the tribune, obtained a moment's
silence. "No scenes of violence," cried he; "let us
reserve our arms for our enemies." Finding it
utterly impossible to obtain any further hearing inside
the Chamber, M. Gambetta, accompanied by the
members of the Left, proceeded to the steps of the
peristyle, and there announced the dethronement of
the Emperor to the people assembled outside. Accompanied by one section of the crowd, they now hurried
to the Hôtel de Ville, and there installed themselves as
a Provisional Government, whilst another section took
possession of the Tuileries—whence the Empress had
that morning taken flight—as national property. A
select band of Republicans, mindful of what Count—now
Citoyen—Henri Rochefort had done to bring Impe-
rialism into disrepute, proceeded to the prison of Sainte
Pélagie and conducted the author of the *Lanterne* and
other political prisoners in triumph to the Hôtel de Ville.

The deputies who quitted the Chamber when it was
invaded by the mob, met that same afternoon at the
President's residence, and sent a deputation to the

Hôtel de Ville, with a proposal to act in common with the new Government. This proposition was, however, declined, on the score of the Republic having been already proclaimed and accepted by the population of Paris. At an evening meeting of nearly two hundred deputies, held under the presidency of M. Thiers, MM. Jules Favre and Simon attended on the part of the Provisional Government to explain that they were anxious to secure the support of the deputies, whom they hinted, however, could best serve their country in the departments. After this unequivocal rebuff, the deputies, who had in the meantime been apprised that seals had been placed on the doors of the Corps Législatif, saw that nothing remained to them but to protest, and protest they accordingly did against the events of the afternoon. The strange respect which the French invariably show for a bit of red wax—excelling our own reverence for red tape— and their belief in the efficacy of procès-verbaux in the gravest situations, was ludicrously exemplified on this occasion. Not one of the two hundred deputies present so much as dared suggest the breaking of the seals and the assembling in the Legislative Chamber.

## IV. THE GOVERNMENT OF NATIONAL DEFENCE.

The Government which grasped the reins of power on the utter collapse of Imperial institutions was a mob-named one in the fullest sense of the term, the names having been chalked by the populace on the pillars of the portico of the Palais Bourbon during that invasion of the Chamber on the Sunday afternoon which resulted in the overthrow of the Imperial régime. The list appears to have been accepted by the principal members of the Left, who, although they

would have preferred disassociating themselves from
M. Rochefort, nevertheless felt that it was impossible
to leave him out of the combination, and therefore
adroitly—and not inappropriately, as the safety of
Paris was especially in their keeping—made it embrace
all the deputies for Paris, save, as M. Jules Simon
observed, the most illustrious—meaning M. Thiers,
who refused to join it—thereby excusing the presence
in it of M. Henri Rochefort to the more timid among
the Parisian bourgeoisie.

The Government of National Defence, as it
elected to style itself, on M. Rochefort's suggestion,
was composed of the following members :—General
Trochu, President ; Jules Favre, Vice President and
Minister for Foreign Affairs ; Emanuel Arago ;
Crémieux, Minister of Justice ; Jules Ferry, Secretary;
Leon Gambetta, Minister of the Interior ;  Garnier-
Pagès ; Glais-Bizoin ; Eugéne Pelletan ; Ernest Picard,
Minister of Finance ; Henri Rochefort ; and Jules
Simon, Minister of Public Instruction.  Subsequently
it associated with it General Le Flô, Minister of War ;
Admiral Fourichon, Minister of Marine ; M. Dorian,
Minister of Public Works ; and M. Magnin, Minister
of Agriculture and Commerce.  These, with Count de
Kératry, charged with the Prefecture of Police, and
M. Etienne Arago, appointed Mayor of Paris, composed
altogether no less than eighteen members, upwards of
two-thirds of whom were Bretons, advocates, or journalists ; so that if in a multitude of counsellors there
really is wisdom—a time-honoured axiom which is open
to dispute, it being notorious that men think singly
but act in herds—it was fairly to be hoped for here.

For some days the new Government was prodigal
of proclamations and decrees.  Its first acts were
to close the doors of the Palais Bourbon and the

Palais du Luxembourg, and dissolve the Corps Législatif and abolish the Senate as *bouches inutiles politiques*, to issue proclamations to the army, or rather the débris of one, justifying the Revolution and appealing to the troops to continue their heroic efforts for the defence of the country, and to the National Guard, thanking them for their past, and asking for their future patriotism. It released all functionaries from their oaths, dismissed the ambassadors at foreign courts, appointed prefects in all the departments, and new mayors in the twenty arrondissements of the capital, proclaimed the complete liberty of the press, ordered all Germans not provided with special permission to remain, to quit the departments of the Seine and Seine-et-Oise within four-and-twenty hours, directed the cemeteries inside the walls of Paris to be opened, and the theatres to be closed, on the plea that the nation was in mourning, and that the fire-brigades ordinarily on duty at these establishments could be better employed in helping to man the ramparts. It pressed forward the provisioning of the city and its works of defence, increased the herds of sheep and oxen and the stores of corn and flour, provisionally abolished all local customs and octroi dues, and fixed the price of butcher's meat, armed the outer forts and the enceinte, blew up or mined all the bridges and fired all the woods in the environs, razed thousands of houses to the ground, felled roadside trees, and constructed huge barricades with them; laid in fact all the beautiful suburbs in waste; listened to the thousand and one wild schemes put forth by patriotic madmen for exterminating the invaders, and launched a huge captive balloon, which hovered daily over Paris to give timely notice of their dreaded arrival.

Besides these acts of the Government in its collec-
tive capacity, each member of it had thrust upon him
his full share of individual duties.   On the morrow of
the Revolution M. Jules Favre, Minister of Foreign
Affairs, had to receive the Dukes d'Aumale and de
Chartres, who came to offer their swords to the
Republic, and politely bow them out of France.   The
day following he proclaimed to Europe the desire of
the nation for peace, which he rendered at the same
time impracticable by his famous declaration, now
become historical, that France would not yield a
single inch of her territory, or a single stone of her
fortresses—Frenchman-like, sacrificing the real interests
of his country for the sake of a happy antithesis,
which in the end cost France a lavish outlay of blood
and treasure, and the partial destruction of its capital.
Subsequently he received the ambassadors of the United
States, Spain, Portugal, Italy, Switzerland, &c., who
had been directed to recognise the new Republic by
their respective governments, besides delegates and
addresses from ultra-Liberals in all parts of Europe.

M. Gambetta, Minister of the Interior, charged
himself with sending out circular upon circular to the
prefects, urging them to stir up the patriotism of the
people, and to give their undivided attention to the
national defence.   Besides which, in a series of laconic
telegrams — the information being the reverse of
pleasant, did not require to be dwelt upon—he had
to keep Paris daily apprized of the nearer approach of
the enemy.   The venerable Crémieux found occupation in displacing the more unscrupulous legal
functionaries, whose advancement had been due
to their subserviency under the Empire, and in
delivering eloquent addresses to fiery young republicans, whom he persistently styled his children,

until his colleagues despatched him as delegate to Tours to air his senile garrulity on provincial audiences.

M. Ernest Picard, Minister of Finance; M. Magnin, Minister of Agriculture and Commerce; M. Dorian, Minister of Public Works; General Le Flô, Minister of War, and General Trochu, Governor of Paris, all had onerous labours imposed upon them in connexion with the defence of Paris. The first in providing the money for the enormous expenditure which the provisioning and fortifying of the capital involved, the second in accumulating the live stock and general alimentary substances requisite for feeding two millions of people for at least several months, the third in organizing the execution of immense defensive works planned by Generals Trochu and Le Flô, on whom devolved the task not merely of constructing fortifications that should prove impregnable, but of disciplining an army that should prove invincible. M. Jules Simon, Minister of Public Instruction, busied himself with the reorganization and extension of the educational resources of France, and by a stroke of his pen abolished the subventions to the Paris theatres; M. Etienne Arago, Mayor of Paris, had the burden of the administration of a city, which was a world of itself, thrust upon his shoulders; and even M. Henri Rochfort, after formally severing himself from the democratic journal the *Marseillaise*, which, suppressed under the Empire, made its reappearance under the Republic, presided over a commission charged with the interior defence of Paris, by a system of scientific barricades; while as for the Count de Kératry, Prefect of Police, after calling on the Parisians by their calm and manly attitude to mount to the dignity of the task which had fallen on them and France, he expressed himself confident that his post would prove a sinecure; saying which, he at once signed an order for the arrest of his predecessor, whose satellites he abolished en bloc. People, however, maintained that the Count's guardians of the public peace, by whom they were replaced, were simply the old sergens-de-ville devoid of their imperials, and disguised in pilot coats with hoods—which rendered them a cross between the monk and the sailor—the same old birds in fact, with a different plumage. During his short term of office, M. de Kératry instituted some fresh raids on the bouches inutiles of the capital, which like the heads of the hydra, only multiplied themselves the more, the more they were got rid of—the irruption of beggars on the boulevards being at this epoch equivalent to one of the plagues of Egypt. In addition he sought, by his proclamations, still further to reduce the population of Paris by urging all who were not prepared to fight to fly the city while there was yet time.

The Revolution was welcomed by the Parisians with paroxysms of joy, which found vent in the decapitation of Imperial eagles, the effacing of Napoleonic ciphers, the smashing of all the plaster busts of the Emperor, the obliterating of all the heraldic insignia of the Empire, and in the rebaptizing of those streets and thoroughfares of the capital which awakened reminiscences of the Imperial régime. Having accomplished these sacred duties, and rendered themselves completely hoarse in vociferating "Vive la République!" "À bas les Bonapartes!" and in chanting the "Marseillaise," which they had latterly given over singing, far into the night, they gave up the morrow of the proclamation of the Republic to enjoyment and repose, and the day following—which ushered in a perfect deluge that naturally delighted every one, as it would certainly delay the advance of the Prussians if it did not rack them with rheumatism as well—to sober reflection, induced in great measure by the eloquent exposé of the situation contained in M. Jules Favre's famous circular, which made its appearance in that morning's *Journal Officiel.* While appealing to the patriotic sentiments of the Parisians, it still nurtured hopes of peace, for, which the majority craved without daring to acknowledge it. The disasters that had befallen France were being constantly brought to their minds by the apparition in the streets, morning, noon, and night, of weary, dejected-looking, travel-stained fugitives, the remnant of Macmahon's army, who kept pouring into Paris in their bedraggled uniforms and damaged accoutrements, marching without order and more or less footsore; so different to their appearance a few weeks ago when with drums beating, bugles sounding, and colours flying, and cheered at every step of their way, they marched proudly along the crowded boulevards, as everybody foolishly believed, on their promenade militaire to Berlin.

After alluding to the "collapse of the Empire under the weight of its faults, and amid the acclamations of an immense people, without the shedding of a single drop of blood, and without any one individual being deprived of his personal liberty," M. Jules Favre reminded the Parisians that "time must not be lost; the enemies," said he, "are at our gates; we have but one thought—namely, their expulsion from our territory. But this obligation, which we resolutely accept, we did not impose upon France. She would not be in her present position if our voice had been listened to. We have energetically defended,

even at the cost of our popularity, the policy of peace ;*
we still maintain the same opinion with increasing
conviction.   Our heart breaks at the sight of these
human massacres wherein is sacrificed the flower of
two nations, that a little good sense and a great
deal of liberty would have preserved from such
frightful catastrophes. . . .   Ready for every emer-
gency, we look with calmness on the position of
affairs, made what it is, not by us but by others.
We loudly condemned the war, and, while protesting our respect for the rights of peoples, we
asked that Germany should be left mistress of her
own destinies.   We wished that liberty should be at
the same time our common tie and our common shield.
We were convinced that these moral forces would for
ever insure peace, but as a sanction we claimed an
arm for every citizen, a civil organization, and the
election of leaders.   Then we should have remained
invincible on our own soil. . . . .   On his side, the
King of Prussia declared that he made war, not
against France, but against the Imperial dynasty.
The dynasty has fallen to the ground.   France raises
herself free.   Does the King of Prussia wish to
continue an impious struggle which will be at least
as fatal to him as to us ?   Does he wish to give to
the world of the nineteenth century the cruel spectacle
of two nations destroying one another, and, in forget-
fulness of humanity, reason, and science, heaping

---

* Truth is held in but small esteem even among the more
honourable Frenchmen. Had M. Jules Favre been perfectly candid,
he would have qualified this assertion.   Of the Government of
National Defence only four members voted against the war on the
vital question of the supplies—Arago, Favre, Garnier-Pagès, and
Pelletan ; whilst five voted in its favour—namely, Ferry, Gambetta
Magnin, Picard, and Simon.

corpse upon corpse, and ruin upon ruin? He is free
to assume this responsibility in the face of the world
and of history. If it is a challenge, we accept it.
We will not cede either an inch of our territory or a
stone of our fortresses. A shameful peace would
mean a war of extermination at an early date. We
will only treat for a durable peace. In this, our interest
is that of the whole of Europe, and we have reason
to hope that, freed from all dynastic considerations,
the question will thus present itself before the
Cabinets of Europe. But should we be alone, we
shall not yield. We have a resolute army, well-
provisioned forts, a well-established enceinte; and,
above all, the breasts of 300,000 combatants determined to hold out to the last. . . . . After the forts
we have the ramparts, after the ramparts we have the
barricades. Paris can hold out for three months and
conquer. If she succumbs, France will start up at
her appeal and avenge her. France would continue
the struggle, and the aggressor would perish. . . .
I sum up these resolves briefly, in presence of God
who hears me, in the face of posterity which shall
judge us. We wish only for peace; but if this disas-
trous war, which we have condemned, is continued
against us, we shall do our duty to the last, and I
have the firm confidence that our cause, which is that
of Right and of Justice, will triumph in the end."

Parenthetically it may be remarked that the King
of Prussia made no such declaration as M. Jules
Favre attributed to him. All he said was that he
made war on the French army, and not on the French
nation. It was the Crown Prince who proclaimed
that war was waged with the Emperor, and with him
alone, which encouraged in the Parisians the illusion
that peace on their own terms was to be secured,

either through the generosity of their enemy or
the intervention of the neutral Powers, and rumours,
now that Austria, now that Russia had volunteered
her good offices in that direction, were current from
one day to another.    Many believed that the
mere transformation of France from an Empire into
a Republic would cause the olive-branch to blossom
and bear fruit.    The less sanguine, however, felt
that Paris ran the risk of being exposed to needless
suffering, and to the prolongation of a struggle which
they believed had become hopeless, simply because
the issue was in the hands of men who, if they gave
in, would fear to see their pet institutions collapse,
their pet theory of government for years to come again
out of favour.    The more thoughtful, with far from
perfect faith in this Government of advocates,
journalists, and Bretons, cast their eyes round far and
near, and asked themselves where was the presiding
mind capable at the present crisis of directing the
fallen fortunes of France—the man who would begin
by resolutely combating illusions and telling the
nation the unblemished truth—

> " Oh God ! for a man with heart, head, hand,
>    Like some of the simple great ones gone
>       For ever and ever by,
>    One still strong man in a blatant land,
>    Whatever they call him, what care I,
>    Aristocrat, democrat, autocrat—one
>       Who can rule, and dare not lie ! " *

---

* The man on whom the general hopes eventually centered
when the question had narrowed itself to the saving of Paris was
naturally General Trochu, president of the new Government—a
soldier of some reputation, the whole tenour of whose life had been
irreproachable.    The fact, however, of his being a known devotee
lessened the confidence which would otherwise have been reposed
in him.    Like several of his colleagues he was a Breton, having

Between the Republic, with its visions of the spectre rouge, and the prospect of being besieged and bombarded in Paris, something like a panic spread among the tranquil and wealthy classes. Disquieting demonstrations, the objects of which were unknown, were made from time to time in the streets by hundreds of men and women, who set off their rags with tricolor ribbons, and who on one occasion after parading the boulevards, crossed the Place de la Con-

---

been born at Belle Isle, in the department of Morbihan, on March 12, 1815. He commenced his military career in Africa, that pernicious school in which the French generals of the present day have been invariably reared, and where he became attached to the staff of Marshal Bugeaud, with whom he was a great favourite. He obtained his lieutenant-colonelcy in 1845, and was subsequently named assistant-director of the ministry of war, in which capacity he was the actual organizer of the Crimean expedition. Appointed one of the aides-de-camp of Marshal St. Arnaud, he seconded the suggestion of Lord Lyons, to carry on the war before Sebastopol rather than in Bessarabia, as the commanders of the expedition purposed. He personally distinguished himself as the commander of a division during the Italian war, at the same time displaying the determination to enforce a strictness of discipline to which French troops had heretofore been unaccustomed. In 1866 he became a member of the Commission on the reorganization of the French army, and the year following published his famous " L'armée Française," a work which went through no less than 18 editions, and in which he dwelt equally upon the falling off of discipline among the French rank-and-file, and the absence of all sense of responsibility on the part of the officers, from the lowest to the highest ranks—denouncing at the same time the disposition the Government had shown to favour brilliancy rather than solid education and signalling the dangers of patriotic illusions, such as volunteering and so-called levées en masse. When the war with Germany broke out, General Trochu commanded at Toulouse, and was to have had the command of the corps d'expédition intended to have been landed in Germany. The sudden disasters at the frontier, however, caused that project to be abandoned, and to conciliate public opinion he was appointed commander-in-chief of the forces in Paris under the Palikao administration.

corde and the bridge, proceeded to explore the deserted halls of the Palais Bourbon, wandering thence into the Faubourg Saint Germain, frightening certain ancient dowagers, who were reminded of some horrible scenes they had heard of in their youth. All this, combined with the dread of the désagrémens, if not the dangers of a siege, caused the different railway stations to be crowded from morn to night—the trains starting anyhow, at all hours—and the streets leading to them to be blocked incessantly with vehicles piled up with luggage. The railway servants were overwhelmed with questions, and people rushed agitatedly from one ticket place to another, or elbowed their way into the already crowded waiting-rooms, while women accompanied by troops of little children wandered distractedly up and down, or sat for hours together, with the resignation of despair, on the trunks and packages crowding the pavement in front of the stations.

The provisioning of Paris was of itself overtaxing the energies of the railway officials, flour, rice, biscuits, preserved meats, &c., arriving from all directions; in addition to which, furniture continued to be sent in by residents on the various lines of railway in the environs. Simultaneously, too, the provincial mobiles summoned up to assist in the defence of Paris, commenced to arrive; while to add to the confusion at the Northern railway station the troops under the command of General Vinoy, who had got to the front too late to take part in Macmahon's engagements before Sedan, and had made good their retreat, also arrived in Paris; and trains conveying artillery, cavalry, infantry, and military stores kept rolling into the station at every hour of the day.

The proclamation of the Republic, moreover, brought

political refugees from all parts of Europe trooping into Paris. Among the more illustrious, MM. Edgar Quinet and Louis Blanc arrived unannounced, and in the quietest manner; but the exile of Jersey, M. Victor Hugo, met with quite an ovation on the part of some couple of thousand demonstrative admirers, who escorted him in triumph along the boulevards at night time, cheering him frantically every step of the way. Addressing them, he said "he had promised to return when the Republic returned, and he had kept his word. He had come to do his duty in the hour of danger; to save Paris, which was more than to save France—it was to save the world, the centre of humanity, the capital of civilization. Such a city was not to be taken by a savage invasion. She must inevitably triumph if they were all united. Fraternity would save liberty" Fine words, designed of course to pander to the national vanity.

### V. PARIS EXPECTANT.

After a brief repose following upon their brilliant victory before Sedan, the German columns leisurely resumed their march on Paris, to allow, as Count Bismarck cynically expressed it, "the Parisians time to stew in their own gravy;" expanding their front at Rheims, where the old king installed himself in the archbishop's palace, northwards as far as Laon, whence they intended sweeping round towards Paris by way of Soissons, Compiègne, Creil, and the valley of the Oise, and spreading over the fertile plains of Champagne from Chateau-Thierry to Montmirail, scaring the vintagers from the vine-covered slopes. From Montmirail the Crown Prince of Prussia's army advanced by Coulommiers, Chaumes, and Corbeil, where the main body crossed the Seine, and eventually took up positions extending from La Lande, near Cœuilly, eastward of Paris, to beyond St. Germain, investing the capital completely on the south and the west; while the army of the Crown Prince of Saxony posted itself in the intervening space east and north of Paris.

For a few days after the proclamation of the Republic, while a general displacement of Imperial prefects was in progress and lawyers and journalists —the place-hunters par excellence in France whenever a "strong" government chances to be overthrown— were struggling to secure the vacant posts, and the official wires generally were changing hands, the Parisians heard but little respecting the movements of the German forces, which in presence of the number of ammunition waggons en route to the detached forts, that at this epoch thronged the streets showing a warm reception in store for their enemies, scarcely troubled them so much as might have been expected  On September 8th however they were awakened to a sense of the imminence of the danger which menaced them, when the Minister of the Interior formally announced that the enemy was advancing on Paris in three distinct corps; adding by way of postscript, that Laon had been summoned to surrender, but had closed its gates, and was prepared to offer a determined resistance.  Next day the fluttering black and white pennants of the ubiquitous Uhlans were reported eastward of Paris, at La-Ferté-sous-Jouarre, in advance of Chateau-Thierry, and spreading out right and left to Vailly-sur-Aisne and Montmirail.  A couple of hours afterwards it was announced that they were expected at Coulommiers, fifteen miles nigher to Paris, that same evening, while news arrived from the north that these venturesome éclaireurs were threading their way through the forest

of Compiègne to the whilom Castle of Indolence of
the ex-Imperial Court.   At this juncture a proclamation of General Trochu's exhorts the Parisians to let
the enemy experience " the formidable surprise of
finding an immense capital which he believes to be
enervated by the pleasures of peace, prepared, in view
of the misfortunes of the country, with one mind for
the fight ;" and to give the population confidence, pro-
nounces the enceinte, " defended by the persevering
efforts of public spirit," and what is rather more to
the purpose, 300,000 rifles, to be inaccessible.   An
official decree launched at the same moment ominously
notifies the removal of the Courts of Criminal Justice and Cassation to Tours.   There is, however, one
faint ray of hope to dissipate the general gloom.
M. Thiers, while refusing to ally himself directly with
a government the exceptional origin of which was
not to his taste, consents to go on a special mission
to London, St. Petersburg, and Vienna, and endeavour
to rouse the neutral Powers to an active interference
on behalf of France ; and everybody agrees the nation
could have no better advocate in the present crisis
than the wily, venerable, and highly respectable ex-
Minister of the monarchy of July

On the morning of the 11th it becomes known that
the citadel of Laon has capitulated to save the town,
and that at the moment of the surrender a powder
magazine had exploded, killing numerous German
soldiers and Gardes Mobiles, and wounding the commanders on both sides—namely, the Grand Duke of
Mecklenburg and General d'Hame.   On its eventually
transpiring that the powder magazine had been blown
up designedly and treacherously, the Paris newspapers,
with scarcely an exception, extolled the deed as rivalling the noblest examples of Spartan heroism.   The

*Gaulois* demanded the publication of the heroes' names, "which ought to be inscribed," it maintained, " in letters of gold in the sacred annals of the country ;" saying which, it proceeded to give a series of strategic rules for the best way of combating the uhlans. One paper had already advised that the Hanoverian legion, in course of formation, should adopt the uhlan costume, and surprise and slay these daring cavalry scouts in detail.

For the next few days the Parisians were absorbed in studying the geography of their environs, and the number of maps of these which filled the windows of the book and printsellers was quite remarkable. On Monday the 12th it was announced that the enemy's adventurous scouts had advanced as close as Meaux, which thousands for the first time learnt was in the valley of the Marne, and only eight and twenty miles from Paris ; just as thousands discovered that Melun, where they made their apparition a day or two afterwards, and commanded the customary déjeuner, including so many cigars per head, in advance, was on the Seine and within a like distance of the capital. These were of course mere corps of observation pushed daringly forward considerably in advance of the main body, to ascertain whether the troops were likely to encounter any more serious impediments than they had hitherto met with as they drew nearer to Paris. At Nogent-sur-Seine the mayor was jubilant over the check he had made them submit to, telegraphing in high glee to Paris that thirty Prussian dragoons had been compelled to retreat in face of " the energetic attitude of the population." The Germans occupied Melun at their leisure, and closed the railway traffic between Paris and Nevers, Dijon, Mulhouse, Lyons, and the Mediterranean, while their occupation of Meaux secured them a like control over the communications eastward of the capital. Paris knew by this time what was in store for it. On Monday afternoon it was placarded from one end to the other with an official notice, which gave the tens of thousands who read and re-read it not to mistake its too evident purport, clearly to understand that henceforth they were dwellers within the walls of a beleaguered city. "Seeing," it said, "that the enemy may be momentarily expected under the walls of Paris, the Government of National Defence give notice that on the morning of the 15th instant, at six o'clock, the gates will be closed, and neither ingress nor egress permitted to any person except by the written order of the Minister of the Interior."

Some news which had evidently been delayed in transmission from having had to travel by a circuitous route, owing no doubt to the general clipping of telegraph wires on the part of the uhlans, arrived the next day, stating that these ubiquitous gentry had been threatening the town of Nogent-sur-Seine with bombardment in the event of the bridge being blown up, and asking for instructions; that eight thousand pioneers of the enemy were at Châlons, and that Count Bismarck's famous regiment of white cuirassiers were billeted at Chauny, towards the north, where they were said to be awaiting the arrival of the main body of the army, which was about to attack Soissons and La Fère. Whatever plan of defence might be adopted with regard to Paris, there was now no time to be lost in putting it into execution. Renewed attempts were made to fire the woods in the environs, which on former occasions had obstinately refused to burn. Stacks and standing crops were frantically committed to the flames. More bridges, both railway and others, were sent bounding into the air, notably that of Creil, which destroyed communications with England by way of Calais and Boulogne. More trenches were dug across the broad Imperial chaussées, and more of the huge trees methodically skirting them were felled to obstruct the thorough-fare—anything to delay the enemy's advance even for half a day. The National and Mobile Guards were also passed in review by the Governor of Paris on the morning of the 13th. There were one hundred and thirty-six battalions of the former, numbering little short of a hundred and eighty thousand men, all armed with either chassepots or fusils à tabatière, decorated at the muzzles with flowers and sprigs of evergreen, or having caricatures of the Emperor stuck on the bayonets. The majority wore some kind of uniform; still, with many thousands the workman's blouse was simply supplemented by the kepi, calling to mind the officer's rejoinder to the barefooted volunteers of 1792 who had demanded shoes before marching against the enemy, "The general says that with bread and steel you can go to the end of the world; he didn't so much as mention shoes." The men were ranged along the boulevards from the Place de la Bastille to the Madeleine, thence down the Rue Royale, around the Place de la Concorde and up the Champs Elysées, as far as the Rond Point; the Mobiles, more than another hundred thousand continuing the line thence to the Arc de Triomphe and being also posted along the quays. A veritable forest of bayonets glittered in the autumn sunshine. General Trochu rode down the entire line accompanied by the Minister of War, the Commander of the National Guard, several admirals called upon to perform military duty in connexion with the defence of Paris—take command of certain of the detached forts, or particular sections of the enceinte—and who sat their steeds in true sailor fashion, and a small staff. A detachment of cavalry of the National Guard formed the escort. The enthusiasm was extreme, General Trochu, in whom the Parisians placed a childish confidence, being very cordially greeted, while the fineness of the day brought all Paris into the streets to celebrate, as it were, its last fête ere entering upon a season of austerity and gloom within the walls of " the greatest prison which the world has ever seen, and nought but desolation and hostility environing it outside."

Many companies of National Guards, when the review was over, defiled before the residence of Mr. Washburne, the United States Minister, and sent in a deputation to thank him for the sympathy which his Government had expressed for France. In his reply, while expressing his desire that the two great Republics might remain united in presence of Monarchical Europe, he was careful to inform them that the nature of the support they might hope to receive from the United States was moral rather than material.

It was at this epoch that the last of those straggling files of vehicles laden with furniture, which, since the hour when M. Chevreau raised the cry of " wolf " had been coming into Paris, entered the capital. To-day however, it was only the very poor, the obstinate, and the dilatory who arrived. The poor, who could not remove their goods until they had paid their rent, an obligation which the Government eventually relieved them from; the obstinate, who until the last moment had determined not to budge come what might; and the dilatory, who had postponed their departure until they had leisurely gathered in their final crops, or not having the heart to tear themselves away from home,

and its familiar everyday surroundings, had delayed
their packing up until the butcher and baker had
quitted the village.  If it was painful to leave, how
much more painful to return after peace had been
proclaimed and find one's home a mass of ruin.

The procession was for the most part a melancholy
one—all these poor households, with everything they
possessed—their shabby bedding, rickety chairs and
tables, broken kitchen utensils, cracked crockery and
baskets, bundles and birdcages, stacked haphazard
either in tottering carts, drawn by poor bony horses
or donkeys, whose spirit had been broken by toil; or
else in trucks, dragged and pushed along by sad and
weary looking men, women, and children, dusty and
travel-stained, all but the very old and the very
young bearing their shares of the burthen.  The
dilatory ones scrambled off as best they could, while
as to the obstinate ones, many of them were forced to
leave their household goods behind.  With a view,
however, of propitiating their unbidden guests, they
made arrangements for receiving them with becoming
attention, hoping—how vainly the sequel proved—by
their delicate consideration to dispose them not to do
unnecessary and wilful damage to their property.
They walled up their cellar of fine wines, it is true,
still they saw that the other was stocked with plenty
of full bottles, and a cask or two as well.  They left
all the keys in the cupboards, in which were stowed
away cheeses, hams, brawn, boxes of sardines, and
pâtés-de-foie-gras, not forgetting sausages, of which
they of course knew their guests to be intensely fond,
nor preserves for the sweeter-toothed, nor even
liqueurs as correctives to acidity.  Candles, too, were
considerately placed in the chandeliers, with lucifer
matches in readiness by the side; fires even were laid in

REFUGEES FROM OUTSIDE PARIS AT A CANTINE.

i. 42.

the grates; sheets moreover were put upon the beds, and tablecloths on the tables. People who had taken all these precautions, of course expected on returning to their property to discover all the good things eaten, but hardly to find their chairs and tables broken, their looking-glasses smashed, their pianos burnt for fire-wood, and their clocks and chimney ornaments carried off to Germany.*

On September 14th Paris heard of the first engagements with the enemy which had taken place since the surrender of Sedan. These were of course mere skirmishes between Uhlans and Francs-tireurs, one of which had occurred at Montereau on the line to Troyes, and the other at Melun. The same day there was an insignificant encounter somewhere between the latter place and Brie-Comte-Robert, so famous for its cheeses and its roses ; and the day following a company of Uhlans captured a train at Senlis ; baulked of similar prey at Chantilly, they gallantly fired into the carriages, but luckily wounded none of the passengers.

The British ambassador having inserted an advertisement in *Galignani's Messenger,* a paper which regular British residents in Paris never see, informing his fellow countrymen that if they remained over the morrow it would be at their own peril, proceeded, in conjunction with the ambassadors for Spain, Austria, and Holland, to address "cordial" letters to M. Jules Favre, intimating their intention to remain in Paris, an announcement which of course gave great pleasure to the French Minister for Foreign Affairs, though, as we shall presently see, not for long. Desperate attempts were made the same day to ignite more of

---

* Sarcey's *Siége de Paris*, p. 75.

the woods round Paris, particularly on the north-east.
News from a distance kept coming in by circuitous
routes along such telegraph wires as had escaped
destruction. Now it was Joinville in the Haute Marne
that was in hourly peril of seeing 15,000 Prussians
arrive there; next, one of the enemy's columns, 10,000
strong, was making requisitions at Nanteuil; and as
a matter of course, from the force of habit, Paris was
appealed to—Paris, who would soon be herself in the
throes of a siege that promised to cast all the great
sieges of ancient and modern times into the shade.
Joinville and Nanteuil were, however, too far off to
interest the Parisians with their insignificant troubles;
and even the knowledge that Soissons was invested
by a considerable cavalry force, and that Villers-
Coterets was occupied by several thousand troops,
failed to move them, so absorbed were they in what
was passing nearer home. When uhlans were
signalled at Dammartin, within twenty miles, and an
hour or two afterwards at Villeneuve-St-Georges
within ten miles, Paris felt that the first act of the
siege, to sustain which such gigantic preparations had
been and were still being made, was not likely to be
delayed for long. An attack on the side of Vincennes
was talked of, and a considerable body of troops was
sent out of Paris in that direction the same evening.
Towards nine o'clock people were startled at hearing
the rappel being beaten at numerous points of the
capital. Cries of "To arms! to arms!" arose on all
sides. Crowds assembled on the boulevards, where
rumours prevailed that the Prussians were attacking
Vincennes and Charenton. Women hastened within
doors, National Guards rushed to the Mairies, and
Gardes Mobiles, shouldering their rifles, ran off, they
knew not where, in search of some rallying point. The

alarm proved to be a false one. A mob of ruffians, who had been forcibly ejected from Paris a few days previously by the Governor's orders, on finding themselves with the Prussians in front of them and the French advanced posts in their rear, determined to re-enter Paris at all hazards, and forcibly invaded the commune des Lilas, adjoining Belleville, and out of which they were eventually chased by the National Guard.

These were some of the ravagers—jackals, as the Parisians expressively styled them — who were a perpetual source of trouble throughout the siege. They commenced plundering the abandoned houses in the environs before the enemy's arrival, and profited by there being no regular police to bring their booty into Paris. It was no unusual thing to see dirty, disreputable looking vagabonds being interrogated by the National Guards at the city gates, respecting valuable articles of property—a handsome clock, a pair of candelabra, or some elegant vases—found in their possession, when they would either reply that they had been employed by the owner to assist him with his removal, or else would boldly assert that they were moving into Paris on their own account, to prevent, as they expressed it, their property from falling into the hands of " ces voleurs, Messieurs les Prussiens." Some of the francs-tireurs were not strangers to the same system of plunder, and used, moreover, to rob any unprotected peasants they encountered coming into Paris of all their loose cash. The cantinière of the "francs-tireurs de Paris," and her husband, were detected pillaging a house, and their cart, on being searched, was found to contain a quantity of stolen property. Subsequently, after the Germans arrived, and the ravagers found their trade dangerous, they used to go

out marauding, as it was called, that is, gathering in
the abandoned vegetables in the environs; in which
capacity many of them kept up regular communications with the enemy, whom they apprized of all
that transpired in Paris.

### VI. THE GERMANS ARRIVE.

While Paris was exclusively depending on the
official telegrams for its information respecting the
steady advance of the German army, which was being
accomplished with fatal regularity, a few scraps of
intelligence were furnished by the newspapers, from
which it appeared that on the evening of September
15th, some Uhlans had been observed endeavouring
to ford the Seine opposite the railway station at Juvisy,
south of Paris, and had been fired upon by National
Guards lying perdu there; and that so stealthy had
been the enemy's advance, that while the forest of
Senart swarmed with German soldiers, the inhabitants of the neighbouring villages were unconscious of
their presence, and had, many of them, fled in dismay
on seeing the troops emerge and ford the river, with
the water reaching to their waists.   Once across,
they had proceeded, it seems, to establish batteries on
the heights of Athis.   At this moment the plain of
Clamart was occupied by 12,000 French troops.

In the north a dozen French lancers were driven
back by a detachment of uhlans, whom they encountered in advance of Le Bourget; and still further
northward, in the direction of Gonesse, some tardy
agriculturists, on the move into Paris a day too late,
had three and twenty cartloads of produce captured
by another body of the enemy's adventurous cavalry.

Early the following morning, September 16th, the
commander of the fort of Vincennes telegraphed to

the Governor of Paris that the bridge at Joinville-le-
Pont having been blown up, he was unable to give
any account of the march of the enemy, whom he
did not believe to be very near. Before his telegram
arrived even, the Germans were between Creteil and
Neuilly-sur-Marne, scarcely five miles from the fort
of Vincennes, and under the guns of Forts Rosny
and Nogent, while their scouts had penetrated to
Creteil, four miles distant from Paris, and under the
guns of Fort Charenton, where it seems they sabred
some marauders. The same day they cannonaded
the Orleans railway, between Ablon and Athis,
eight miles from Paris, and destroyed the station at
the latter place : after which they proceeded to cross
the Seine with fifty cannons. Lower down the river
still, nearer to Paris, others of the enemy's columns
encamped that night on the heights of Brunoy and
Villeneuve-St.-Georges, and at dawn the following
morning were observed constructing a bridge at the last
named place, where, as well as at Choisy-le-Roi, only
four miles from the enceinte and almost within range
of the guns of Fort Ivry, they crossed the river
throughout the day in swarms. Along their line of
march their advance had been practically unmolested.
Up to this moment Vinoy's corps of five and thirty
thousand men which escaped the disaster of Sedan had
not ventured to dispute a single road with the invader.
The barricades and other obstructions were not
defended ; and even behind the shattered bridges and
railway tunnels not a single man was posted. At
whatever point the Germans sought to cross the
Seine they encountered no impediment ; in no one
instance did they find their passage of the river on
a bridge of boats contested ; not a cannon, not a rifle
even opened fire upon them. They were thunder-

struck and puzzled by the tactics of the defence.
Like all the rest of the world they were ignorant at
that time that the Governor of Paris had a "plan"
on which he was relying.

" In the towns, villages, chateaux, and villas at a
distance of more than twenty miles from Paris,"
wrote Herr Wickede, " almost all who possessed
anything and were able had fled, but women, children, and men not in uniform were seen, though only
those of the lower classes.  The nearer we approach
the capital the more we perceive the traces of the
war.  All the houses in the streets were empty ; no
human being not belonging to our army was visible
for miles.  The flying French had repeatedly blown
up the bridges, dug up the streets, felled poplars on
both sides for barricades and obstructions, which they,
perhaps, had wished to defend.  These had been
erected in so strange a fashion, and the obstructions
were so easy of removal, that even their defence, had
it been attempted, which was never the case, would
have involved a useless sacrifice.  They showed how
the French are now carrying on the war, without any
method or central direction.  Although a few French
troops fight us with the greatest self-sacrifice, the
French on the whole, are waging the war in a
wretched style, and there can be no doubt that in no
long time we shall come out of this terrible struggle
as victors.  The picturesque Villeneuve-le-Roi was
totally forsaken, and in the other suburban villages
none but soldiers were visible, except here and there
a peasant who had been impressed with his waggon,
and who walked by his horse with bitter rancour, carefully watched by soldiers.  The troops had quartered
themselves in the splendid chateaux and elegant villas,
sleeping on luxurious couches, libraries serving as

stables, and the kitchen fire being fed by bearded soldiers with costly works of art or with orange trees. Fruit, grapes, potatoes, and vegetables were found in abundance; rice and coffee were supplied by the commissariat, and men and horses were in good condition, the fatiguing marches having ceased. Eggs, milk, cheese, and butter are unattainable. How the people will find subsistence on the departure of the troops in a region which will be as devoid of provisions as the desert of Sahara is a puzzle. Yet this circle of from twenty to five and twenty miles belongs to the richest and most luxuriant district in Europe. The whole region round Paris has become an immense camp of 250,000 men. In the immediate neighbourhood of Versailles one first remarked old women sitting before the houses, or saw in the street a small group of children at play. I was two whole days travelling without seeing a single female form, a child, a domestic animal not belonging to the army, or a man without a uniform, or who did not belong to the troops. And this is one of the most populous, active, and affluent districts in all Europe !"

Whilst all this was transpiring, and with the enemy almost at the gates, the *Journal Officiel* of September 16th announced that the elections to the Municipal Councils throughout France would be held in a fortnight's time, and a Constituent Assembly elected in three weeks, instead of at a later date, as had been originally determined on. The Government seemed to have a dim notion that Paris might possibly be invested before this time, in which case Nestor Crémieux, who was almost an octogenarian, might not be able to support the entire burden of governing provincial France, overrun, as it promised to be, by almost a million Germans, and what was even of more consequence, of rousing up the departments to come to the relief of Paris, they thereupon joined with him a septuagenarian deputy, and a sexagenarian admiral, MM. Glais-Bizoin and Fourichon, who left for Tours that evening.*

It was only on Saturday the 17th that the French

---

* Isaac Adolphe Crémieux, born of Jewish parents, at Nîmes, in 1796, and called to the bar in 1817, displayed much ability at the political trials on which he was subsequently engaged. In 1830, spite of his well-known liberal opinions, he did not hesitate to defend M. Guernon-Ranville, one of Charles X.'s ministers, whose acquittal however he failed in securing. During the reign of Louis Philippe, he defended several newspapers against proceedings brought by the Government, and on his election as deputy for Chinon in 1842, commenced a vigorous warfare against M. Guizot's ministry. At the revolution of 1848, although in favour of the regency of the Duchess of Orleans, he was induced to form part of the provisional government and to accept the post of Minister of Justice. He brought about the downfall of the Ministry shortly afterwards, by opposing in his capacity of Minister of Justice, the proceedings against Louis Blanc. Still continuing to act with the democratic Left, he nevertheless showed but little sympathy towards the Government of General Cavaignac, and was the only deputy of Indre-et-Loire who favoured the candidature of Louis Napoleon ; after whose election, however, he again became a member of the opposition, and one of its most vehement orators. At the *coup d'état* he was arrested and confined in Mazas, and when released resumed his profession as a barrister, until re-elected to the Chamber.

M. Glais-Bizoin, born at Quentin, in the Côtes-du-Nord, Brittany, in the year 1800, was called to the bar in 1822, and immediately joined in the struggle carried on by the liberal opposition against the Restoration. After the revolution of July, 1830, he became a member of the Chamber of Deputies for Loudeac, and sat with the Extreme Left, a perpetual thorn in the side of the Government. He took an active part in the affair of the Reform banquet, and signed the act of accusation presented by M. Odillon Barrot, against the Guizot ministry. Upon the proclamation of military authorities seemed to recover from their stupor, when General Vinoy crossed the Marne just before noon, at Charenton, with several regiments of infantry, a battalion of chasseurs and a battery of mitrailleuses, and advanced in front of Mesly, where he encountered the enemy posted as usual in the woods on the high ground, and who received him with a sharp fusillade, followed by discharges of artillery, to which he replied with his mitrailleuses, sending some superior officers scampering off in various directions. After half an hour of this work, suspecting the enemy's batteries to be established in fixed positions, and perceiving the adjacent woods to be bristling with motionless bayonets and cavalry concealed there remaining perfectly still, the general withdrew his troops into Paris, which he reached before dusk. At the same time this engagement was going forward, a party of some forty uhlans, posted along the banks of the Seine in front of Choisy-le-

---

the Republic he was chosen one of the representatives for the Côtes-du-Nord, and always voted with the party of the Extreme Left. After the elevation of Louis Napoleon to the Presidency of the Republic he violently combated the policy of the Elysée. Subsequently he retired into private life, but in the 1863 elections was again returned by the Côtes-du-Nord, and was chosen deputy for Paris in 1869. The vivacity of his attacks against the Imperial Government generally caused his voice to be drowned by the members of the Right, whenever he rose to speak.

Vice-Admiral Fourichon, born in 1809, had attained the rank of captain in 1848, when he was appointed Governor of the penal colony, Cayenne. His unobjectionable fulfilment of the duties of this function, has been a standing reproach against him in the eyes of the extreme democratic party. His naval services appear to have been limited to commanding at several European naval stations, and at one period he filled the post of director of the navy in Algiers.

Roi, fired upon a railway train and compelled it to beat a rapid retreat.

The second secretary of the British Embassy, who had been on a mysterious mission to the Prussian head-quarters, returned to Paris on the morning of the 17th, and in the afternoon the *Patrie* assured its readers that an interview was almost certain to take place between M. Jules Favre and Count Bismarck. Having brought matters to this point, Lord Lyons, in spite of his "cordial" letter to M. Jules Favre a couple of days since, ordered his portmanteau to be packed up, and with the Ambassadors of Russia and Austria, and the personnel of the British Embassy, quitted Paris for Tours that very evening by the circuitous route of the Chemin de fer de l'Ouest, the only line on which trains were running outside the walls ; considerately, however, leaving behind him an amiable though unenergetic secretary of legation, and the ornamental rather than useful military and naval attachés,* to attend to the interests of some two or three thousand British subjects remaining in Paris. The consul, Mr. Falconer Atlee, who of all functionaries was bound to remain at his post at such a juncture, had prudently withdrawn aux eaux some three weeks previously, at the first intimation of the possibility of Paris being called upon to sustain a siege.

At this moment the German columns were advancing to their posts round the doomed city, every regiment

---

* Colonel Claremont, the military attaché, appears to have told the "Besieged Resident" that he had no intention of going outside the ramparts. Under these circumstances, as he quitted Paris before the bombardment commenced, his report on the siege, none of the military operations of which he could have seen, will be invested with a value peculiarly its own.

taking up its appointed place with the same facility, as if merely moving from Berlin to Potsdam rather than operating before an enemy's capital. The intrepid uhlans who had first set foot on the left bank of the Seine, "spread themselves out," says Mr. Michell,* "according to their custom, in small scattered companies, and made their way rapidly and methodically from point to point. Threading their way, by the aid of their wonderful campaigning maps, without mistake or hesitation, they had pushed on before evening half-way upon the journey to Versailles. The by-paths and cross-country roads seemed as well known to them—perhaps often better known—than to the peasant natives of the place. Skirting the line of southern forts, so as to be out of range of their guns and mitrailleuses, they reconnoitred all the country for a mile or so on each side of the highroad leading from Choisy-le-Roi to Versailles. Not a soldier, not a solitary franc-tireur, to dispute their way: it was a pretty autumn ride through the glades and bridle-paths.

" Meanwhile the main body, their way thus prepared and guarded in advance, made the passage of the river leisurely. Descending in dense battalions upon Choisy and Villeneuve, they prepared to cross the last barrier that separated them from the provinces of western France. The bridges were all destroyed: was the passage then to be disputed? Not a bit of it : they were left to throw across their pontoon bridges thoroughly and completely at their ease. Four or five hours, and the close continuous stream of soldiers began to pass from bank to bank. For days that stream flowed on almost in uninterrupted line of march. Slowly, like

---

* Siege Life in Paris, p. 6.

a migration of black ants, passed on the columns of the infantry, along the broad avenue beneath the grand old trees. Little did the great Louis think, when he laid down that splendid road, and for the first time rode along it with his gay court and gorgeous equipages, that a time would come when the Goths of Prussia should ride along it unchallenged and un-hurt, to plant their hostile banners in the demesne of France. But Versailles is no longer royal; and French loyalty is dead. To their Most Christian Majesties have succeeded Committees of National Defence.

"While the legions continued their Sabbath-day's journey through Thiais and Chevilly towards Versailles, the éclaireurs pushed on their willing horses through the beautiful woods of Meudon and Verrières. On all sides of them were straggling coverts, made as if by nature for an ambuscade. The woods disposed themselves, as if out of pure love for France, as natural fortresses and barricades. Mutely they seemed to invite—almost to ask for—their proper garrisons of francs-tireurs. At every turn the uhlans expected a volley to salute them from some thicket on one side. But not a shot—not an opponent to encounter. The pheasants fluttered up before the horses' hoofs; the hares raced away before them down the forest glades. These were the only living things that crossed their path. On they went, silently, swiftly, and fearlessly, into the royal town of Versailles."

## II.

## THE DEFENCES.

———

### I. FIRE, AXE, PICK, SPADE, AND TROWEL.

WITH her armies overthrown or beleaguered and her
capital menaced, and abandoned in the hour of her dire
distress by every European power—even by Italy, on
whom she had an ineffaceable claim—France, or rather
so much of her as was represented by Paris, which is
the heart of the nation, offered a picture of courage
and resolution which no reverses seemed to damp.
Admitting that she still continued a prey to illusions,
and again took to singing "Aux armes, citoyens! formez
vos bataillons! marchons jusqu'à Berlin ; égorger les
Prussiens!" and to talking bombastically of compelling
the enemy by means of a levée en masse, that vaunted
panacea for all disasters, to evacuate the national soil,
it was nevertheless impossible for painful sacrifices to
have been more cheerfully made, or for greater earnest-
ness to have been shown than was displayed by the
Parisians, with regard to the defence of the capital.
Trade became utterly at a standstill, as something
like three hundred thousand men were taken from
their usual avocations to be transformd into soldiers.

The sacrifice of property too was enormous.   The
houses demolished within the zone of the fire of the
detached forts and of the enceinte, and the inhabitants
of which had been enjoined to evacuate them by an

order of General Trochu, dated the 8th of September, might be counted by thousands—not merely complete streets, but entire villages were destroyed, besides a considerable number of isolated factories and piles of warehouses. Capital and labour will soon replace these after the peace, but neither capital nor labour will readily replace the magnificent trees forming the grand avenues leading out of Paris to Asnières, Neuilly, St. Cloud, Sèvres, Versailles, Sceaux, Fontainebleau, Choisy, Vincennes, and Bondy, which had to be sacrificed to the exigencies of the defence. In the Bois de Boulogne, the foliage of which almost brushed the ramparts, and the Bois de Vincennes, trees moreover were felled by the acre, while the more distant woods of Bondy, Fontenoy, Meudon, Clamart, Bellevue, Verrières, St. Cloud, and Montmorency were given up to the flames; and wherever fire failed to do its work, the axe was brought into requisition to effect enormous openings. On September 10th, General Trochu issued a decree announcing that inasmuch as the forests, woods, and plantations which surround Paris at all points of its circumference afford the enemy a cover, of which he will undoubtedly avail himself, to mask the movements of his armies, to arrive under shelter within range of the fortifications, and to manufacture fascines and gabions for the siege of the capital, all those woods which may be injurious to the defence of the city would be burnt down on the approach of the enemy. Proper precautions would be taken to isolate towns, villages, hamlets, and homesteads from the ravages of the fire, and the inflammable material requisite for causing such masses of green wood to ignite would be collected and transported to the spot with every precaution. The fosses of the fortifications, moreover, were to be supplied with faggots and brushwood, steeped in inflammable material, and which were to be fired when the occasion demanded it.

This last announcement was highly approved by the *Opinion Nationale.* " Since scientific barbarism," it remarked, " is being hurled against us, it is the task of civilized science to defend us." The labour of destroying these woods was confided to bands of francs-tireurs and Gardes Mobiles, who, under the direction of the military engineers appointed to superintend the work, applied first petroleum and then lighted torches to the more pleasant suburban promenades and holiday haunts of the Parisians. But nature, we are told, revolted at the sacrifice of these sylvan glades. However this may be, it is quite certain that at the outset, in spite of the desperate attempts which were made, hardly any quantity of petroleum sufficed to coax the trees to ignite and consume, owing possibly to the amount of rain that had recently fallen, and to the trees being still full of sap. Subsequent efforts proved, however, more successful, and for days huge fires might be discerned blazing in the broad sunshine in every direction ; the vast masses of flame and dense clouds of smoke cutting sharply against the clear blue sky, while at night-time the heavens were illumined with a ruddy glow, arising from the reflection of one or more of these suburban conflagrations. Besides the sylvan girdle encircling Paris, ricks of hay and straw and acres of standing crops, which the owners, through want of assistance— every one being engaged with the harvest at the same moment—had failed to gather in, were set fire to to prevent them from falling into the hands of the enemy, who, from this circumstance, was obliged to impose heavier requisitions on the inhabitants of

the towns and villages surrounding Paris than otherwise need have been levied.

It was the knowledge of the defeats which French
arms had sustained at Weissenbourg and Wörth that
first threw Paris into a state of consternation, silenced
the vain boasting of the boulevards, and aroused the
Parisians to a sense of their own immediate danger.
During the few hours of office that remained to the
Ollivier Ministry, hurried steps were taken with regard
to provisioning the capital and placing the fortifications in an efficient state of defence, and ere long
twelve thousand excavators were at work day and
night—the electric light illumining the scene of their
labours whenever necessary—digging out the platforms and embrasures of the detached forts, and carrying the fosse across the sixty-nine roads leading into
Paris.   Masons were simultaneously set to work to
block up the subordinate entries, and contract the
width of the remainder by building stone piers to
which the huge drawbridges were to be hung, and
raising massive stone walls with loopholes in the
intervening space between them and the flanks of the
bastions.   Platforms for the guns, together with
embrasures for the cannon to point through, had then
to be dug out on the green turf of the ramparts, and
vast spaces excavated for the construction of casemates ; next, traverses were thrown up to protect
guns and gunners from a cross fire, redoubts were
formed to shield alike sentinels and artillerymen,
and bomb-proof places of refuge were burrowed out
for the men off duty.

But these were not the only excavations made outside and inside the ramparts ; rifle-pits were dug
around the detached forts, and breastworks thrown
up to connect in some degree the latter.   The road-

ways of the broader thoroughfares into Paris were
mined, and the footpaths honeycombed for several
hundred yards with deep octangular-shaped holes, a
yard in diameter, at the bottom of which short stakes
were thrust with their sharp points upwards, just as
though the Prussians were so many wild animals
likely to blunder in the dark into these convenient pitfalls. In advance of the drawbridges a species of
tête du pont, an extensive angular-shaped earthwork
with covered way, and shut in with stockades in the
rear, was thrown out some couple of hundred feet in
advance of the bastioned enceinte, and the sloping
sides of which were covered with planks, studded with
tens of thousands of tenpenny nails, points upwards,
and almost as close together as quills on a porcupine's
back, and intersected moreover with stout invisible wire
designed to trip up intruders, and bring them on their
knuckles, knees, and noses unawares. As though,
however, with the humane view of keeping their
antagonists off this Tom Tiddler's ground, where far
more bullets and bombs were likely to be picked up
than gold and silver, in advance of it was a most
menacing chevaux-de-frise, formed of huge branches of
trees, which thrust forward their thousand-and-one
spiculated arms, as though each were a Briareus lying
perdu, mutely signifying to the advancing Prussians,
" Thus far shalt thou advance, but no further."

Within the ramparts and immediately opposite the
drawbridges, the golden-tipped iron railings which
used to form the city barriers were cased with sheet
iron pierced with loopholes for musketry, and forming a veritable armour-plated barricade. Occasionally
in its rear a stone barricade crowned with sand-bags and
having apertures for chassepots would be constructed.
But this was not all. Supposing the luckless Prussian

to have triumphed over the countless impediments which beset his path from the moment he entered the French lines, to have carried the barricades at the outposts, evaded the advance redoubts, slipped past the rifle-pits, eluded the big naval guns of the detached forts, the miles of mined thoroughfares, the thousands of pitfalls and other man-traps which Parisian ingenuity had prepared for him, to have escaped the cannon balls of the enceinte, shunned the many-armed chevaux-de-frise, the incline sown liberally with ten-penny nails, and the invisible wires—to have leapt the tall stockades, crossed the moat with its blazing petroleum, passed the drawbridge flanked with loopholes, through each of which a chassepot is pointed, the armour-plated barricade with more chassepots, the stone barricades with chassepots again, the chances are that he would find himself assailed with cannon shot from a stone redoubt at the upper end of the avenue, which at Port Maillot was a veritable cul-de-sac, all the outlets being blocked up, and every dead wall, on both sides of the road, being loopholed, whence more chassepots might direct their murderous fire upon him. Perhaps the most formidable labour of all that devolved on the Parisians was the levelling and clearing away of the trees, houses, outbuildings, walls, fences—every mortal obstacle, in fact, within the limit of 800 feet from the guns of the ramparts and also within a certain range of the detached forts—that the precision of their fire might not be interfered with, and the enemy might be deprived of every kind of cover. In certain districts beyond these limits, the upper stories were removed from entire streets of houses to admit of the guns firing over them. Before the fortifications were constructed, handsome houses, villas, and other erections already lined the sides of the principal avenues leading

out of Paris, and more recently thousands of buildings
had sprung up almost within the shadow of the ramparts—just as in the Middle Ages the houses of the
bourgeoisie and the hovels of the peasants used to
nestle under some lordly castle's walls—although the
law expressly provided that no compensation was to be
accorded for any building erected within the military
zone since the 1st of February, 1841, in the event of
its destruction being determined on should Paris be
menaced by a foreign enemy; so little did the too confident Parisian propriétaire dream of the possibility of
Paris ever being called upon to submit to a siege. The
lofty mansions, the miniature chateaux, the charming
villas, the coquettish maisonnettes of the aristocratic
Avenues de Neuilly and des Ternes, and other
fashionable thoroughfares westward of Paris, were
given up to the pick of the demolisher quite as in-
exorably as the dingy factories and warehouses, the
gloomy houses, and the miserable guinguettes, with
their so-called jardins et bosquets in the Grenelle,
Montrouge, Gentilly, and La Villette districts.

While this seemingly endless task of destruction
was in progress and a wide circuit around the walls was
being converted into a desolate waste, and the green
turf of the glacis, with the outlying gardens, fields,
and hedgerows were smothered with fine white dust
arising from the powdered mortar, crowds of well-
dressed people daily assembled to watch the demolishers
at work; poverty-stricken women and children
gathered up for firing such scraps of wood as had
not been carted away, and chiffonniers turned over
the rubbish heaps with their hooks in search of bits of
old metal and rusty nails. As fire was called into
requisition to consume the woods and standing crops
in the environs of Paris, so was it had recourse to to

destroy the fences, palings, sheds, and other rickety
constructions which lined many of the waysides.*

## II. THE ENCEINTE AND THE DETACHED FORTS.

If the advance of the German legions on Paris was
scarcely retarded by the blowing up of bridges and
tunnels, the digging of trenches, the felling of trees,
the piling of barricades, the burning of woods, and
the devastating of the environs generally, the defences
of the city at any rate brought the enemy to bay.
Paris, as every one knows, is indebted for its fortifi-

---

* A report issued by the Government of National Defence a few
weeks after the investment, thus sums up the defensive works
executed in advance of the enceinte under its auspices.

The military zone was cleared; the Bois de Boulogne and
Vincennes were partly cut down, and the approaches to the forts
were provided with palisades, on a line nearly 33 miles in extent.
At the same time it was found necessary to bar the four canals and
place stockades in the Seine.

To close the 69 gateways and establish drawbridges, upwards of
11,000 workmen were employed. That portion of the enceinte
near Point-du-Jour, which appeared exposed to the fire of the
enemy, has become by means of works executed in front of the
village of Billancourt, and by entrenchments erected inside, one of
the strongest points of the defence.

These works were completed by the exploration of numerous
quarries, which by certain prudent dispositions combined with a
vigilant surveillance are protected against any attempt of the
enemy; by mining the sewers of Boulogne, Billancourt, Neuilly,
Clichy, etc.; by the erection of electrical apparatus of great power
in the forts, and by a system of military observatories; by the construction of dams destined to maintain the level of the river within
the walls, so as to assure the circulation of the armour-plated gunboats, and the full action of the water-works of Chaillot; and lastly,
by occupying in force the villages adjacent to the ramparts.
From Vitry to Issy, on the one side; between St. Denis and the
canal de l'Ourcq, in another direction, the houses have been
loopholed and the streets barricaded.

cations to M. Thiers. After the revolution of July, 1830, the question of fortifying Paris began to be agitated, and three years subsequently Marshal Soult asked from the Chamber of Deputies a first credit of thirty-five millions of francs, for surrounding Paris with permanent defensive works; but the project being disapproved of on technical grounds by various military authorities, had to be withdrawn, and for seven years the question remained in abeyance.

In 1840, at a period when France found herself at issue with the principal powers of Europe on the Eastern question, and was in dread of a new coalition being formed against her, M. Thiers profited by the occasion to revive the proposal for fortifying Paris; and eventually, after considerable discussion, a law was passed authorizing the construction of an enceinte, flanked by sixteen detached forts, together with a certain number of redoubts. And these works, commenced in 1841, were completed within three years, at a cost of one hundred and forty millions of francs.

The enceinte continue, or fortified wall, which encircles Paris, is an irregular pentagon in form, upwards of twenty miles in circumference, its five sides, which are of unequal length, having ninety-five bastioned fronts, sixty-eight of which are on the Tuileries side of the Seine, and twenty-seven on the left bank. Fifty-nine of these bastions are constructed after an uniform type, that is, with four sides of unequal length—namely, two faces and two flanks, the former, which are longer than the latter, meeting at the centre of the bastion, where they form a more or less acute angle, technically known as the salient. There being no demi-lunes between the bastions, the fronts consequently have no cross fire. The revet-

ment of the scarp—as the wall facing the steep side
of the rampart on which the parapet stands, and where
the guns are mounted, is called—is thirty-two feet in
height, and is but partially covered by the glacis.
Behind the facing of millstone, built in courses of
from eight to ten inches, is a mass of rubble masonry,
giving to the wall an average thickness of upwards of
twelve feet. The fosse is forty-eight feet wide, and
its outer boundary, on the side facing the enemy,
known as the counterscarp, is not only not revetted,
as is commonly the case with permanent fortifications,
so as to render descent into the ditch difficult, but its
slope has no more acute angle than forty-five degrees.
The fosse had been carried across all the roads conducting to the city, the principal of these thoroughfares being provided with massive drawbridges, while
the subordinate ones were permanently closed with
solid masonry loopholed at given distances. In advance of these drawbridges demi-lunes with covered
ways and combining all the paraphernalia of stockades,
chevaux-de-frise, piéges-à-loups, mines, &c., had been
constructed. The ramparts were continued to the
banks of the Seine, which in their turn were defended
by a series of advanced earthworks, stone redoubts,
loopholed walls, and palisades, while the passage of the
river, barred with piles and booms alike at Auteuil and
Bercy, was placed under the protection of a flotilla of
gunboats and armour-plated floating batteries.* In
addition the Chemin de fer du Ceinture encircling Paris
immediately in the rear of the ramparts, was capable

---

* According to the report already cited, very few of the cannons
with which the enceinte was to be armed were in position on
September 4th. On the ramparts as in the forts, everything, it
is said, was wanting. Traverses and shelter places, with seventy

of being turned largely to the advantage of the defence by facilitating the accumulation not only of men, but of heavy warlike material, on particular portions of the works which might be subjected to attack.

At the epoch of the siege, the bastions of the enceinte were grouped so as to form nine sections, each of which, under the command of either a general or an admiral, had its own distinctive character. Thus the first section comprehended Bercy and Reuilly, the former a special district with its port, its immense wine and spirit stores, and its population of coopers, tasters, merchants, clerks, and carters. The second section comprised Charonne, noted for its market-gardens and orchards, and, above all, for the cemetery of Père La Chaise, Menilmontant and Belleville ; the latter the principal site of the so-called battle of Paris, fought on March 30, 1814, and of late years inhabited almost exclusively by the surplus working population of the capital, driven from the crowded quarters of the city by Baron Haussmann's improvements, and credited with strong bellicose propensities. Belleville is joined to La Villette by the lofty Buttes Chaumont, formerly an extensive waste, but of late years transformed into an ornamental park for the recreation of the neighbouring population, and having adjacent to it the famed Carrières d'Amérique, the scene of many a melodrama of misery and crime, and whose constantly burning limekilns render them the habitual resort of Parisian vagabondage during the long cold nights of winter. Section three included La Villette and La Chapelle,

---

vaulted magazines to store away powder and warlike material, had to be constructed, in addition to which the parapet was crowned with two millions of sandbags.

manufacturing suburbs, inhabited exclusively by the labouring classes, and the former being noted for its vast cattle-market and slaughter-houses and its immense warehouses bordering the Canal de l'Ourcq. Section four embraced Montmartre, with its steep winding streets and its redoubtable Butte dominating the city, and keeping guard over the adjacent plain of St. Denis, and whose inhabitants on the side nighest to the centre of Paris, together with those of Batignolles, which also forms part of the same section, are principally composed of small employés, rentiers, and shopkeepers, while its outskirts are occupied exclusively by the labouring classes. Section five comprised the quarter of the Ternes, which links by degrees the bourgeoisie of Batignolles to the grand monde of the Place de l'Etoile and the Champs Elysées. The sixth section included Passy, Auteuil, and Point du Jour, abounding in pleasant villas encompassed by delightful gardens, and long since favourite places of resort with well-to-do men of letters, artists, and savants. The seventh section embraced Grenelle and Vaugirard, the first redolent of nauseous odours arising from its numerous chemical works and infectious manufactories, and noted for its metal foundries and rag-warehouses, around which the chiffonniers muster in force. Section eight included Plaisance—a name apparently ironically bestowed on a locality where few of the streets are paved or lighted, and sewers are unknown—with Petit Montrouge, another refuge of that working population forced to retreat in face of the improvements effected in various parts of the capital. The ninth and last section, including the district of the Maison Blanche and extending to the Seine, comprised certainly one of the most miserable quarters of Paris, where poverty exists under peculiarly harrowing aspects, and families crouch in cellars or hovels open to the elements, and the chiffonnier revels in drunken dissipation in his so-called Cité Doré.

The distance of the detached forts from the enceinte varies from about a couple of thousand yards to more than three miles. On the north-east and south sides the city is encompassed by a complete chain of forts, the intervals between which are invariably within the range of rifled guns, enabling them to support each other by their artillery fire.* The extreme area of the space contained within the chain measures about twelve and a half miles from east to west, and ten miles from north to south, with an approximate circumference of five and thirty miles. The advanced works subsequently thrown up in front of several of these forts enlarged the circumference to between forty and fifty miles. A strategical road runs round and connects them all, and telegraphic communication moreover was established between the different forts as well as between these and the capital.

------------

* Subjoined are the exact distances of the various detached forts from the enceinte and the distances of the forts and of the principal redoubts from each other. Distant from the enceinte in English yards:—La Briche 5574, La Double Couronne 5465, L'Est 3828, Aubervilliers 2078, Romainville 1585, Noisy 3280, Rosny 5082, Nogent 5356, Vincennes 2296, Charenton 3607, Ivry 2732, Bicêtre 1640, Montrouge 1694, Vanves 2296, Issy 2405, Mont Valérien 4372.

Distant from each other in English yards:—La Briche and La Double Couronne 984, La Double Couronne and L'Est 1641, L'Est and Aubervilliers 3172, Aubervilliers and Romainville 3062, Romainville and Noisy 1859, Noisy and Rosny 2406, Rosny and Nogent 2844, Nogent and La Faisanderie 2515, La Faisanderie and La Gravelle 766, La Gravelle and Charenton 1969, Charenton and Ivry 2625, Ivry and Bicêtre 2406, Bicêtre and Montrouge 2297, Montrouge and Vanves 2242, Vanves and Issy 1531, Issy and Mont Valérien 7655, Mont Valérien and Gennevilliers 9187, Gennevilliers and La Briche 1312.

The stream of the Seine issues through the main ramparts of Paris at the south-western corner, and soon bending northwards, covers the whole west of the city, including the Bois de Boulogne, running in fact almost parallel with the fortifications, about a mile and a half from them, until it reaches the north. Here it turns still more northwards and, at about four miles' distance from the ramparts, washes the suburb of St. Denis, with its famous cathedral, the sarcophagus of the kings of France, wherein so much of the ashes of the Merovingian, Carlovingian, and Capetian dynasties, including the branches of Valois and Bourbon, as were rescued from the Cimetière des Valois at the Restoration, are interred. The Seine, which here forms a wide loop, subsequently winds in a south-westerly direction, and runs nearly parallel to its former course, but this time about four and a half miles from it. By its means a water defence is formed to the entire west of Paris, and only one fort, that of Mont Valérien, is placed on this side of the city.

The three forts grouped around the town of St. Denis, situated at the point of the loop made by the Seine mentioned above, form the most northerly defence of Paris. A portion of the town itself is fortified, while to the east of it, and actually touching the Seine, stands the Fort de la Briche, which covers the branch of the Northern railway to Pontoise. Due north of St. Denis, and about two-thirds of a mile from it, on the opposite side of the Creil branch of the Northern railway, is the Double Couronne du Nord, within the walls of which all the roads from the north, north-east, and north-west leading to the suburban town, and through it to Paris, meet. The Fort de l'Est lies to the south-east of St. Denis, and is a regular bastioned square, while about a mile and three-quarters further to the south-east is the Fort d'Aubervilliers, an irregular bastioned pentagon which rests upon the main road to Lille, and closes it against an enemy. Within these forts runs the canal of St. Denis, having three redoubts established on its banks in rear of the intervals between the forts in question.

So far the defences of Paris are situated in a plain, which is, moreover, commanded by the lofty Buttes Montmartre and Chaumont, comprised within the enceinte, and where as well as at St. Ouen, equidistant from the forts of St. Denis and the ramparts, batteries of huge naval guns were established during the siege. South of Fort d'Aubervilliers and the Ourcq Canal, however, there commences a plateau which extending beyond Vincennes covers all the east of Paris. If an enemy succeeded in establishing his guns upon the plateau he would be able to command the city and its ramparts, but fortunately for the defence the plateau slopes steeply down on its side furthest from Paris, and several works had been constructed at the summit of the slopes. The first of these is the Fort de Rômainville, dominating the pleasant village of that name with its little wood, the paradise of Parisian grisettes in years gone by and the favourite resort of Paul de Kock's lovers—a bastioned square with advanced outworks, composed of a series of entrenchments and a couple of redoubts, extending to the road from Paris to Metz and the Ourcq Canal. The artillery fire of the fort and its outworks commands all the plain as far as the Fort d'Aubervilliers, and helps to cover the north-east angle of the Parisian system of defence where it was possibly the weakest. Next in order, on the plateau mentioned, are the forts of Noisy, Rosny,

and Nogent, bastioned squares with outworks. The
fort of Noisy, as well as that of Romainville, covers
with its fire the Ourcq Canal and the Eastern Railway, while Rosny, in advance of the villages of Bagnolet and Montreuil, noted for their fruits, and especially
famed for their peaches, protects the Mulhouse branch
of the same line, and commands a spur of the plateau
running in an easterly direction, which would otherwise be occupied by an enemy. The fort of Nogent,
which is nearly south of the fort of Rosny, and
distant about two miles and a half from it, also commands the railway to Mulhouse, as well as the roads
from Paris to Coulommiers and to Provins; besides
which, it covers the River Marne. Moreover, the
intervals between the forts on the plateau are not left
vacant. Between Romainville and Noisy is the
redoubt of Noisy, and between the fort of Noisy
and that of Rosny are the redoubts of Montreuil and
of La Boissière, while the redoubt of Fontenay has
been constructed between Forts Rosny and Nogent.
A road on the summit of the plateau passes behind
the forts and redoubts, and keeps up their communication. Altogether this group of works on the
plateau constituted a very formidable defence, indicating that any enemy who came to attack Paris
was to be expected from the Rhine, but at the same
time rendering it improbable that the city would ever
be seriously assailed between the Marne and the Ourcq
Canal.

The next regular fort, that of Charenton, in advance
of the village of that name, noted for its immense
lunatic asylum, is nearly four and a half miles from
Nogent, and is larger than most of those already mentioned. It is also a bastioned pentagon, and stands
within the angle formed by the junction of the Seine

and the Marne, at no great distance from the celebrated Veterinary School of Alfort. The long interval
between Charenton and Nogent is covered in front
by a salient loop of the Marne, which is here 100
paces in breadth, and forms of itself a natural defence, fortified moreover by an intrenchment 2800 feet
in length, consisting of a parapet and ditches covering
the isthmus of St. Maur, where a bridge crosses the
Marne. The two extremities of the intrenchment are
flanked by the redoubts of La Faisanderie and La Gravelle, close to the former of which runs the suburban
railway to La Varenne. All these works enclose in a
semicircle the feudal Château de Vincennes, skirting
the famous wood of that name, and which flanking
alike the forts and the south-east angle of the enceinte,
has within it the principal arsenal of Paris, on the edge
of the great field for manœuvring artillery close to the
Marne. The Lyons railway-bridge, as well as the
bridge across the Marne leading to the Lyons road, are
close behind Fort Charenton, and are both covered by
the fire from the main ramparts of Paris and the
Château de Vincennes.

We now come to the left bank of the Seine, which
enters Paris at the south-east corner, and encounter
the southern defences of the city. The first is the fort
of Ivry, another bastioned pentagon, little more than
a mile and a half from Charenton, and commanding
the Lyons railway and road, with the passages of the
Seine and Marne, and occupying a plateau between
Ivry, the country retreat mostly of chiffonniers and dé-
bardeurs, and Vitry, at no great distance from the
railway to Orleans, which it also protects. The next
fort is that of Bicêtre, which is also a bastioned pentagon situated upon a plateau. Placed within a mile
of the enceinte, between Gentilly and Villejuif, and near

to the historical madhouse of Bicêtre, which occupies
the site of an ancient château of one of our bishops of
Winchester, this fort covers the short line of railway
to Orsay and the road to Fontainebleau, and is,
together with the fort of Ivry, just mentioned, situated
on the peninsula formed by the Seine and the Bièvre
brook. On the opposite side of the Orsay railroad,
and in close proximity to it and the road to Toulouse,
is Fort Montrouge, a bastioned square, nigh to the
Bièvre valley and in advance of innumerable abandoned quarries, in whose dark depths the artificial cul-
tivation of mushrooms goes on upon an immense scale.
Next comes the fort of Vanves, an irregular bastioned quadrangular work protecting the Chevreuse
road and the Versailles railway; and lastly, the fort
of Issy, a bastioned pentagon close to the western
slopes of the plateau, also commanding the Versailles
railway and the road to Versailles, and near to the
Seine at its first bend after issuing from Paris. The
villages of Vanves and Issy, after which these forts
are named, are two miserable suburbs, the first inhabited principally by laundrymen ; the other plea-
santly enough situated and noted for its handsome
château and park, formerly one of the most charming residences in the environs of Paris, and of late
years transformed into a hydropathic establishment.

The five forts just mentioned, on the left bank of
the Seine, are not so fortunate as those protecting the
east of Paris ; for the plateau on which they are
situated extends southwards to a considerable distance,
and includes elevations which actually command them.
The forts of Vanves and Issy, which since the intro-
duction of rifled cannon are more particularly exposed
to attack from these heights, are both weak of
their kind, their bastions being small and cramped

and having no demi-lunes between them. To protect them an earthwork was constructed on the plateau of Chatillon, 250 feet above the level of the ground on which these forts are erected, and rather more than a mile in advance of them. Redoubts were moreover thrown up at Hautes-Bruyères and the Moulin Saquet, in advance of the forts of Montrouge and Bicêtre.

Parenthetically mention may here be made that six of these detached forts—namely, Romainville, Noisy, Rosny, Ivry, Bicêtre, and Montrouge—were garrisoned by the sailors, who had been summoned up to Paris to assist in its defence. On being installed there they found not only numerous supplementary works, such as screens in front of the entrances, traverses in the bastions, and reducts in the courtyards had to be executed, but that after years of neglect extensive repairs were requisite to place the existing works in a state of efficiency. Embrasures too had to be opened and platforms constructed for the guns, the stands of which, moreover, had to be mounted. The requisite fascines and gabions had also to be made and miles of palisades erected; all was nevertheless accomplished with rapidity and precision. Once installed inside the fort the sailors looked upon it as their ship, and hastened to make all taut. In about a couple of weeks, and long before the other forts were in a perfect state, the transformation of those in charge of the sailors was complete. At Fort Bicêtre they met with unexpected auxiliaries in the aged savant Dr. Milne Edwards, and his corps of sixty volunteers belonging to the Museum and the College of France. Officers and men were appointed to their respective bastions as to the batteries of a ship; and it was curious to note the points of variety which they presented: in some everything was rigidly confined to the purely useful;

in others certain sacrifices were made to the agreeable.
Here each one had his special observatory, there beds
of flowers figured among the cannon. And yet with
all this not a single duty was neglected; whilst one
half of the men were working, the other half were
going through their manœuvres; and at dusk one saw
the sailors employed on the exterior works, regaining
the forts in bands, neither club nor cabaret having
power to turn them aside. As the men were, so
were their commanders, one of whom issued this
laconic proclamation to the garrison under his orders
when the Germans first made their appearance: "My
lads, here one does not surrender, but blows up!"

With regard to the western side of Paris, the
whole of it, from Issy on the south, to St. Denis
on the north, is protected by the first return of the
Seine, and within the peninsula formed by the second
bend of the river, and nearly due west of the centre of
Paris, is the large bastioned pentagon, the fortress or
citadel of Mont Valérien. In close proximity to the
railway to St. Cloud, it rises in solitary grandeur
above the plain, dotted over with the pleasant villages
of Suresne, Rueil, and Nanterre—the latter renowned for its rosière—as if scorning all aid from
its smaller neighbours and impregnable in its own
strength. The designers of the fortifications of Paris
appear to have considered that the reach of the Seine,
extending from St. Denis to Sèvres, would suffice
as an exterior line of defence for the portion of
the enceinte which it covered; for while guarding the remainder of the enceinte with a cordon
of forts each within gunshot of its neighbours on
either side, they only placed the single fort of Mont
Valérien on the fourteen miles of enceinte defended
by the Seine, which here forms in fact a gigantic wet

ditch, covering that portion of the ramparts at an average distance of eleven furlongs, and which could be nowhere crossed by an enemy out of easy range of the guns. Possibly it may have been contemplated that the defenders of the city should be assisted by a field force encamped to the westward between Versailles and St. Germain, and having a part to play similar to that of the Russian army during the siege of Sebastopol. The duty of such a force would be to hold itself ready to strike a blow at any convenient moment at the siege works of the enemy, or to operate against his communications. It would have the advantage of moving upon interior lines, and if attacked might always seek refuge within the zone of forts. Should an enemy oppose to it an overwhelming body of troops, some of its divisions might be transported rapidly by means of the Chemin de fer du Ceinture, to attack any point wherever the besieger had especially weakened himself. As the French, however, could command no such army as this, it was sought to fill up the gap existing in the exterior cordon of forts between Issy and Mont Valérien, by the construction of four important redoubts, one at the Château of Meudon, others at Brimborion and Les Bruyères, near Sèvres, and the fourth at Montretout, north of St. Cloud, the whole intended to sweep the heights and valleys which the fire of Mont Valérien could not attain, and where the enemy concealed in the unburnt woods afterwards fortified himself at leisure. To protect the city on the northwestern side, between Mont Valérien and the forts of St. Denis, several redoubts were constructed in the plain of Gennevilliers, and a battery established at St. Ouen, on the right bank of the Seine, a mile or so south-west of St. Denis.

The forts themselves were evidently planned not so much with the view to a passive as to an active defence. The garrison of Paris was expected to come out into the open, to use the forts as supporting points for its flanks, and by constant sallies on a large scale to render impossible a regular siege of any two or three of these works. Thus whilst the forts protected the garrison from a too near approach of the enemy, the garrison would have to protect the forts from siege batteries, and constantly to destroy the besiegers' works. The defences of Paris possess the same advantage as those of Mayence, inasmuch as they cover the junction of two rivers—the Seine and the Marne—which necessitates the separation of the besieging force into three distinct parts, so as to watch three several fields of action, any one of which it is at the option of the garrison to select for a sortie in force. Moreover, to assault the city either on the east or west the besieging army would have to cross rivers, the passage of which is defended by one or other of the detached forts; the angle formed by the junction of the Seine and the Marne is also a wide one, and these rivers defend quite one-half of the eastern side of Paris, while the loops of the Seine, as already remarked, cover the city effectually on the west.

### III. THE ARMAMENT.

Fortunately for the defence of Paris, prior to the investment, the Government was able to get up by railway a considerable number of naval guns from Toulon, Cherbourg, Brest, and Lorient, as well as additional field-pieces from the provincial arsenals, with which to arm the detached forts and redoubts and the bastions of the enceinte. The naval guns, which were principally placed in the former, were chiefly cast-iron breech-loaders, cast hollow, and strengthened with steel hoops, and were capable of throwing projectiles of great power; moreover, their breech mechanism was generally admitted to be the simplest and strongest known.

These cannon were originally deposited at the Palais de l'Industrie, which was converted for the time being into a perfect arsenal, crowded with artillery and military stores. Eventually the batteries of Montmartre, St. Ouen, and the Buttes Chaumont were exclusively armed with them, and a certain number of pieces were mounted on the detached forts, excepting those of Aubervilliers, Vincennes, and Nogent, the remainder, save some few kept in reserve, being appropriated to the more important bastions of the enceinte, like those at Point du Jour, the junction of the Seine and Marne, and where the Orleans railway intersected the ramparts. The transport of these huge naval guns from the Palais de l'Industrie to their several destinations was a most laborious task; the larger pieces, when a steep ascent such as that presented by the Buttes Montmartre had to be surmounted, requiring as many as four-and-twenty horses to drag them along. As they went rumbling over the stones, causing the most solidly built houses to vibrate, crowds would accompany them a considerable distance on the way, and whenever a halt was necessary spectators would gather round to admire alike the size and solidity of these formidable engines of war which were to keep their dreaded enemy at a respectful distance. In the working quarters men in blouses would scientifically scan the steel hoops, and thrusting their brawny arms down the muzzles, would pass their fingers over the rifled grooves; while giggling girls would pat, as if approvingly, the huge clumsy-looking objects, strive to encircle them with their arms, and peer into their big black muzzles with curious eyes.

The French had found it impracticable to transport to Paris in time any of their largest naval guns weighing nearly two and twenty tons, and throwing projectiles, ranging from three to more than four hundred weight, a distance of upwards of five miles. The ship guns on which Paris relied to defend itself were simply of three classes ; of the lightest, weighing just under five tons and throwing shells between four and five miles, some were breech and others muzzle-loaders.* The larger Seine gunboats were armed with cannon of the latter type which were peculiarly adapted to the purpose by reason of their comparative lightness, involving no great draught of water, and their great length of range.

The next, a rifled piece weighing nearly eight tons, had a range exceeding four miles, and threw projectiles from a hundred weight and upwards beyond four miles. Unfortunately the authorities had succeeded in getting up only fifteen pieces of this description, and not more than a couple of heavy ship guns of the class known as the perfected model of 1864, throwing projectiles weighing from two to three hundred weight a trifle under five miles. The principal Seine gunboat, known as the *Canonnière Farcy*, was armed with one of these formidable pieces; and the other, known as the Joséphine, was installed at the battery of St. Ouen.

Mont Valérien boasted the most formidable piece

---

* The muzzle-loaders, according to M. Reybaud (see *Revue des Deux Mondes*, vol. xci. p. 133), were pieces of an old model which had been subsequently rifled. Other authorities say that all the naval guns brought up to Paris for the siege were breech-loaders.

of artillery the French were in possession of—a huge
cannon christened the Marie Jeanne, which had been
accidentally discovered at Vincennes, and which was
reported to be capable of throwing a projectile weighing between three and four hundred weight a distance
of five miles. It was mainly by means of this insignificant number of guns of heavy calibre that the
Parisians hoped to save the capital.

There were a considerable number of mortars in Paris
of various sizes suitable for curved or vertical firing,
and an ample quantity of siege howitzers, together
with some small smooth-bore howitzers, which served
to arm the flanks of the bastions; while with regard
to field-guns with which the smaller redoubts and
even the bastions of the enceinte were principally
armed, owing to the number of naval guns brought
up to Paris being limited, these were all bronze rifled
muzzle-loaders, converted from the old smooth-bore
cannons by grooving them with three spiral channels,
and comprised respectively what the French style
cannons of 4, 8, 12, and 24. Of the cannon of 8, which
had only been recently introduced into the French
service, there appeared to have been merely a limited
number. At any rate, but few pieces of this description were mounted on the ramparts; while as regards
the short pieces of 24, which had a three miles range,
these were transformed into light guns for the purpose of arming the field works with.*

The Palikao administration, to calm the apprehen-
sions of the population of Paris, announced, on the

---

* Some technical details on the armament of the Paris fortifications are here appended. Of the three kinds of naval guns with
which the forts, ramparts, and gunboats were armed, the lightest
weighed just under 5 tons, the bore $6\frac{1}{4}$ inches, was smooth, and
with a charge of 11 lbs. of powder, it would project an oblong shell

24th of August, that there were already 600 cannons in battery, served by no less than 8000 naval gunners, under the command of Admiral de La Roncière Le Noury. If this statement were true these cannons must have been mounted almost exclusively in the detached forts, as the Government of National Defence asserted that, on September 4th—eleven days later— the enceinte was armed with very few pieces. Of the guns found in the detached forts many were worthless, others without stands, and a considerable proportion required some kind of repair. The majority were of an ancient model, with a smooth $6\frac{1}{4}$ inches bore, the remainder being recently rifled cannon of 12 and 24,

---

weighing 68 lbs., or with a charge of $15\frac{1}{2}$ lbs., a steel ball 94 lbs. in weight. Its extreme range at an elevation of 35 degrees was about four and a half miles. This is the gun with which the Seine gunboats were principally armed.

The next was a rifled piece, weighing nearly 8 tons, the bore of which was $7\frac{4}{10}$ inches. With a charge of 17 lbs. it was capable of projecting a cast-iron shell 114 lbs. in weight, or with a charge of $26\frac{1}{2}$ lbs., a steel ball weighing 165 lbs. The longest range it was known to attain was slightly beyond four and a quarter miles. The largest ship guns transported to Paris were rifled like the preceding, and the weight was almost 14 tons, while the stand, which admitted of an elevation of 21 degrees being given to the gun, weighed $6\frac{1}{2}$ tons. The bore was $9\frac{1}{2}$ inches, and with a charge of $35\frac{1}{4}$ lbs. of powder the piece would project an iron shell weighing 220 lbs., and with a charge of 44 lbs., a massive steel ball weighing no less than 316 lbs., little short of 3 cwt. The extreme range it was capable of attaining was 8525 yards, or close upon five miles; its best results were, however, produced at a range of a mile and a quarter.

The largest French naval guns, which weigh nearly 22 tons, and have $10\frac{1}{2}$ inches bore, played no part in the siege. These pieces are capable of firing oblong shells 316 lbs. in weight, with a charge of $52\frac{3}{4}$ lbs. of powder, or a cannon ball weighing 475 lbs. with a charge of 66 lbs., a trifle over five miles.

The mortars were of four sizes, and of $5\frac{1}{4}$, $8\frac{3}{4}$, $10\frac{3}{4}$, and $13\frac{1}{2}$ inches bore respectively, while the bore of the siege howitzers was but mounted on their old stands, and consequently only able to carry a limited distance in spite of their rifled bore. By means, however, of wooden beds and the adoption of an oblique line of fire, an extra length of range of 1000 yards was attained. At the epoch of the investment there appears to have been no less than 2627 garrison and siege guns in Paris, of which 2140 were eventually placed in position on the detached forts and on the ramparts, leaving nearly 500 pieces—of which about two-thirds were serviceable—in reserve for such points of the fortifications as might require to be reinforced.*

During the year 1868, a mixed commission, com-

---

8¾ inches. With respect to the rifled field-guns, the cannon of 4, as it is called, weighed no more than 6½ cwt., and had 3⅖ inches bore. It would throw a 9 lbs. projectile with a charge of rather less than 1¼ lbs. of powder, a maximum distance of nearly two miles. The cannon of 8, weighing 11½ cwt. with 4¼ inches bore, with a charge of 1¾ lbs. of powder, threw a projectile weighing 16 lbs., and attained a maximum range of two miles. The cannon of 12, weighed 12½ cwt. and had 4¾ inches bore. With a charge of 2⅛ lbs. of powder, the extreme distance it would throw a projectile weighing 25 lbs. was 2 miles 260 yards, while the cannon of 24, was capable of throwing a projectile weighing nearly half a hundred weight, with great precision, upwards of 3 miles.

* The original intention was, that the enceinte should be armed with 1226 cannons, and the detached forts and redoubts with 982, or 2208 pieces in all; consequently the actual armament fell but little short of the proposed one, so far as the number of pieces was concerned, and was, in reality, far more effective when the calibre and range of the guns was taken into consideration. The number of cannons intended to have been mounted in each of the detached forts, which comprised in the whole 75 bastions, was as follows:—

La Briche 61, La Double Couronne 52, L'Est 38, Aubervilliers 66, Romainville 49, Noisy 57, Rosny 56, Nogent 55, Vincennes 117, Charenton 70, Ivry 70, Bicêtre 60, Montrouge 43, Vanves 45, Issy 64, Mont Valérien 79, Redoubts 10. Total, 982.

posed of artillery and engineer officers, had decided
upon the precise number and class of cannon to be
mounted in each bastion of the enceinte, and had
moreover determined the rôle of each gun, indicating
the places which could be reached by its projectiles,
and their respective distances from the ramparts,
together with the particular elevation to be given to
the piece according to the point aimed at. Considerable use is understood to have been made of these
instructions during the siege.

Beyond the armament of the fortifications, there
were in Paris 92 field and 4 mountain batteries, comprising in all 576 cannons and mitrailleuses,* and
forming, with the siege artillery, a total of 3203 guns.
Each of these pieces, whether field or siege, was provided with at least 400 rounds of ammunition, the
cannon of the forts being furnished with as many as
500 rounds, while as regards the store of powder, this
had been increased to 2560 tons.†

It was decided to take advantage of the command-

---

* These last were all after the Meudon model, the joint invention
of Commander de Reffye and Captain Pothier, and which, at a little
distance, closely resembles a breech-loading field-gun. Instead,
however, of one large mouth, it has twenty-five small ones, disposed
in a square, five on a side. Its breech piece fitted with the cartridges lifts in and out, and screws up, and when once the piece is
loaded, the simple turning of a handle explodes successively the
twenty-five cartridges as quickly or as slowly as may be desired.
At a short range, the bullets fly too close together to produce their
full result, but at a distance of from a thousand yards to a mile,
they are said to spread out and cover a large space, when their effect
is most deadly.

† Report on the armament of Paris by the Government of National Defence, dated Oct. 17, 1870 :—" L'Artillerie avant et depuis
la Guerre," par le Général Susane, directeur de l'artillerie au
Ministère de la Guerre. *Revue des Deux Mondes*, vol. 91, article,
" La Marine au Siége de Paris," etc.

ing position of the two-storied bridge at Point du
Jour, to provide it with an armour-plated locomotive
battery which should run along the rails of the
Chemin de fer du Ceinture, and be armed with no less
than thirteen long-range cannon or mitrailleuses,
capable of showering shells or bullets on to the
opposite heights of Meudon, and the iron sides of
which, some 2¾ inches in thickness as well as the
compartment sheltering the engine-driver and stoker,
were to be proof against the most powerful projectiles.
It was also to be provided with a smoke-consuming
furnace, to obviate the necessity for a chimney, such
little smoke as issued from the furnace making its
escape through the interstices of the plating.

The aggregate weight of this formidable moveable
battery was about thirty-five tons. Its construction
commenced in the Government factory at Meudon,
under the superintendence of Captain Pothier, the
associate of Commander de Reffye in the invention of
the Meudon mitrailleuse, had been interrupted owing
to the necessity which arose for abandoning this
establishment on the approach of the German armies,
but was subsequently resumed at the works of
M. Cail, the well-known engineer and metal founder
on the Quai de Billy, Grenelle.

To defend the Seine and Marne, the flotilla of gunboats and floating batteries drawing very little water,
which had been constructed at St. Denis to operate on
the Rhine, and had been sent to Toulon to be equipped
and armed, were had up by rail to Paris after being
taken to pieces for the convenience of transport,
and transferred to the Ile des Cygnes, opposite
Auteuil, there to be put together again and launched
on the Seine.

The floating batteries, five in number, were almost

6—2

square in shape, and provided with double screws impelled by smaller screws of 20-horse power. They had also two rudders, and were armed with a couple of cannons of 5¼ inches bore, carrying a distance of three and a half miles, placed in a "reduct" or iron blindage at the head of the vessel, together with a field-piece of 4, and two blunderbusses. Each of these batteries was commanded by a naval lieutenant, and had a crew of forty men. Owing to their shape, the speed they were capable of attaining was not more than between three and four knots an hour, which was, however, sufficient to enable them to make way against the current, excepting at points where the river was dammed. Their armour, three inches in thickness, afforded them efficient protection against an enemy's projectiles. It was otherwise, however, with the gunboats, the hulls of which, constructed simply of sheet-iron, could easily be pierced by a cannon ball. Such advantages as they offered lay in their armament, consisting of a breech-loading naval gun of the type we have already described, carrying upwards of four and a half miles. Ordinarily they drew nearly 5½ feet of water, which was increased to upwards of 6 feet when they were fully armed. Their crews consisted of twenty men, and, like the floating batteries, they were commanded by lieutenants in the navy.* The flotilla also comprised half a dozen little steamers of ten tons burthen, drawing 4¼ feet of water, and which, armed with a small cannon weighing scarcely more than half a ton, attained a speed of seven knots.

---

* The following were their names—*La Bayonette*, *La Caronade*, *La Claymore*, *L'Escopette*, *L'Estoc*, *Le Perrier*, *La Rapère*, and *Le Sabre*.

There remains one other gunboat to be mentioned, belonging altogether to a different category, a very superior vessel, built under the superintendence of its designer, by whom it was commanded, and after whom it was, moreover, named. This was the *Canonnière Farcy*, which, owing to the little water it drew, spite of its heavy armament, was able to ascend the arms of the Seine, where the floating batteries could not penetrate. It carried, as we have already mentioned, a huge naval gun, weighing nearly 14 tons, mounted on a revolving stand almost half that weight, and capable of throwing a 210 lb. projectile just under five miles. The merit of Commander Farcy's invention lay in securing stability while carrying its principal weight above the centre of gravity, with a draught of not more than 3¼ feet of water; he succeeded, moreover, with a 10-horse power engine for 50 tons burthen, in securing a speed of six knots per hour.

The Government of National Defence gave orders for the casting of a certain number of mortars, and the manufacture of additional mitrailleuses after the Meudon model, and others upon the Montigny and Gatling systems. Of the two latter the one has no less than 35 barrels, while the other has only 10, but of considerable diameter; the ten round shot being moreover projected at a single discharge. The piece is also provided with a shield protecting those who serve it against the enemy's projectiles. All the percussion muskets in stock were ordered to be transformed into fusils à tabatière pending inquiries as to whether it would not be possible to manufacture chassepots in Paris, in the event of communication with the provinces being completely interrupted. The Government also gave directions for the construction of what were termed terrestrial torpedoes, a formidable engine of destruction which exploded under the pressure of the foot, and the first specimens of which were buried around the detached forts. The manufacture of projectiles of all descriptions alike for artillery and small arms, and also of fulminating powders, was pushed forward with the utmost vigour, the staff of the Conservatoire des Arts et Métiers, as well as the Chemical Society, having placed their services at the disposition of the authorities with that object.

The Commission of Barricades, of which Citizen Henri Rochefort, no longer the orator of the mob, but a hard working member of the Government of National Defence, had been appointed president, and his intimate friend Citizen Gustave Flourens, vice-president, sedulously occupied itself in connexion with the corps of engineers of roads and bridges in constructing an additional line of defence within the ramparts, which was designed to render Paris impregnable in the event of any breach being made in the latter.

Such were the practical means of defence which the new Government had initiated within the short space of a fortnight, besides listening to the importunities of inventors of all manner of formidable implements of destruction, and to the proffered counsels of patriotic fanatics. The employment of dynamite, picrate of potass, and petroleum appears to have been largely recommended to them. One enthusiast proposed, by means of fulminate of picrate of potass, to blow the entire German army off the face of the earth, or, with another preparation which he had discovered, to asphyxiate it regiment by regiment, and then reduce it to cinders. He moreover asserted that he was in

possession of a secret for transforming water into
liquid fire, but did not suggest how he proposed
utilizing it to the detriment of the invaders.

Possibly this was the same invention subsequently
described in the *Presse*, a perfectly serious newspaper,
and which, according to this authority, consisted of a
new kind of projectile far surpassing anything yet
heard of for its murderous effects. Indeed, it would
seem to have been of so terrible a character that the
dreaded Greek fire must have been child's play compared with it. It was a rocket, costing little to manufacture and easy to fire, and was said to have a range of
four or five miles. Experiments with it, conducted
by a commission consisting of engineer and artillery
officers and professors of the Conservatoire des Arts et
Métiers, gave, it was said, the most satisfactory results so far as its destructive properties were concerned. It seems that during one of the trials, a
rocket fired into a large iron tank filled with
water, placed in the centre of a large piece of waste
ground, burst the instant it came in contact with the
liquid, and caused it to boil over and run along the
ground in a sheet of fire. A violent detonation rent
the air, the tank and its supports were thrown sky-
wards and descended again, broken into small frag-
ments. Luckily for the Prussians, and perhaps for the
French too, the commission were so overcome by the
results of this experiment that they hesitated to
recommend the adoption of such a terrible weapon for
fear of placing France beyond the pale of civilized
nations.

A similar murderous missile submitted to the
authorities, was christened the Satan Fusée. Filled
with petroleum, the explosion of which was regulated by a time fuse, it was said to be capable of

covering the ground for a considerable distance
around with a perfect sea of inextinguishable fire.
The commission in this case, while bearing testimony to the efficacy of the invention as a means of
destruction, were troubled, we were told, with much
the same scruples, and declined to recommend the
Government to have recourse to it. One amateur
exterminator suggested the collecting together of all
the stores of inflammable rock-oils in the neighbourhood of Paris, and burying them in the earth a certain
distance in advance of the detached forts, which the
enemy being encouraged to assault, the oils were
to be exploded at the right moment by means of
electric wires. A more puerile suggestion was the
providing of every franc-tireur with a big bottle of
petroleum, which he was always to carry about with
him, so as to be prepared to fire the woods in which
fatigued uhlans might be discovered sleeping after a
hard day's work in plundering the châteaux and
villages in the environs. With most of these amateur
strategists petroleum appears to have been a favourite
medium of destruction. One of them proposed that in
the event of a breach being made in the ramparts
straw should be stacked in the opening, and then
saturated with petroleum, which was to be set fire to
at the moment the enemy sought to enter. A huge
fire-engine was, moreover, to be employed, not in
extinguishing, but in feeding the flame anew, by
directing a stream of petroleum at such points where
it showed signs of expiring.

The inventor of another terrible war machine,
termed the Faucheuse, maintained it to be equal to
at least fifty mitrailleuses. Perfectly portable and
requiring only three men to direct it, without noise
or smoke, it was capable, he said, of exterminating 1800

men per minute, at a range of 500 yards. It was, moreover, as economical as it was efficacious, the cost of propelling 500 balls being no more than a sou.

A citizen, to whom the authorities had turned a deaf ear, advertised in the newspapers for a patriot of wealth to lend him the trifle of 100,000 francs, to enable him to construct a machine the deadly qualities of which required to be witnessed to be appreciated; and even women came forward in print with crazy suggestions for exterminating the enemy. One amiable creature proposed not merely poisoning all provisions which the Germans might requisition in the villages around Paris, but insisted upon the wholesale poisoning of the waters of the Seine. The suggestion only met with disfavour because it was thought that more Parisians than Prussians would fall victims were it put into practice.

A sober newspaper, the *Français*, gravely maintained that the only thing which could save France was the air-balloon, freighted with monster bombs, to be launched by aërostatic artillerymen. "By this means," it said, "not only might France be saved, but Germany might even be conquered. If the nation resolutely sets itself to the work, and the balloons are got ready, neither Trèves nor Mayence nor Cologne will stop us." It seemed as though the dream of the poet were about to be realized, and we were really to have "the nation's airy navies grappling in the central blue."

It was at the clubs that some of the most extravagant suggestions for combating and extirpating the enemy were propounded. A very determined patriot was accustomed to visit one club after another and exhibit a hand bomb of his own invention, which, according to him, he had merely to let drop on the floor to blow up the entire assembly. Accompanying his assertions with demonstrative gestures, he flung about the particular hand in which he grasped the bomb every instant, and created in the minds of his hearers a visible inquietude. Naturally every one hastened to recognise the value of his invention, and begged him to submit it without further explanation to the proper authorities. It was, moreover, a club tactician who proposed raising the blockade of the capital and driving back the German invasion by simply constructing a redoubt under the fire of one of the forts, another redoubt under the fire of this, and so on; and then turning out the Parisian and provincial National Guards en masse, spreading them as sharpshooters all over the occupied districts of France; lastly, that most original suggestion of letting loose the ferocious wild beasts of the Jardin des Plantes in the woods round Paris, where the enemy was certain to be hiding in accordance with his usual habit, was first developed at a Paris club.

## III.

## THE GARRISON.

ONE of the earliest acts of the Palikao administration was to call out the Garde Mobile, and to summon up auxiliaries of all kinds from the provinces. The appeal was promptly responded to, now that not France alone, but Paris, "the sacred city," which in the eyes of many Frenchmen is even more than France, was menaced with danger. At this epoch the capital was swarming with an infinity of diverse uniforms, those of the regular army and the auxiliary troops being intermingled with the novel and more or less bizarre costumes of countless improvised defenders of the national soil, who for the most part occupied themselves in strutting about the streets, or lounging outside the wine-shops and cafés, evidently proud enough of their warlike plumes. The puny-looking Parisian Mobiles found themselves thrown into the shade by the stumpy sapeurs-pompiers of the provinces in their fantastical and over-capacious brass helmets, by the dashing francs-tireurs, in operatic tenue, the sedate-looking marines, the tall gensdarmes, the acute douaniers, the smart men-of-wars' men, the naval gunners, and the volunteers of all classes, grades, and ages (from sixteen seemingly to sixty) in Alpine hats and kepis, blue and white blouses, high boots and gaiters, with red stripes down their trousers, red bands round their kepis, and red sashes round their waists, who had their uniforms at any rate, which seemed to satisfy them, and a certain percentage of whom were armed ; though few of these raw levies submitted to any regular drill.

The fundamental idea of the military engineers who planned the fortifications of Paris was, that an army more or less considerable, while unable to hold the field against the enemy, should yet contribute to the defence of the city, and by manœuvring in the open prevent anything like a regular investment of the place. No portion of the armed force, however, which composed the motley garrison of Paris at the moment the German armies arrived before the city could lay claim to any such distinction.  Of all those redoubtable forces sent by the French into the field since the commencement of the war, and which had previously been a perpetual menace to the peace of Europe, one army had been well nigh destroyed after three great battles, another had capitulated at Sedan, and a third was shut in under the walls of Metz.  All that remained was Vinoy's corps, composed in a great measure of the garrison withdrawn from Rome, the fugitives from Macmahon's army, and some raw troops in the depôts at Paris, Versailles, and neighbouring garrison towns, out of which, and of the gendarmerie, the gardes municipales, the douaniers, the gardes forestiers, the sergens de ville, the marines, the sailors, and the mobiles, an active army was hastily formed.

The gendarmerie and the douaniers had been summoned up from the provinces during the early days of the Palikao administration, and within a day or two after the overthrow of the Empire, Vinoy's corps, and the débris of Macmahon's troops who had escaped being made prisoners at Sedan, arrived in Paris. The sight of these latter, principally soldiers of the line, Zouaves, and Turcos, straggling into the capital, travel-stained, harassed, haggard, and hungry, during a down-pour of rain, looking the reverse of burning to avenge their chief and their companions in arms, as the newspapers pretended, was sufficient to depress all amateur martial ardour, and the Parisians judiciously received them with sympathetic silence. If they were not acclaimed, however, they were certainly not uncommiserated: money was slipped into many of their hands, and when the rain had moderated, the blouses and the gamins vied with each other in marks of attention, relieving many a wearied warrior of his musket, and marching with it by his side during the defile along the boulevards. They camped for the night in the Avenues de l'Impératrice and de la Grande Armée, many among them asking and receiving charity at the neighbouring houses. They all appeared to have formed the same estimate of the enemy who had routed them. " Detestable infantry," said they ; "one French regiment is worth three Prussian— excellent and daring cavalry and numerous and powerful artillery." The corps commanded by General Vinoy arrived under different conditions, this officer after effecting his retreat from Mézières with all his artillery and cavalry in good order, having finally succeeded in getting alike his troops and his matériel brought up to Paris by rail.

At this epoch all Paris flocked to the Avenue de la Grande Armée, to see the troops encamped there. " On each side of the broad carriage-road in the centre stretched a double avenue of young plane-trees, under which were pitched the tentes abris in picturesque

array. There was clean straw in abundance spread
over the ground, and the light gravel drained the rain-
water away almost as fast as it fell.    Subsequently
the men moved to the Champ de Mars, and encamped upon the gravel there, leaving the avenue
to be occupied by their comrades, who arrived later
from the march.    In the evenings these camps were
a striking sight, and a popular one, till the novelty
wore away.    Carriages crowded down past the Arc
de Triomphe to have a look at the army of our hopes;
throngs of pedestrians hurried there to satisfy their
curiosity by a chat with soldiers actually returned
from the war.    Round the embers in their little brick
grates you could see them chattering, as the French
alone know how to chatter.    The soldiers were always
ready to answer questions, and never bothered themselves about arresting anyone as a spy.    There is
something in a French private soldier which makes
him popular almost everywhere. Subordination, regular work, and constant exercise, remove or modify
to a considerable extent the national vanity and levity.
He retains his bonhomie without arrogance, his good-
nature without self-conceit.    In his camp life he is
serenely happy, idling contentedly the hours away.
In a few days the Champ de Mars was covered over
half its space with rows of the pointed tentes abris.
Along the edges of the rows of tents were piled the
glittering white chassepots, their tall bayonets shining
from afar.    Immediately outside the Ecole Militaire,
and opposite its central entrance, was drawn up a
large square of baggage-wagons. On one side the bag-
gage horses were picketed;   on the other, a line of
wooden huts were being hastily run up.    Soon the
tents would be changed for more substantial lodgings,
and the sides of the broad space, where so lately stood

the great Industrial Exhibition, would be converted into military barracks, and stored with the practical implements of war.

"What the Champ de Mars was for the infantry troops, the Tuileries Gardens were for the returned artillery. The whole of that beautiful enclosure, lately so quiet and undisturbed, was converted, as if by magic, into a busy, noisy, bustling camp. Inside the railings were drawn up, in densely-packed array, the short field-pieces, with their various belongings. Beyond them the tents stretched in a long dusty row; the tall tents of the officers rising here and there in clusters above the more humble tentes abris. Close along the private gardens, at the other end, the lean horses stood in pitiable rows, gazing wistfully on the bright green grass out of their reach. The lovely statues seemed to stare from their pedestals in mute surprise upon the changed and barbarous scene. But here, too, the 'barrackments' had been commenced. The solidity of the materials, the substantial way in which these wooden buildings were erected, would have indicated to any but the most partial mind, that no early end to the siege was expected by the military authorities."*

Paris, to which the sea and all pertaining to it, offers that kind of charm which the unknown usually inspires, was in ecstacies with the ships' crews which kept arriving one after the other. It admired the lithe and sturdy figures of the men, their open and resolute demeanour, the picturesque appearance they presented in their large black leathern hats, with curled-up brims, their huge shirt-collars turned over half way down their backs, and their broad belts, in which

---

* Michell's "Siege Life in Paris," p. 19.

their revolvers were stuck. Out of these men nine battalions of six companies each were formed; in addition to which there was the bataillon école of marine fusiliers from Lorient, and the Louis XIV. vaisseau école of gunners, numbering 1000 men, and making eleven battalions in all. Each battalion was commanded by the captain of a frigate, and each company by a lieutenant and an ensign. A company was composed of 120 men, so that the effective strength of each battalion was 720 men. Taking into consideration the excess of the Louis XIV battalion, some extra contingents of ships' carpenters and helmsmen sent up from various ports, and about a couple of hundred retired sailors who had volunteered in Paris, it raised their strength in round numbers to 9000 men, and to them the defence of the detached forts was entrusted. In addition to the foregoing, there were 1200 men belonging to the marine artillery, who, with the exception of a limited number reserved to fire off the mortars in the various forts, were attached to the field batteries, then in course of organization; and four battalions of marine infantry, numbering altogether 3200 men, the whole being under the command of Vice-admiral de La Roncière Le Noury. By the month of October the artillery had been raised to an effective of 13,000 men, of whom 7000 were sailors.*

No official intimation was ever given of the exact strength of the armed force congregated within the ramparts of Paris and occupying the detached forts, and the various positions outside the walls at the moment the Germans invested the city. A thorough

---

* *Revue des Deux Mondes*, article, "La Marine au Siége de Paris;" also the official report on "L'Armament de Paris."

sifting of the contradictory evidence on this point only enables us to arrive at an approximate idea of the military forces of the besieged at the epoch in question, and which in round numbers may be estimated as approaching 400,000 men. To arrive at this total, the army proper, concerning which there is but little reliable information, would have to be taken at fully 90,000,* including some 35,000 men belonging to Vinoy's corps, the remaining 55,000 being composed of troops in the various depôts, the fugitives from Macmahon's army, the gendarmerie, the douaniers, the gardes municipales, the gardes forestiers, and the sergens de ville, which last numbered some 3600 men. With respect to the number that each arm comprised, nothing whatever is known ; but regarding the sailors, naval gunners, and marines, we have precise information, enabling us to fix these at 13,400 men,† the Gardes Mobiles, local and provincial, were officially estimated at 90,000, and the numerous special and volunteer corps at 20,000; while the National Guards, at the period we are speaking of, may be computed at about 180,000, giving a total of 393,400 men, which was eventually raised to something like half a million by increasing the number of National Guards, by re-enlistments into the artillery, and by the enrolment of additional volunteers.

---

* If the official return of the number of votes said to have been given by the regular troops and the mobiles on the occasion of the Plebiscite of November 3rd is to be relied upon, the effective of the army at the date of the investment must have been considerably in excess of our estimate. The number of voters is set down at 245,676, and if from these 90,000 mobiles, and say even 30,000 of the different volunteer corps are deducted, we have still upwards of 125,000 left.

† *Revue des Deux Mondes,* article, "La Marine au Siége de Paris."

Less than one-fifth of this number were sufficient to man the 170 bastions of the detached forts and the enceinte, which according to recognised military principles required 500 men each, or 85,000 in all.

Vinoy's corps was composed of average troops, greatly dispirited, however, at the immensity of the recent disaster, which they only escaped participating in by the lucky accident of being too late for the conflict, for the French soldier, whose courage has more the element of dash than of resistance, needs success to cheer him on. Frenchmen themselves admit that reverses depress, defeat finishes him. As for the men in the depôts they were, with scarcely an exception, all young soldiers, while as regards the sailors, the marine infantry, the gendarmerie, &c., they might be considered as corps d'élite. The thoroughly demoralized men of Macmahon's army were justly regarded with extreme suspicion, and it was believed the Mobiles would require to undergo many a " baptism of fire" before they would stand their ground against disciplined troops in the open. As for the National Guards, all that was expected of them at this time was the performance of rampart duty, which nevertheless left over a couple of hundred thousand men of one kind and another—but on scarcely more than a third of whom real reliance was to be placed—for garrisoning the forts and active operations in the field.

## II. THE GARDE MOBILE.

The Garde Mobile professed to include in its ranks all Frenchmen from twenty to twenty-five years of age, who by drawing a good number or providing a substitute, had managed to escape the conscription ; the only exemptions being widows' sons and sons who were the support of their families. The officers had been named by the Imperial Government, and were principally retired officers of the army, gentlemen, or members of the liberal professions. Prominent among the defenders of Paris were the Mobiles of the Seine, comprising no less than eighteen battalions of from 1100 to 1500 men each, as well as two detachments of artillery from St. Denis and Vincennes, and forming altogether an effective force of upwards of 25,000 men. Raised for the most part in Paris, the majority had all the dissipated habits which youth too readily contracts in that city of delights, all the national conceit, and the most perverse sentiments respecting honesty. Their apologists pretend that they united in themselves all military qualities except the essential one of discipline, the lack of which was attributed to a general ignorance of military affairs, and laxity on the part of their officers, who were so unaccustomed, it is said, to habits of command, that many of them on their first appointment used to address their men as " Messieurs."

At the camp of Chalons, to which they were sent shortly after being called out, they are said to have been guilty of endless acts of insubordination ; hooted the General who passed them in review, refused to mount guard when called upon, sacked the neighbouring hotels and auberges, and mixed themselves up in other disgraceful disorders. Marshal Macmahon declining to be troubled with them, sent them back to the capital, whereupon they were encamped in the environs at St. Maur, where they can hardly be said to have conducted themselves more creditably, deserting as they did their posts en masse at night time and returning into Paris, some forty only out of a hundred answering on the following

morning to the roll-call. Shortly before the investment, General Trochu, equally embarrassed as to what
to do with troops who set an example of insubordination which was certain to prove contagious, issued an
order of the day, calling upon them within a delay of
forty-eight hours, under pain of military punishment
for abandoning their posts in presence of the enemy,
to repair to what he termed the " post of honour,"
meaning the detached forts among which they were
distributed, and whence many of them still made a
point of escaping to Paris for several days at a time
whenever a favourable opportunity presented itself.
At the very moment the arrival of the German forces
was signalled, and it was believed the defenders of
the capital were impressed with a stern sense of the
duty cast upon them, Paris was scandalized at hearing
of a hideous saturnalia enacted by some Gardes Mobiles
of the Seine at a village adjacent to the fort where they
were garrisoned. After pillaging the church, some
dressed themselves up in the ecclesiastical vestments,
and eat and drank the sacramental bread and wine;
while others, mounting the pulpit, indulged in the
most scandalous blasphemies. Whether or not a
baptism of fire would cleanse the Paris Mobiles of
their peccant ways remained to be seen.

The provincial Mobiles arrived in Paris during the
fortnight preceding the investment, and remained
there representatives, so to speak, of the departments
from which the capital was isolated during the siege.
The battalion of Villers-Coterets, La Ferté Milon, and
Château Thierry, the only one belonging to the department of the Aisne which came to the relief of
the capital, was the first to arrive. The men were
assembled at Villers-Coterets, whence every one was
flying before the advancing enemy, who had passed

Rheims, and before whom General Vinoy was in full
retreat. In the confusion that prevailed the battalion of
Mobiles, comprising some 1600 men, stationed in this
little town, seemed to have been quite forgotten. The
rearguard of Vinoy's corps was passing through when
the commander of the Mobiles, of his own accord,
determined to direct his men upon Paris, quitting Villers-Coterets on the evening of the 5th of
September, and marching as far as Dammartin, twelve
leagues distant, the same night. Here they waited
in a pouring rain nearly the whole of the following
day for a train to be got in readiness to convey them
to Paris, where they arrived during the evening,
creating quite a sensation as they passed along the
Boulevard Sebastopol in their white blouses, each
with his bundle slung on his back, and a fowl or a
bunch of vegetables on the tip of his bayonet, to the
Lycée St. Louis, where they were provisionally barracked. Few imagined from their rustic appearance that many of these young men carried in their
pockets the diploma of their bachelor's degree, and
yet such was the fact, for they came from one of the
best educated districts in all France.

The Seine-et-Marne and Seine-et-Oise battalions
which were among the most soldier-like that arrived
in the capital, comprised in their ranks the young
peasants of Montereau, Provins, Meaux, and their environs, whose fathers had more than once witnessed the
passage of foreign troops, and had had painful experience of the ravage they created. Most of the departments of France were represented at the siege of Paris.
From the north Picardy sent its battalion of stalwart
young fellows, all well equipped, who had quarters
allotted them in the College of Sainte Barbe ; while
Normandy sent the battalions of the Seine Inférieure.

The east of France furnished a battalion of the Marne from Chalons, the oft-invaded Champagne country, the peasantry of which have a well-known rallying song—

> " A quoi bon la poudre et l'épée ?
> L'ennemi vient, notre sang bout ;
> La faux est large et bien trempée :
> Paysans de France, debout !"

also the battalions of the Aube and others from Burgundy, coming from the departments of the Ain, the Saone-et-Loire, and the Côte d'Or, the young men of which have all the exuberancy and vigour of their wines. The commander of the battalion of the Côte d'Or made excellent soldiers of his men in a couple of months. They were called out on the 13th of August, and on the 13th of October were fighting bravely at Bagneux. The centre and the south of France spared but few battalions for the defence of Paris. Of these several were from Orleans ; the young men composing which had already a military air, and in their white blouses and gaiters looked like so many francs-tireurs. Some few detachments only arrived from Poitiers, Châteauroux, Valence, and Ambert ; but the contingents of the Herault and the Tarn were complete. The men of Languedoc showed themselves ordinarily grave and reserved ; their own soft patois alone seemed harmonious to their ears, and when they did speak it was generally in praise of the rich fruits and wines of the south, which they sorely missed in the beleaguered capital.

The Breton battalions appear to have excited the most interest. When the Mobiles of Finisterre marched into Paris with their bignons playing the favourite air of " En ani gous, e zo men dous," the Parisians,

while regarding them with a curiosity not devoid of
emotion, hardly expected that these unenlightened
young peasants and their compatriots of Ille-et-Vilaine
and the Côtes-du-Nord, would subsequently prove
themselves the heroes, so to speak, of the siege. They
were looked upon as partisans of Henri V., and it
was asked, would they fight for the Republic? Empire
or Republic, it mattered not to them; they were
simple soldiers, and had come up to defend Paris,
without knowing it, and caring nothing for its vaunted
high civilization. They had been told that France
had need of them to repel the invader, and they
responded cheerfully to the call. The Mobiles of
Finisterre and the Côtes-du-Nord were raised principally from among the seafaring class, and it was the
same in a less degree with those of Morbihan; but
while the two former were remarkable for a certain
gaiety, on the latter something of the silence and
mysteriousness of their native landes and druidical
remains seemed to be impressed. The battalions of
Ille-et-Vilaine, composed of calm, resolute young
fellows, guided by a profound sentiment of duty,
were among the first arrivals in the capital. They
had been called out on the 15th of August, and were
in Paris on the 7th of the following month, having
already learnt how to manage their fusils à pistons.
All the Breton battalions, without exception, were
accompanied by their priests, who, receiving no pay,
marched none the less cheerfully with the young men
of their parishes, repeating the old Breton motto,
" Avec l'aide de Dieu pour la Patrie," and convinced
that they would fear death the less by believing in
the life to come.

The provincial Mobiles appear to have had their
uniforms served out to them by degrees, com-

mencing with the kepi, which was afterwards supplemented by the belt. On arriving in Paris only a few companies had cloth tunics, the others being simply provided with linen blouses, and as the September nights were becoming cold, and the men had already to do duty on the ramparts, the officers were empowered to treat directly with the wholesale army clothiers. The uniforms were turned out with the utmost speed, but presented some remarkable dissimilarities of both colour and cut—the trousers, for instance, were of all shades, from the deepest blue to the palest grey ; indeed, only one rule appeared to be observed—uniformity was maintained in the different battalions, and every man wore a red band round his kepi, and a red stripe down his trowsers.

At the commencement of the siege all the Mobiles were armed with rifled muskets converted into breechloaders, and termed fusils à tabatière, or snuff-box rifles, from the form of the lock case, altogether an inferior weapon to the chassepot, but preferred by many of the men on account of its being easier to learn the use of. The Mobiles used to sing a song àpropos of this weapon, of which this was the refrain :—

" J'ai du bon tabac
Dans ma tabatière,
J'ai du bon tabac,
La Prusse en aura,
J'en ai du bon et du râpé,
Bismarck, ce sera pour ton fichu nez."

At Paris no kind of arrangements appear to have been made for the reception of this immense body of men coming from the provinces. The battalion of Seine-Inférieure had to bivouac the night of its arrival in the Galerie d'Orléans of the Palais Royal, while other battalions were barracked in the empty lycées; the majority, however, of these provincial visitors were billeted on the inhabitants. In all quarters of Paris one encountered them wandering about with their billeting papers in their hands like so many lost sheep, seeking for streets the whereabouts of which they knew not, and which it was not always possible to explain to them, many, like the bas-Bretons, not understanding a word of French. While the latter were thus dispersed in different houses, it was found difficult to get them to recognise the customary trumpet call until one of their chiefs conceived the happy idea of replacing it by the national air "En ani gous," which brought every man to the rendezvous. Eventually long wooden huts were constructed along most of the exterior boulevards for the accommodation of the Mobiles, who were exercised several times a day, and for a couple of hours at a time, in the open spaces and broader thoroughfares contiguous to these localities. Their pay during the siege was at the rate of a franc and a half per day.

### III. THE NATIONAL GUARD.

When, subsequent to the coup d'état of Dec. 2nd, 1851, Louis Napoleon dissolved the National Guard, he organized a pretended semblance of the institution under its original name, but with none of its ancient attributes, and exercised moreover every precaution that only staunch Bonapartists should be enrolled in it. Regarding even this precaution as insufficient, he retained in his own hands the appointment alike of all the officers and sub-officers of this emasculated corps. The position of the force, which having lost all its ancient popularity had been for years, equally with the sapeurs-pompiers, the standing butt of vaudevillists, continued the same down to the commencement of the war, when its effective strength averaged no more than 32,000 men divided into 51 battalions. After the French reverses, one of the first steps of the Government was to increase this number to 80,000 by the formation of new battalions, and by additions to the companies of the old ones. Twelve companies of auxiliary working engineers were likewise created, which gave a supplementary effective of 2500 men. Subsequently, when it became a question of associating the National Guards in the defence of Paris, General Trochu impressed upon the Palikao administration the necessity of restoring to them the privilege they formerly enjoyed of electing their own officers, and a Bill was passed in all haste according this demand; but before the day of election arrived the Empire was overthrown.

On September 6th, a couple of days after the proclamation of the Republic, which imposed upon every citizen his share of military service, the formation of 60 additional battalions was decreed, the maximum strength of each of which was fixed at 1500 men. No sooner was this decree published than men of all ages hastened to inscribe their names at the various mairies, and there was certainly no diminution of zeal on the part of these new recruits when the battalions were regularly constituted. All the public places of the capital, every open space, square, garden, carrefour, quay, avenue, or boulevard, wherever there was sufficient room to assemble a company, was transformed into a manœuvring ground, where savants, authors, artists, politicians, financiers, merchants, manufacturers, shopkeepers, clerks, and working men, some in full uniform, others merely

NATIONAL GUARDS IN THEIR QUARTERS ON THE RAMPARTS.

i. 106.

wearing the kepi, who, closing their lecture-rooms, studios, theatres, warehouses, factories, and shops, went through a regular system of drill for several hours daily—served a hasty apprenticeship, so to speak, to the art of war. Here some old sergeant might be seen instructing a company of young fellows in the management of their muskets, while beside him a juvenile corporal would be putting grave looking fathers of families, whose beards were already grey, through the phases of the goose step, conveying the impression that the Parisians who with all their partiality for the "pride, pomp, and circumstance of glorious war," have really peaceful tastes, dearly love their ease and are loth to forego their habitual enjoyments, were earnestly devoting themselves to stern courses of discipline; all seemed so docile and anxious to learn. When their drill was completed they practised firing on the ramparts, the guarding of which was confided to them, and they were afterwards exercised, several battalions at a time, in shooting at the target, and platoon firing, at Vincennes, Mont Valérien, and the Ecole Militaire.

The force speedily became imbued with a most warlike spirit, and proclaimed aloud—if not on all the housetops, in all the cafés—the principle of "No surrender." If the forts were taken they would defend the walls, driven from the walls they would fight behind barricades, and dispute with the enemy every inch of the city, street by street, house by house, step by step, rather let it become one mass of ruins than fall into the hands of the Prussians. No sooner had this bellicose spirit become general than it was sought to render it universal and all exemptions from military service were regarded with extreme jealousy. The Mayor of Paris actually felt himself

constrained to issue a proclamation on behalf of the
Paris cabdrivers, who, he said, had been menaced and
even struck on the pretext that they ought to be
carrying a musket rather than a whip, and be doing
duty on the ramparts instead of lolling at their ease
on a coach-box.

The peaceful bourgeoisie shared in the national
enthusiasm, and in simply donning their uniforms, of
which they were especially vain, fancied they were
making the most praiseworthy sacrifices in their
country's behalf. There was this in their favour,
if deficient in real pluck, they were patient and
amenable to discipline, which is more than could be
said with regard to the battalions of the working faubourgs, the men of whom, believed not to be wanting
in pluck, showed a remarkable distaste for obeying
orders. Most disquieting of all, however, were the
fears early expressed by many that a certain result of
this general armament of the population would be an
attack by the proletaires upon property — which
Proudhon had taught them to consider as merely
stolen goods—at the first favourable opportunity, and
visions were conjured up of a saturnalia of pillage in
the midst of the horrors of an incessant bombardment.

At the epoch of the investment the number of
battalions of National Guard had been increased to
136, the effective strength of which was estimated at
about 180,000 men. From that period up to the
30th of September, no less than 118 additional
battalions were formed, but as the whole were not
armed, the effective was only raised to 280,738 men.
The unarmed battalions, with others subsequently
enrolled, were converted into auxiliary battalions of
working engineers. Ten batteries of artillery were
moreover formed. One discouraging feature of this

expansion of the force was, according to the testimony
of General Trochu, the absorption into the National
Guard of no less than 25,000 released convicts and
6000 ultra-revolutionists. "Bad passions," remarked
the General, "were in a minority it is true, still the
absence of discipline, the entire neglect of work and
the prevalence of drunkenness brought about wide-
spread demoralization."

Shortly after the siege commenced, National Guards
in necessitous circumstances, were empowered to draw
the same pay as the Mobiles—namely, a franc and a
half per day, and eventually an extra allowance of
75 centimes was made to the wives of such of these
men as were married, it being especially directed that
the woman herself was to draw this allowance.

### IV. THE VOLUNTEER CORPS.

The number of volunteer corps organized for the
defence of Paris was legion, and the uniforms adopted
were almost as diverse as the titles of the various
corps. Some were certainly simple enough; others,
again, more than verged on the gay and showy.
Gaiters, white or brown, appeared to be the grand
essential; and next to these a broad red or blue sash.
Tall Tyrolean hats, with peacock's feathers, were
naturally prevalent, though many corps contented
themselves with the less pretentious and more convenient kepi. Principal among these free corps of
éclaireurs, tirailleurs, volontaires, guerillas, francs-
tireurs, chasseurs, and carabiniers, as they indiscrimi-
nately described themselves, and which were formed
at Paris in response to the incessant appeals made for
every one to rise and chase the invader from the soil,
were the Volontaires de la Seine, which numbered four

battalions of infantry and a squadron of cavalry, composed almost exclusively of men who had already served in the army, and many of whom had been decorated for services in Mexico, Italy, China, and the Crimea. Their uniform was simple enough—a dark blue kepi and pea-jacket, rough linen trousers and gaiters. Like the rest of the volunteers, with some rare exceptions, they were not armed with chassepots, but fusils à tabatière. Another corps of note was the Eclaireurs à cheval de la Seine, composed of picked men all possessed of means, who were mounted, so far as these served, on horses from the imperial stud, and whose dashing young commander, M. Franchetti, did not hesitate to push his reconnaissances well into the enemy's country. The Francstireurs de la Ville de Paris, one of the earliest volunteer corps formed, and equipped and paid by the municipality, comprised in its ranks members of good families, old soldiers, professional men, students, and others. After having passed it in review, General Trochu remarked to the officers, that he recognised among them some grey moustaches as well as beardless faces : some breasts covered with decorations, and others which had yet to gain them. This admixture of men of resolution of all ages and all classes inspired him, he said, with confidence, for the excellence of a troop depended upon the mingling of the youthful and ardent element with the experience and sangfroid which belongs to the old soldier. The crack corps of Tirailleurs de St. Hubert, which had taken for its motto "The first to advance, the last to retreat," admitted into its ranks none but young men of family and fortune and first-rate shots withal, on which latter account they were provided by the Government with chassepots. Its members equipped themselves at their own cost, and the corps had its own field ambulance. The Carabiniers Parisiens were men occupying a respectable station in life, who took upon themselves the more adventurous outpost duties and often formed the advanced guard in dangerous positions beyond the posts. The Légion des Amis de la France was composed exclusively of foreigners, and reckoned amongst its members representatives of every European nationality save the countries with which France was at war. Incorporated in its well disciplined ranks were Belgians, Swiss, Italians, Englishmen, Irishmen, Dutchmen, Americans, Swedes, Austrians, Spaniards, Poles, Russians, and Greeks, with a single Dane, the Count Schmelton, huntsman to King Christian and a painter of talent, and a single Turk. The corps, which, moreover, included some Wallachians, South Americans, and natives of British Colonies, had for its commander General Van der Meer, a Belgian, and former minister of war to King Leopold.

The corps of Francs-tireurs de la Presse, a more than ordinarily undisciplined body of volunteers, was formed at the instigation of M. Gustave Aimard—the Fenimore Cooper and Mayne Reid among French novelists— whose appeal to arms was quite of a piece with his other literary compositions. "The hour," he announced, "has struck to conquer or to die. The supreme struggle has commenced. The barbarian hordes of the modern Attila murder, violate, burn, and sack, throughout our richest departments. They even dare to menace Paris, the holy city; the capital of the civilized world. The chassepot must replace the pen. Let every one rise: journalists, men of letters, artists, workmen, &c. All rise for your country—for France in mourning, and shrieking with

pain—for civilization, rise! The press has already
its ambulance, and it shall have its soldiers. Forward
for our country."

Among the numerous volunteer corps organized
for the defence of Paris, were five different ones,
describing themselves as free shooters: four others as
sharpshooters, three as skirmishers, three as volunteers,
three as free corps, and two as guerillas; there were
moreover four companies of gunners, a free corps of
artillery for the service of the mitrailleuses, a corps of
cavaliers, one of carabineers, one of chasseurs, one of
sappers and miners, and one of forest guards. In
addition, there were the Soldats du Bâtiment et du
Terrassement, originally employed on the fortifications
and in demolishing the houses within the military zones,
afterwards on the barricades, and who subsequently
exercised a supervision over the catacombs and the
sewers, into which the Parisians were terribly afraid
the enemy would succeed in penetrating. Then there
were the Sauveteurs Francs-tireurs, with their somewhat contradictory motto of "Save, conquer, or die,"
who professed especially to charge themselves with
defending the banks of the Seine; the Compagnie de
Travailleurs, whose mission was to open communications through party walls of houses which it might be
necessary to fortify in the event of the enemy penetrating within the city; the Légion des Vétérans,
and the Volontaires de l'Interieur, who, while offering their co-operation in the defence of Paris, proposed
charging themselves more particularly with night
police duty in their respective quarters, and protecting
property against, as they said, the "Prussians of the
interior."

All the foregoing corps—in which, among men of
the highest character actuated by genuine patriotism or

military ardour, a considerable number of unmistakable scoundrels were enrolled—had been duly recognised by the French Ministry of War, and all wore distinctive uniforms of some kind or other. Nevertheless, the threat contained in the proclamation issued by the Crown Prince of Saxony at Clermont, appears to have been carried out, and, as may be supposed, provoked reprisals ; so that during the siege quite as many German soldiers as francs-tireurs were shot in cold blood. The proclamation in question set forth : " It having come to the Crown Prince's knowledge that bodies of francs-tireurs were being formed to act separately from the French troops and to kill sentries and detached bodies of men, notice was given that orders had been issued to the German troops to shoot down without mercy all persons acting independently of the French regular army, and not really forming part of it." It is difficult to justify this barbarous decree, especially, too, in face of the Prussian law, dated August 21, 1813, which enacted : " that the Landsturm should not wear any uniform or peculiar dress, so that they might not be recognised and hunted after by the enemy ; that where there was a levée en masse the nature of the contest sanctified all means employed in it ; and that it was the duty of the Landsturm to deprive the enemy of all facilities for invasion or retreat ; to cut off his supplies, posts, and recruits ; suppress his hospitals, attack him by night, harass him and not let him sleep, and destroy both single soldiers and detachments wherever possible."

Shortly after the investment, a volunteer battalion of gavroches was raised, under the designation of the Pupilles de la République, the members of which were employed on the barricades and at the ramparts, and in connexion with the fire brigade and the

ambulances.    Among certain corps which were
suggested, but never completely organized, may be
enumerated the Enfants perdus de La Chapelle, a
republican battalion tinged with the deepest scarlet ;
the Anciens Proscrits et Détenus Politiques, tinged,
as may be supposed, with the same objectionable
shade ;  the Légion de Guttenberg, intended to have
been composed of printers out of employ ;  the Bataillon de Chiffonniers, which was to have included all
the hale members of the rag-picking fraternity, who
found their occupation gone the instant Paris
was invested, the wholesale dealers in refuse of
every description having closed their warehouses,
and ceased their purchases when a market was no
longer open to them.    A Compagnie humanitaire
Italien, was partially organized ;  and so was a
Polish Legion, at the instigation of a certain Colonel
Dombrowski who will be heard of again, and which
proposed to fight the enemy under the national
banner ;  but permission to complete the organization
was eventually refused on political grounds, vague
hopes of Russian intervention in favour of France
being at that moment entertained.    Another corps
which the Government of National Defence refused
to countenance, had been suggested by some of our
American cousins domiciled in France ;  it was to have
been composed of American volunteers, raised, of
course, among the fraternity of filibusters, who were
at their own cost, risk, and peril, to capture Count
Bismarck, dead or alive, and to receive a certain
premium, either from the French Government, or
out of funds raised by public subscription, on the
successful termination of their enterprise.

# IV.

## THE PROVISIONING.

---

### I. HOW PARIS WAS ACCUSTOMED TO BE FED.

THE victualling of a besieged city, containing a couple of million souls within its walls, was of course felt to be second only in importance to the efficiently fortifying and garrisoning it; but certainly no one believed when Paris was first threatened, that it was actually of primary consequence, and that famine would play a more decisive part in the siege than the famous Krupp cannon with which the Parisians had been so freely threatened. The food question having proved the vital one, a resumé of the method by which Paris was ordinarily provisioned, as well as of the steps taken to feed the city, when its habitual sources of supply were cut off, will consequently not be out of place. It is indeed only by a knowledge of all the ramifications of the system ordinarily pursued with reference to the provisioning of the French capital that a correct idea can be formed of the magnitude of the task which devolved upon the authorities of laying up sufficient stores to feed its immense population for such a long period of time.

It was fortunate for Paris, when it was evident it would have to sustain a siege, that the old restrictive laws which were the cause of periodical famines throughout France were no longer in force. In the good old days of absolute monarchy the free transport of grain was prohibited by all manner of contradictory decrees, the result being that, while one province was famishing, grain was rotting in the granaries of its neighbour. Add to this that taxation was so oppressive that the sack of corn frequently paid more than its intrinsic value in local dues before arriving at market, and that no matter how abundant the harvest might be, the cultivators of the soil could hardly live by their labour. Imposts were progressive, but in an inverse sense, for the farm of 4000 francs rent was taxed at 10 crowns, while the farm of 400 was taxed at 100 crowns, or a hundred times as much as it fairly ought to have been.

When Turgot sought to bring about the free circulation of corn throughout France, his efforts were met by popular risings. Some of these movements were spontaneous, others were fomented by interested parties—holders of large stocks of grain who for a money payment had acquired a sole right of exporting corn from France. Louis XV was himself a partner in this iniquitous association to the extent of ten millions of francs; and many of the highest personages at Court were also secret shareholders in it. The mode of proceeding was to buy up the corn in the French markets and transport it to Guernsey or Jersey, where the company had enormous granaries. When corn rose high in price owing to these manœuvres, it was re-imported from time to time, and sold in the open market at enormous profits. The setier of wheat bought by the association at 10 francs in 1769 was resold by it the year following for 30 and 35 francs. It was not prudent to expose these nefarious transactions, as M. de Beaumont found to his cost, for he was privately kidnapped, and nothing was heard of him for two-and-twenty years, until he was found within the walls of the Bastille on the day of storming that fortress. Every one knows the fate that befell the chief forestallers when the tide of revolution fairly set in. Both Foulon and his son-in-law, Berthier, were massacred by the populace, and a week afterwards their associate Perret was found in the wood of Vesinet with his skull battered in.

After the downfall of the Monarchy it was in vain that the different assemblies which succeeded accumulated laws upon laws, decrees and police ordinances. France was doomed to the inheritance of hunger left to it by the ancien régime. It was in vain that the bakers were persecuted alike by the State and by the populace, that forestalling was made a capital crime, that only a single kind of bread, the "pain d'égalité," was permitted to be made, and that a maximum price was fixed by the Government. Scarcity and want continued to be the normal condition of the Paris populace during the whole of the revolutionary epoch.

To-day the trade in corn in France is almost free. There are no longer restrictions on its export, and only on its import to the extent of a duty of 50 centimes the hectolitre (about a third of a quarter), and what is called the "décime de guerre," which was imposed under the first Republic as a temporary measure, but has been continued to the present time.

It was the duty of the prefects, under the second Empire, to address annually to the Minister of Agriculture five several reports on the state of the grain crops in the departments over which they presided— the first at the moment the plant sprouted out of the ground, the second when it was in flower, the third at the period of the harvest, the fourth when the harvest

had been got in, and the fifth after the corn had been
threshed.    The object of these reports was to enable
the Government to adopt precautionary measures to
avert anything like general distress in the event of
the harvest being a bad one.    Instead, however, of
buying up wheat, or fixing an arbitrary maximum
price, as used formerly to be done, the Government
contented itself with devoting an increased amount to
the execution of public works.

Paris, with a population of 1,825,274 souls, consumed
during the year 1867, 277,781,580 kilogrammes (equal
to 263,520 tons) of bread, being at the rate of 328 lb.
per head, or 14½ oz. per head per diem.    This was
exclusive of 81,299 kilogrammes calculated by the
authorities to have been eaten by strangers attracted
that year to the Paris Exhibition.    About a hundredth
part of the bread consumed in Paris came from the
provinces and the environs, and paid an octroi duty of
about a farthing for every 5½ lb.    The remainder was
made within the fortifications, at the 1201 bakeries
licensed by the Government, and was retailed at these
establishments and at 526 subordinate depôts.    Until
within a few years the Paris baking trade was subjected to the most oppressive restrictions.    It was not
necessary only to obtain permission to engage in it and
to furnish certificates of good character, sufficient apprenticeship, and knowledge of the trade, but every baker
was obliged to keep a stock of flour in the Government
magazines, together with a stock at his own shop
sufficient for three months' consumption ; to carry on
business at the spot fixed on by the authorities, to
keep such quantity of bread in his shop as they might
order, and to sell his loaves at the price they might
determine; he was, moreover, prohibited from abandoning his business without giving six months' previous

notice, and from selling elsewhere than at his shop. Formerly the prefect or mayor had the power of imprisoning without trial bakers who had suffered their stock of bread to become exhausted.

The municipal authorities of Paris, under certain circumstances, continued to exercise a control over the price of bread, which used to be regulated every fifteen days by the price of wheat according to the published average, adding thereto so much for grinding, and about 3 francs per cwt. for the cost of kneading and baking. When, according to the price of wheat, the kilogramme (2 lb. 2 oz.) of bread became chargeable to the public at more than 50 centimes (almost 5*d*.), the municipal authorities intervened, and paid the baker any excess beyond the half-franc out of a fund deposited in the Caisse de Boulangerie, and arising from a supplementary octroi duty established in 1853. In November, 1867, the price of bread in Paris was in excess of the regulation maximum, whereupon the Prefect of the Seine published a decree announcing the amount of compensation which would be paid to the bakers, and in a few days bread was down to the accustomed rate. As the terms of the decree were not obligatory on the bakers, many of them at first refused to accept the compensation offered, on the plea of its being insufficient, whereupon it was intimated to them that they would be compelled under penalties to weigh every loaf of bread sold by them in presence of the customer, whether delivered at their shops or at the customer's apartments. As this would have involved carrying sets of weights and scales up endless flights of stairs and giving, moreover, correct weight, the rebellious bakers were reduced to one of two alternatives —either to refuse to deliver bread at the apartments of their customers, or to accept the compensation offered by the municipality. Gradually one and all submitted to the latter.

In Paris the working classes, who as a rule eat far less meat than their London brethren, have an instinctive aversion from bread of an inferior quality; and the middle and the lower classes for the most part eat precisely the same kind of bread. Some years ago an attempt was made to introduce among the poor of Paris bread manufactured at the municipal bakery, such as was supplied to the Paris hospitals and prisons, and depôts for the sale of it were opened at all the markets. Although the bread cost about $\frac{1}{4}d$. per pound less than ordinary bread, the scheme met with but slight success, only 2,085,971 kilogrammes of it being sold during the year 1867, against 295,716,908 kilogrammes of the better class of bread. With the exception of this municipal bread, there was only one price for household bread all over Paris. Five sous per pound was alike the price to the chiffonniers at the Barrière de Fontainebleau, and the financiers of the Chaussée d'Antin.

In the same year only 9,398,348 kilogrammes of wheat paid the Paris octroi duty, against 221,508,557 kilogrammes of flour, which is accounted for by Paris possessing at that epoch only two or three insignificant flour-mills, rendering it necessary that its supplies of breadstuffs from the provinces should be for the most part in the form of flour. Beauce, Brie, and Picardy seem to have the Paris market pretty much to themselves. The flour of the first is white, that of the second dark, and that of the third an intermediate shade. The Paris bakers usually mix these flours together in proportions according to their fancy. Certain flours, the source of which is known, are more sought after than others, and find an immediate sale.

These are the flours long known as of the four marks,
each mark being that of some particular miller.
Some years ago two others were added, which raised
the number of marks to six.

The Paris corn market—the Halle au Blé, as it is
styled—is within a stone's throw of the grand Halles
Centrales. The building is heavy-looking without
being imposing, and is anything but graceful. The
large dome which surmounts this vast rotunda, is supported by four and twenty semicircular arcades.
Just as all the other Paris markets are noisy and animated, the Halle au Blé is ordinarily quiet and, as it
were, asleep. One saw piled up within it numerous
sacks of corn and flour, some few of which, together
with sacks of beans, maize, lentils, &c., were open,
with the view of displaying their contents. A weary-
looking sergent-de-ville promenaded up and down
with his arms behind his back; some flour porters,
in short blue blouses, lolled on their benches chatting
among themselves, with the copper-studded sticks
they commonly carry slung to their wrists, and their
broad-brimmed felt hats lying at their feet; a few
pedestrians made a short cut through the central
avenue, taking care as they did so not to come in contact with the flour sacks, and some women might be
seen knitting at their little retail stalls; but as for
encountering any one buying or selling there, you
might have visited the place a score of times without
witnessing even a single transaction.

Spite of all the efforts of the management, it was
found impracticable to induce the millers, the corn
and flour merchants, the bakers, and the jobbers to
transact their business beneath the dome of the Halle
au Blé. They preferred to repair to the neighbouring
cafés in the Rue de Viarmes, and make their bargains

over cinquièmes of wine or gouttes of eau-de-vie. As is the case in every corner of Europe where corn is trafficked in, the chief part of the transactions at the Halle au Blé was between jobbers, who made colossal fortunes or ruined themselves without so much as a handful of corn passing through their fingers, rather than between regular dealers. A deposit receipt for flour, known as a "filière," which was transmitted by endorsement like a bill of exchange, often changed hands several hundred times before the flour which it represented was removed from the magazines and converted into bread.

The municipality of Paris has of late years given great attention to the increase of facilities for provisioning the city, and to-day the French capital counts eight wholesale and fifty-seven retail markets, one cattle market, and four slaughter-houses. At these seventy establishments there are no less than 30,000 people employed, who, so far as the duties they had to discharge there were concerned, used all to be under the authority of the prefecture of police. There was, first of all, the administrative staff, composed of 275 employés, fifty-five facteurs, charged with the sale of market produce, the "forts," or porters of heavy loads, the ordinary porters, the guardians, the superintendents of the abattoirs or slaughter-houses, the drovers, the stallkeepers, with their assistants, &c. Placed over every branch of this active commissariat were the inspector-general and his assistants, having under their immediate orders numerous subordinates, who were always on the move, seeing that rules were observed and order was maintained in that busy world, the Paris Halles.

The prefecture of the Seine had charge of the

construction and maintenance of the fabrics of the markets, regulated the tariff, the service of the public ways, the standing places for vehicles, &c., and collected the municipal dues. With the view of attracting supplies to the Paris markets the octroi duties levied on all produce consigned direct to them were lower than those enforced at the barriers, and varied, moreover, according to the market rates of the day. For instance, a pheasant brought into Paris in the ordinary way paid the fixed duty of a franc and a half, and whereas if consigned direct to the Halles, it paid a duty of ten per cent. upon the amount it realized, or about half a franc. All carters conveying produce to the markets were prohibited under severe penalties from stopping after they had once passed the barrier of the octroi until they had arrived at their destination, the object of course, being to prevent their leaving articles on the way, and by so doing defrauding the municipality of its dues. To enforce this regulation all market carts and waggons were escorted by agents of the octroi until their arrival at the Halles, when they were placed under the inspection of other agents, one of whom watched the sale of the produce. During the year 1868 the octroi duties levied at the Paris markets amounted to 5,584,000 francs (223,360*l.*)—no insignificant amount; but still a mere bagatelle, in the budget of the city of Paris, which derived in the same year no less than 68,189,538 francs (2,727,580*l.*) from octroi duties collected at the city barriers. The whole of these duties amount to a tax of 1*l.* 12*s.* 4*d.* on every man, woman, and child in the capital.

The Paris markets derived their supplies from upwards of 6000 producers, the bulk of whom were represented by fifty-five facteurs or salesmen appointed by the prefect of police, who had to deposit a certain amount of caution money, and were responsible alike to consigners, buyers, and the authorities. They kept the former apprised of the current prices of provisions, of particular articles that were in demand, and of the prospective gains or losses likely to arise on their consignments. By means of their agencies and their correspondence they may be said to have stretched all over France, in addition to which they had relations with most of the countries of Europe, all of which contributed in a greater or less degree towards the provisioning of Paris. No previous knowledge of or communication with these facteurs was necessary; it was sufficient to consign a side of beef, a hamper of game, a tub of butter, or a basket of fruit to the Halles for it to find its way to one or other of them, who would sell it, pay the octroi duties, and within four and twenty hours account to the sender for the balance of proceeds due to him. The commission charge varied, according to the nature of the articles sold, from 1 to $2\frac{1}{2}$ per cent. Of these fifty-five facteurs, twelve were for grain and seeds, twelve for flour, three for meat, eight for poultry and game, eight for salt-water fish, three for oysters, one for fresh-water fish, five for butter and eggs, one for cheese, and two for fruit and vegetables. They were absolutely forbidden, on pain of instant dismissal, to buy or sell on their own account, and their probity was proverbial; indeed, they were held in such confidence, both in Paris and the provinces, that after the Revolution of 1848, when the notes of the Bank of France circulated with difficulty and at a discount, the commercial paper of the facteurs of the Halles was everywhere accepted without deduction and as freely as specie.

The Paris consumption of meat is considerable. During the year 1867 it amounted to 121,707,599 kilogrammes, or 115,460 tons of beef, mutton, and veal, and to 13,646,959 kilogrammes, or nearly 13,000 tons, of pork, giving a total of upwards of 135,000,000 kilogrammes, or about 128,400 tons, being at the rate of 158 lb. per head per annum, and $6\frac{9}{10}$ oz. per head per day on a population of 1,825,274 persons. 20,310,308 kilogrammes of the above quantity came as dead meat from the provinces; the remaining 15,000,000 kilogrammes were supplied by 2,477,745 head of live stock consigned to the various Paris markets. Of these 314,253 were bullocks, cows, and bulls; 219,641 calves; 209,615 pigs, and 1,707,266 sheep. During the year 1868 the consumption of butcher's meat in Paris had risen to 146,359,932 kilogrammes, or upwards of 144,000 tons, which increased the daily rate of consumption per head of the population to $7\frac{3}{4}$ oz. To this has to be added a considerable quantity of horseflesh. And yet with this large consumption of nearly $\frac{1}{2}$ lb. per head per diem, meat is a comparative rarity among the working classes of Paris as compared with those of London.

From local customs, resulting from old habits that date back to the Middle Ages, the supply of cattle from the various provinces arrives by turns at the Paris markets. Thus Normandy sends its bullocks from June to January; Maine-et-Loire from October to March; the Nivernais, the Charolais, and the Bourbonnais from March to June; the Limousin, the Charente, and the Dordogne from November to June. It is the same with the sheep: those that come southwards of Orleans arrive from May to September; those from Maine-et-Loire between July and November; Aisne, Oise, Somme, &c. January and May; Berri,

May and September; the Soissonnais, February and May; Champagne, August and December; and those from the neighbourhood of Paris between harvest and seedtime. In addition to the foregoing many sheep are imported from Germany between September and January The more important departments of France, such as Calvados, Nièvres, Sarthe, Seine-et-Oise, and Maine-et-Loire, send the most regular and largest quantities. Paris, however, was accustomed to lay half Europe under contribution for its supply of provisions. During the year 1868 Germany forwarded no less than 629,342 sheep; Italy, 1950 bullocks; Spain, 1501 bullocks and 2604 sheep; Hungary, 178,280 sheep; the Tyrol, 2183 sheep; and Switzerland, 1239 calves. In addition to which, arrangements were in force for the transit of a portion of the immense herds that graze on the plains of Roumania for the supply of the Paris markets.

Formerly, when the trade was restricted, only 500 butchers' shops were permitted in all Paris. Immediately preceding the siege, there were upwards of three times this number—namely, 1574, besides 268 stalls in the different markets, and 847 pork butchers, or altogether 2689 establishments.

Paris, until a comparatively recent period, was indebted for its entire meat supply to the markets of Poissy and Sceaux—to the first of which the bullocks of Normandy and to the other the sheep of Brie were sent—and the calf market on the Quai des Ormes. About ten years ago an Imperial decree declared the construction of a central cattle market for Paris to be of the first necessity, and in due course a new market was erected upon a vast plot of ground at Villette, which, opened nearly three years since, soon promised to absorb the entire cattle trade of the capital. A

convention entered into by the Prefect of the Seine
and the directors of the Chemin de fer du Ceinture, a
line which connects all the railways that run into
Paris, resulted in the construction of a branch line,
which conveyed the animals arriving from the provinces
into the market itself. The cost of transport from the
various Paris termini was fixed at about $1\frac{1}{2}d$. per mile
for a bullock, a trifle over a halfpenny per mile for a
calf or pig, and rather more than a farthing per mile
for a sheep, with an extra charge of $5d$. for carting
and uncarting a bullock, $2d$. for a calf or pig, and $\frac{1}{2}d$.
for a sheep.

The company, who have constructed both market
and railway, have a fifty years' lease of their privileges.
According to the conditions of their contract, they are
empowered to charge at the rate of two francs fifty
centimes per bullock, one franc per calf, fifty centimes
per pig, and twenty-five centimes per sheep for all
animals brought to the market; in addition to which
every animal, sold or unsold, pays from ten to fifty
centimes, according to whether it is a sheep or a
bullock, for every night it passes in the market.

Behind the iron entrance gates of this vast establishment, which accommodates 4600 bullocks and 22,000
sheep, besides calves and pigs, is a large yard railed off
by barriers, through which the animals have to pass
in order that they may be more easily counted by the
agents of the octroi. Preceding the three immense
halls with glazed roofs where the cattle are exposed
for sale are a couple of watering places, approached by
a gentle slope. The three halls, paralled to each other,
are separated by wide thoroughfares, which enable the
trucks conveying the smaller beasts to be unloaded on
the very platform of the market. The central hall,
destined for bullocks, is upwards of 700 feet long and

nearly 300 feet broad; that on the right hand, devoted to pigs, is of the same width, but less than half the length; the left-hand hall, which is of the same dimensions, contains the calf and sheep pens. Beyond these halls are the sheep and cattle sheds, where animals are housed for the night, and where more than 850 bullocks and several thousand sheep and calves can be accommodated. The buildings all have lofts above them, and are so arranged as to leave a courtyard in the centre furnished with drinking places. The calf pens are provided, in addition, with a supply of lukewarm water, so essential to the comfort of these animals.

When a drover enters the market with his herd he makes a declaration of the number of the animals under his charge, and receives a numbered ticket in return. Before the sales commence all these tickets are collected, and the places for the cattle are drawn by lot. The bullocks, cows, and bulls are carefully separated. The sales are arranged in order, according to the different species of animals, between the hours of eleven and two. Paris cattle-dealers are, however, great loungers; they come and go, walk up and down, speak of indifferent matters while keeping their eyes on the animals they covet, retire to some café, return to the market, whistle in a disinterested manner, as though the idea of bargaining for a bullock or a sheep was the last thing in their minds. Thus one hour, two, and even more, pass by. At last the bell which signalizes the closing of the market is about to sound. Only a single quarter of an hour is left. Everything then changes, a sort of fever prevails, and in a few minutes bargains are struck, hands shaken, and the transactions of the day are concluded. The drovers make their appearance, followed by their dogs, the

different lots are separated and conducted towards the
adjacent abattoir, the barriers, or the sheds, according
to the fate in store for them. The market is gradually
emptied, the sweepers set to work, and soon only
distant lowings, lost in the murmur of the great city,
are heard.

To encourage provincial butchers to send meat to
Paris, a sale by auction was organized at the Halles
Centrales. The pavilion in which it takes place is
divided into two distinct parts, one being for wholesale,
the other for retail sales. Between one and two
o'clock in the morning the trimmed meat arriving
from the abattoirs or the railway stations is hung up
on pegs, sorted, according to the proprietors to whom
it belongs, into a certain number of lots. As soon as
the different pieces are numbered, the inspectors commence their rounds, and stamp each piece which they
approve as wholesome with a V   It is then placed
upon an enormous balance overlooked by the agent of
public weights, and a slip of paper marked with a
corresponding number, and on which the weight is
recorded, is fixed by a pin to the joint. These preli-
minaries accomplished, the sale by auction commences.

All meat pronounced by the inspectors to be unsound was at once put on one side, while that which,
despite a bad appearance, still retained some nutritive
qualities, was reserved for the wild beasts at the Jardin
des Plantes, which during the year 1868 received
nearly 134 tons of condemned butcher's meat. The
thoroughly unsound meat, after being sprinkled with
spirits of turpentine, the odour of which cannot be
got rid of, was sold for certain industrial purposes.
The quantity of positively diseased meat in the year
1867 exceeded that confiscated for the benefit of the
carnivora in the Jardin des Plantes by about 23 tons.

In Roman Catholic countries where, according to the Church calendar, there are no less than 166 days on which the faithful should abstain from meat, fish, the "nourriture maigre" par excellence, is necessarily largely in demand, and especially in the more populous cities. In France in bygone times, when restrictions were imposed upon the free transit of nearly all kinds of food, an exception was made in favour of fish so far as Paris was concerned, and, with the view of insuring to the capital an adequate supply, the drivers of the fish carts coming from the northern coast were interdicted from unpacking and disposing of any portion of their merchandize along the line of route. Paris of late years has derived its salt water fish supply by railway from the remotest points of the French coast, and even lays Belgium, England, and other foreign countries under contribution.

The arrival early in the morning at the Paris Halles Centrales of the long pile of railway trucks laden with salt-water fish was invariably the signal for an exciting scene. The waggons were quickly divested of their different loads, and the baskets, bearing the names of their owners, and of the salesmen to whom they were consigned, were sorted out by the porters and unpacked, the fish being placed on large flat baskets preparatory to being submitted for sale by auction. Regard was, of course, had to the grouping fish of the same species together, and to making the lots as nearly as possible equal in size. The "verseurs," some sixteen in number, who performed this duty, were, moreover, careful to display the fish to the best advantage. When the sorting was over the several lots were passed on to the criers, between thirty and forty of whom were employed, and whose business it was to shout out a description of each lot as it was submitted to the assembled bidders, and to report the names of the various buyers to the salesman's clerk, who generally belonged to the fair sex. Whenever some remarkable specimen, such as a gigantic salmon or a monster sturgeon, was about to be put up to a bidding, men were sent round the pavilion where the sales took place to announce the fact at the top of their voices, which invariably had the effect of bringing together numerous competitors for the prize.

Fresh and salt-water fish were sold under the same roof, a considerable proportion of the former being brought to market alive in large tanks filled with water, from which they were transferred to stone troughs, where a constant current was kept up to restore them to a brisk and lively condition. The sales of fish at the Halles were conducted as rapidly as possible, time in this case being really money, as every hour the day advances the value of the commodity invariably decreases.

In spite of the suppression of the oyster market in the Rue Montorgueil, the quantity of oysters—those essentials to all well-regulated menus—sold at the Halles Centrales was in some degree limited, owing to the indisposition of the trade to depart from old customs and traditions. The oyster season in France extends from the 1st of September to the end of April, and the price of the fish, which is invariable throughout the season, is always arranged beforehand between the dredgers and the agents of the Paris salesmen. In the same manner the principal Paris restaurateurs fix a uniform price to be charged to their customers. In 1867 the salesmen paid forty francs the thousand, or nearly 5*d.* the dozen; in 1868 the price advanced to 71 francs 90 centimes, or upwards of 8½*d.* per dozen. It is needless to say that at the Paris restau-

9—2

rants oysters were retailed at almost double that amount.

The quantity of salt-water fish that arrived at the Halles Centrales during the year 1867 amounted to 18,283 tons, which realized 16,441,000 francs, or 657,640*l.*  There were only 1626 tons of fresh-water fish, which produced 1,925,900 francs, or 77,036*l.* In 1868 the quantity of salt-water fish had increased to 19,350 tons, still the returns were upwards of a million of francs less than they were the year preceding.  The fresh-water fish mounted up to 1907½ tons, and produced nearly 200,000 francs beyond what it did the year before.  Upwards of one-fifth of the salt-water fish came from abroad, principally from Belgium and England, while Holland, Prussia, Italy, and Switzerland supplied fully three-fifths of the fresh-water fish that was consigned to the Paris markets. During the year 1867 there were sent to Halles Centrales 26,750,755 oysters, the larger portion of which came from the oyster beds of Courseulles and Saint Waast.  In 1868 the supply fell to 25,496,752, and, strange to say, among these the Ostend oysters, which are held in such high estimation by Parisian gourmets, presented the insignificant figure of 5350. It is true that a much more considerable quantity may have been forwarded to Paris, as beyond the oysters sent direct to the Halles no less than 215 tons, together with some 64 tons of salt and fresh-water fish, entered the barrières de l'octroi of the capital during the same year.

In 1867 the game and poultry forwarded to the Halles amounted to 14,650,000 head ; 3,114,000 of these being ranked as game, which in France comprises such birds as larks, of which there were no less than 1,110,000.  The partridges amounted to 540,000, the pheasants to 37,400, the snipes only to 30,000, in addition to which there were quails innumerable. The hares were some 270,000, and the deer 13,300. Twice or thrice every week consignments of game, including blackcock, hazle-hens, and ptarmigans, arrived at the Halles Centrales from Russia, packed in oats and stowed in baskets woven of pine-bark, such as ordinarily serve as cradles for Muscovite babies. About three-fourths of the poultry consisted of fowls, ducks, and pigeons, the remaining fourth being composed of geese, turkeys, and tame rabbits. To the pigeons, which are invariably sent to the market alive, the semblance of plumpness is imparted by women known as " gaveuses," each of whom has an assistant to hand the pigeons to her one at a time from the basket or coop in which they are confined, while she opens their beaks and ejects some soaked grain from her mouth down their throats. This operation, which is performed with extraordinary rapidity, is paid for at the rate of 3*d*. the dozen birds, each gaveuse being required to provide her own grain. The 14,650,000 head of game and poultry consigned to the Paris Halles in 1867 realized about 28,000,000 francs, or at the rate of almost a couple of francs per head all round. But beyond the foregoing there were no less than 2100 tons of poultry and game that paid octroi duty at the city barriers during the same year and never found its way to the markets at all.

An enormous quantity of butter, principally from Normandy and Brittany, used to be sent to the Halles Centrales, every parcel of which was weighed, and marked with a particular number and its exact weight, by the market inspectors, before being submitted for sale. The name of the sender and the weight of his consignment were, moreover, indicated alike to the salesman entrusted to dispose of it, to the agent of the octroi, and to the chief inspector of the market. In 1868 the quantity of butter sold at the Halles was upwards of 11,090 tons, producing nearly 32,000,000 of francs, being at the rate of about 1s. per pound on the average. In the same year there were some 4670 additional tons of butter that paid duty at the barriers. Paris is unquestionably far better off than London with regard to the general quality of its butter, the dealers, having a wholesome dread of punishment, do not dare adulterate the article with all manner of filthy substances, but content themselves with mixing various kinds together, after duly subjecting them to immersion in lukewarm water. The kneading which the butter undergoes during this process renders it white and chalky-looking, a disadvantage which is obviated by the judicious admixture of a dye composed of annatto, such as is used by London milkmen to conceal the quantity of water they have added to the pure country milk they vend. The finer kinds of butter are sent to market in wicker baskets containing rolls of 1 lb. each, which circulate with inconceivable rapidity from buyer to buyer along the large platform on which they are grouped. The quantity of cheese of all descriptions forwarded to the Halles Centrales in the course of the year 1868 amounted to 3599 tons, and produced, according to M. Maxime du Camp, 3,454,612 francs, or at the rate of less than 3d. per lb. on the average, which is an evident error. Besides the foregoing there was the cheese that paid the octroi at the various city barriers, and which amounted to upwards of 4000 tons.

The eggs consigned to the Paris Halles from the departments are forwarded there in large baskets, holding on an average about 1000 each; and owing to the skilful way in which they are packed they manage to arrive unbroken, spite of the shocks to which they are subjected during their transit by rail. No less than 229,000,000 of eggs reached the Halles in 1868, and realized 17,045,013 francs, or only a fraction under 9*d*. per dozen. They are, however, invariably sold by the hamper, and according to the number indicated by the sender ; people being speci-ally employed to verify not merely the contents of each basket, but the quality of the eggs as well. This duty is performed in a dark cellar by the aid of a single lighted candle, in front of which every egg is held to ascertain that it is in a perfectly wholesome condition. Those which are spotted or opaque or are discerned to be stale by the vacant space at the broad end are put on one side to be disposed of to manufac-turers, who use them for gilding and other purposes, while such as are recognised to be in a putrid state are immediately destroyed. The high price that eggs commonly command in the Paris markets was attri-buted to the immense exportation which went on to England, thirty-two egg merchants sending thither no less than 50,000,000 of eggs annually.

Fruit and vegetables are the only commodities that remain to be alluded to. The sales of these at the Halles Centrales in the year 1868 realized 3,349,700 francs, or 132,788*l*. One is unaware of the exact quantity of fruit and vegetables that paid octroi duty at the city barriers ; all one knows is that there were 6920 tons of grapes consumed in Paris beyond those sold at the Halles.

Having finished with the solids, it now remains to speak of the equally essential liquids, for the Parisians are a most bibulous set, imbibing not merely unlimited quantities of such mild drinks as coffee, eau de seltz, cocoa, &c., but their full share of more stimulating beverages. If all the fermented liquors that pay the octroi duty are consumed in Paris, its inhabitants manage to dispose in the course of the year of no less than 365,000 tuns of wine—equal to 44 gallons per head of the population, or almost a pint a day for every man, woman, and child in the French capital; and this, too, in addition to 225,000 barrels of beer, nearly a couple of million gallons of cider, and more than that quantity of spirits. Startling as these statistics may appear, we have official authority for them, as also for the statement that to supply a population of less than 1,860,000 souls there were upwards of 25,000 establishments at which wines and spirits were sold, or at the rate of 1 to every 74 inhabitants. Of this number, 14,000, or almost three-fifths, were wine-shops and cafés; 4600, or nearly another fifth, re-staurants and traiteurs, the remainder consisting of wholesale and retail establishments where liquors are not consumed on the premises.

These establishments derived their supplies from a couple of entrepôts, one situated at Bercy, just inside the Paris fortifications, and the other, known as the Halle aux Vins, more within the city, on the Quai ·St. Bernard, adjoining the Jardin des Plantes. The latter owes its origin to a decree of Napoleon I., who designed that it should receive the wines, spirits, oils, and vinegars forwarded to Paris from the provinces. The buildings cover twenty-five acres of ground, and comprise eight extensive piles of warehouses, separated by six roadways and two courtyards. Four of these piles of building are devoted to wines, three to spirits and vinegars, and the remaining one to olive oils. They are capable of storing upwards of 100,000 tons of wine, 3,500,000 gallons of brandy, and 133,000 gallons of oil. The vast granite blocks of building where the wine is stored contain 158 cellars on a level with the ground, 49 subterranean cellars, and a couple of warehouses divided into 116 cellars and 312 bays. The detached buildings in which the brandies are stored contain 69 cellars, which are let out at the rate of 8 francs per annum the square metre (39 square inches). The rent of the wine cellars varies from 3 to 6 francs for a corresponding space. The aggregate rental of the entrepôt in the year 1867 was 600,000 francs, which was increased to 726,000 francs in 1868.

At the Halle aux Vins drays are perpetually passing in and out, barrels are for ever being rolled, branded by the excise, stacked, stamped, filled, and emptied. In front of his particular cellar each dealer has a little wooden hut, not unlike a wide sentry box, where he receives his customers. Every precaution is taken against fire ; of an evening, as soon as the establishment is closed, one-half of the staff engaged there make a careful inspection of the warehouses, to assure themselves that there is no chance of a disaster.

No " piece " of wine or other liquor can be removed from the entrepôt without having been first inspected by the agents of the octroi. A declaration signed by the owner is furnished to the carman, who hands it to the agents on duty at the gate through which he passes. If the cask contains wine it is measured by the aid of a graduated scale called a bâton d'octroi, which gives the quantity sufficiently near, and in order to ascertain whether there are more than the 18 degrees of alcohol allowed by the regulations the liquor is tasted. In front of the guard house where the drays draw up the pavement is of a violet hue, and exhales an insupportable odour of wine lees. If the cask contains spirits a certain quantity is taken from it and tested with the alcoholometer, which gives at a glance the number of degrees. All liquids containing more than 18 degrees pay the same duty as is imposed on spirits. In the event of any disputes arising between the owner and the octroi agents with reference to the precise alcoholic strength of either wines or spirits, recourse is had to the " dépotoir," an instrument of precision which is admitted to be infallible. In 1867 there were rather more than 18,000 casks of spirits and some couple of thousand casks of wine tested by means of this instrument, for which the owners had to pay the authorities about 30,000 francs.

An immense trade is carried on at the Halle aux Vins in common wines, the sale of fine wines being extremely limited. Almost all the business done is wholesale, and of course by the "piece." Owing, however, to certain provincial customs, the barriques are not of uniform size, and the practised eye will recognise at a glance the locality whence the wine comes by the size of the cask. The Maconnais and Beaujolais casks, for instance, contain only 212 litres, or 47 gallons, whereas the Bordelais barrique used for the Bordeaux wines holds 225 litres, or nearly 50 gallons, and the Burgundy 271 litres, or close upon 60 gallons.

In constructing the entrepôt, the intention was that it should be a receptacle for alimentary liquids in general; but at the present time oils and vinegars do not appear to be stored there in any quantity. The returns for 1868 show that about 76,000 gallons of oil and rather more than 81,000 gallons of vinegar were taken from the magazines in the course of the year, whereas there were nearly 4,300,000 gallons of various descriptions of alcohol and 83,500 tuns of wine removed from them.

It is very rarely that wine undergoes adulteration while stored at the Halle aux Vins. Of the 83,500 tuns above-mentioned only about 3300 gallons were seized, and these for the most part through the wine having turned during its transit to Paris or from being badly stored. Wines unusually deficient in alcohol, and those that have already become sour, are mixed with a certain quantity of vinegar and returned to the owners, who can convert them entirely into vinegar and then dispose of them. Wine that is pronounced to be decidedly bad and unwholesome is emptied without further ado into the Seine. Although wines may not be adulterated at the entrepôt, they do not always leave the magazine in the same state in which they entered it. Certainly water is not added to them, but it is a common practice to mix different " crus " together. This operation, known as the " soutirage," is performed in the face of day, with no kind of mystery attending it, the practice being alike recognised by the authorities and by the trade. What passes as good ordinary Bordeaux is produced by mixing a couple of pieces of vin de Blaye, a sound but flat red wine, two pieces of the thin white wine styled "vin d'entre deux mers," which comes from the neighbourhood of the Bec d'Ambez, and a piece of Roussillon, the wine which goes in England under the name of French port. These different wines are poured into a large vat, where they are thoroughly stirred to render their amalgamation complete, after which they are left to ferment slightly, and then placed in casks again. In the same way much of the wine sold as Macon is produced by a mixture of the wines of Beaujolais, Tavel, and Bergerac.

Formerly colour was imparted to pale wines by elderberries, mulberries, and logwood. Nowadays these clumsy ingredients are superseded by a natural wine of the Loiret called " vin noir." At Cette, in the south of France, are regular wine manufactories, at which all kinds of wine are produced from the strong wine of the district by the addition of certain compounds. Most of the wine sold in France as Sherry, Lunel, and Frontignac comes from these establishments. Madeira, too, certainly does not export to France a thousandth part of the wine that is consumed there under that name. Cette, in fact, supplies Madeira to half the world.

The brandy sold at many of the Paris wine-shops and at some of the cafés does not contain a particle of the juice of the grape, but is usually composed of potato spirit of 90 degrees of strength, mixed with water to reduce it from 47 to 49 degrees, and coloured with caramel and sweetened with treacle. Good brandy, that which is really obtained from wine, has no more than 41 degrees of strength. It will sometimes happen by reason of a too recent or too rapid fabrication that brandy remains what is called green and rough. Recourse is then had to a process which is perfectly harmless to soften it. To eleven and a half gallons of spirit is added less than half a gallon of boiling tea, in which some spirit of marshmallow has been dissolved. The keenest palate is deceived by this means; the brandy becomes oily and acquires an apparent age of twenty years in half as many minutes.

Such adulteration of wine as takes place in Paris is almost invariably performed by the retailers. Their habit is out of two pieces of wine to make three by the addition of the requisite quantity of water. To guard the Parisians against frauds so easy of perpetration, the prefecture of police has in its service

twenty-eight tasters, under the orders of a chief
taster and his assistant, and whose mission is to taste
the wines and liquors vended at the 25,000 establishments of which we have spoken, and to denounce any
frauds they may succeed in detecting. These agents
are only engaged after undergoing a rigid examina-
tion. Twelve specimens of wine are presented to all
candidates for the post, the particular "cru" of which
they are required to recognise off hand. Some of
these agents are able to accomplish veritable prodigies
by reason of the extreme delicacy and sensibility of
their organs of taste, and will, it is said, name the
half-dozen different kinds of wine composing a mixture. Their duties, as may be supposed, are no
sinecure. Formerly it was the practice to empty all
adulterated wine seized by the agents into the gutter
in front of the door of the delinquent tradesman,
which brought the poor people of the neighbourhood
to the spot armed with saucepans, jugs, sponges, &c.,
to collect all they could of the unwholesome purple
fluid as it flowed on its way to the sewer; latterly,
on the principle one may suppose of rendering unto
the Seine that which belongs to the Seine, it has been
the practice at once to restore all confiscated wine to
that river, from which so large a portion of it has
usually come.

With regard to milk, the commodity not being sold
at the Paris markets, but supplies being consigned direct to those who deal in it, no statistics
exist to guide us as to the quantity ordinarily
consumed in the French capital. It would appear,
however, that Paris is scarcely better off as regards
the purity of its milk than London itself, although a
strict supervision is supposed to be exercised by the
municipal authorities over the milk on its arrival

from the country by the railway trains, and also at the various establishments where it is retailed to the public. Spite of this watchfulness, it is commonly considered that milk is ordinarily adulterated with 18 per cent. of water before it reaches the hands of the retail dealer, who, after skimming the cream off, and adding a considerable additional quantity of water, mixes some bicarbonate of soda with it to prevent it from turning. Paris milk, it seems, undergoes no more deleterious adulteration than this, which is certainly more than can be said of the London article.

In Paris, beyond the wine-tasting agents already mentioned, there were under the control of the prefect of police, a tribe of inspectors charged to examine and certify the wholesome and unadulterated condition of all food offered for sale, not only within the various markets, but at every shop, stall, cabaret, and hand-barrow even, all over Paris, and to verify the hundreds of thousands of weights and measures in use, reporting all tradesmen who fail to get them duly stamped with the official stamp of the year, and proceeding rigorously against all the more dishonest ones, who were punished by fine for venial offences, and invariably by imprisonment when any deleterious substance was detected in their adulterations and who by a wholesome clause in all decisions were bound to expose a copy of the judgment given against them in a conspicuous part of their shops and in their shop windows, in view of the general public, for the space of fifteen days—a practice that might be advantageously imitated on the other side of the Channel.

## II. HOW PARIS WAS INTENDED TO BE FED.

Even before the downfall of the Ollivier administration on the 9th of August, the Paris municipality, more foreseeing than the Imperial Government, had turned its attention to the provisioning of the capital, in anticipation of its being besieged, and as a preliminary measure had had the stock taken of all the wheat and flour stored in the public magazines, and had required each of the 1200 Paris bakers to furnish an exact statement of the quantity of flour in his possession. At this epoch there were, according to the official return, 293,289 quintaux of flour in the magazines, which, increased by the moderate stock in the bakers' hands, would scarcely have amounted to more than 30,000 tons, equivalent to about 45 days' supply.

When M. Clément Duvernois became Minister of Agriculture and Commerce, one of his first acts was to direct the Prefect of the Seine to require every baker to lay in a stock of flour sufficient for fifteen days' average consumption, and which was to be deposited either at the Halles Centrales or in the municipal granary; his next was to cause considerable purchases of wheat and flour to be made on Government account, and at the same time to interdict the exportation of these articles. The municipal council, which sat en permanence during the latter half of the month of August and the commencement of September, busied itself with the expedition to Paris by railway, and the storage, of large quantities of wheat disembarked at Havre and Marseilles from the United States, the Danubian Principalities, and Algeria, together with many thousand barrels of flour from Chicago and other ports of the west, and

innumerable sacks of this commodity from the principal agricultural districts of France.

The Government purchases appear to have been
made either abroad, or in the more distant departments, with the view of interfering as little as
possible with the regular course of trade; the consequence was that although the Paris markets were
glutted with wheat, buyers were rare; and at one
period the panic was such that the lower the price fell
the scarcer the purchasers became. This evidently
arose from the absence of flour-mills in the capital, and
from many of those in the adjacent departments having
ceased to work, owing to the war rendering it doubtful
whether the grain could be transmitted to the miller,
and received back in the shape of flour before Paris
was invested, as while wheat found purchasers with
difficulty, flour commanded high prices, and was
bought up with avidity. The Government having
insured a stock of breadstuffs on its own account, and
obliged the bakers to lay in an extra supply, directed
its attention to the standing crops and stores of corn,
&c., in the environs, and issued a notice apprizing the
farmers round Paris that corn, flour, dried vegetables,
and forage would be warehoused within the city walls
free of charge. Simultaneously with these steps being
taken, large purchases of horned cattle, sheep, and
pigs were effected on the Government account at the
Paris and neighbouring markets, the number of
animals arriving at which increased considerably
towards the end of August, when the quantity of
sheep sold at La Villette each market day ranged
from 23,000 to 25,000 against 11,000 the week preceding; the number of oxen and pigs had likewise
largely increased, although not in the same proportion.

On August 26th, the day on which the Minister of the Interior informed the Corps Législatif that no longer any doubt existed as to the enemy having resumed his march upon Paris, M. Thiers pressed upon the authorities the expediency of taking immediate steps to secure the outstanding harvests and stores of grain and forage in the environs, which the farmers, refusing to believe in the imminence of the danger, delayed transporting within the walls. The Government notified its willingness to purchase this agricultural produce at a fair price, or to provide warehouse room for it free of charge, in accordance with the notice it had already given; and intimated that failing its removal on the approach of the Prussians being signalled, energetic measures would be had recourse to : meaning that it would be burnt to prevent it falling into the enemy's hands. " We shall not recoil," said the Baron Jerôme David, "before these acts of grave necessity ; convinced as we are that with union, energy, and determination France will be found invincible!" M. Clément Duvernois then explained the steps he had taken for the victualling of Paris, and said that he had originally contemplated laying in a large store of salted and preserved provisions, but had found the markets insufficiently stocked with these commodities ; in addition to which there were obvious objections to a population of two million souls being reduced to animal food exclusively of this character.

A couple of days afterwards a notice appeared apprizing the agriculturists of the environs that, in addition to the warehouse room already offered them, a certain number of enclosed spaces in different quarters of Paris—among others the arches of the railway viaduct at Auteuil, where cattle could be stalled under cover, and corn and forage stacked—were at their disposal free of charge. Intimation was at the same time given that cattle would have to be accompanied by persons who would remain and attend to them, and be moreover provided with forage and litter for at least five-and-twenty days.

At this epoch the exterior boulevards and several of the principal thoroughfares were frequently rendered impassable, owing to the huge droves of cattle and immense flocks of sheep which were being incessantly directed towards the Bois de Boulogne, where they were provisionally installed and formally inspected by the Minister of Agriculture and Commerce. Long files of waggons laden with sacks of flour, and railway vans piled up with casks and cases of provisions of all descriptions, moreover, thronged the streets. In the neighbourhood of the Halle au Blé the thoroughfares were more or less blocked by the number of vehicles arriving with wheat and flour, the unloading of which the privileged "forts" found themselves unequal to, and advertisements appeared daily in the papers for robust men to assist at this work.

In due course the Halle au Blé and the 10th pavilion of the Halles Centrales were piled up to their roofs with corn and flour, and it was announced that considerable stores of these and other commodities were amassed in the Grenier d'Abondance as well as in different private magazines. Nineteen new posts of sapeurs-pompiers were moreover established in the neighbourhood of these various provision depôts, to guard against any outbreak of fire. At this epoch the newspapers were jubilant over the abundant stores of food laid up for the day when Paris should be invested; and one and all proclaimed that whatever else might happen the city would certainly never succumb through famine. The Parisians having ocular evidence of the vast accumulations of alimentary substances made for their benefit, appreciated the prudent forethought of the paternal Government under which they then lived, while such as could afford it none the less observed the recommendation of the prefect of the Seine, and laid up according to their necessities and their means a special stock of provisions of their own. The prefect at the same time, in the interest of the defence, as he expressed it, enjoined all those who were unequal to facing the enemy at once to quit the city. It was necessary, it seems, to get rid of the " useless mouths " by persuasion as well as by force.

During the latter part of August something like a couple of hundred thousand sheep, and between thirty and forty thousand oxen—the pigs, of which a considerable stock had been laid in were not admitted within these aristocratic precincts—were installed in the Bois de Boulogne, and about the same time the animals belonging to the Jardin d'Acclimatation were transferred thence to the Jardin des Plantes. Henceforward this charming park à la Watteau, which the Parisians owed to the genius of M. Alphand, with its artificial lakes, counterfeit rocks, and sham cascades, and the mazy green alleys and shady avenues of which were already doomed to be devastated at a signal from the military engineers, ceased to be the favourite afternoon promenade of the meilleur and the demimondes of Paris, of that long train of brilliant equipages—victorias, landaulettes, calèches-à-huit-ressorts, mysterious satin-lined coupés, petits paniers-sans-anse, stanhopes, dog-carts, and four-in-hands : that réunion at which rank and high social position engaged in a tournament with the insolent display of elegant vice dominant in the French capital. The Bois de Boulogne had become transformed into a vast cattle park, an immense sheepfold. From Neuilly to Auteuil, from Passy to Suresnes, it was nothing but a succession of hillocks of wool terminating in horizons of horns. There were long-legged sheep from Brie, Picardy, Touraine, Berri, Champagne, and Limousin ; and long-tailed black sheep from Gascony and Guienne; bulls from Limagne, Poitou, and Normandy; oxen from the Dordogne, Nivernais, Charolais, Gâtenais, Beauce, and Charente, and miniature cows from Brittany. Sheep baaed and oxen bellowed in all manner of dialects as they roamed adown the avenues, strayed through the hedges, rambled over the grass, or rushed to the margin of the lakes to drink. The arrival of all these flocks and herds gave rise to a paraphrase of Victor Hugo's poem, " Les bœufs qui paissent," the concluding stanzas of which ran thus :—

> " Le temps n'est plus à vos œillades,
> Filles aux manteaux cramoisis,
> Rentrez, folles amadryades,
> Nous attendons les ennemis !—
> Vos cheveux roux qui se déplacent
> Effrayent bêtes et bouviers—
> Enfants, voici les bœufs qui passent,
> Cachez vos rouges tabliers.

> " L'éclat du canon purifie
> L'air souillé de poudre de riz,
> Votre influence est bien finie.
> La guerre a pris vos Amadis.
> Nos enfants de honte se lassent,
> Les saules se font peupliers—
> Enfants, voici les bœufs qui passent,
> Cachez vos rouges tabliers."

The scanty herbage of M. Alphand's artificial lawns, lacking as it did the succulency and the racy flavour of their native pastures, proved scarcely to the taste of these animals, and furnished them, moreover, with insufficient nourishment. At first they fared but sparingly off it, but finding there was nothing else for them, in the course of a few days they ate every tuft of grass down to the roots, and then commenced to devour the young shoots from the bushes and the trees. Not only was there an insufficiency of pasture for all these flocks and herds, but being crowded together, as they were in such dense masses, they could only reach the drinking places with difficulty, and one heard them lowing and baaing piteously from morn till night; added to which experienced herds to tend them were lacking. This want was eventually supplied by telling off a certain number of mobiles from the agricultural districts who had been accustomed to similar duties; still the animals wasted perceptibly; the oxen showed far more of their anatomical development than is pleasing to the eye of a butcher, while as regards the sheep they commenced to die off, rendering it requisite for a professor and numerous pupils of the Veterinary School of Alfort to instal themselves on the spot. The newpapers advised the Minister of Agriculture and Commerce at once to disperse the animals in the environs, and when the enemy approached to have them driven in again; instead of which it was decided to pack and stall them within the walls—in the Jardin du Luxembourg, the Jardin des Plantes, on some waste ground in the Avenue Suffren, near the Champ de Mars, at Montrouge, and other places; also in the sheds of the cattle market at La Villette, the stables of several of the cavalry barracks, the empty stores of various railway stations, the vast courtyard of the College Rollin, and in temporary sheds erected on the Boulevard Montparnasse adjacent to the cemetery.

Here they appear to have fared scarcely any better,

for the cattle might be seen with their hoofs sunk deep in the mire gazing languidly at the visitors who came to satisfy themselves of their true condition, or with their muzzles in the air bellowing long and mournfully. Among them were some cows, which the mobiles would milk, and gallantly offer the warm frothy fluid to the ladies, who, catching up their petticoats and picking their way daintily through the mud, would laughingly drink the milk out of wooden bowls, showing their pretty white teeth meanwhile.*

A few days after the revolution of September 4th, the Government of National Defence—to whom, by the way, none of the credit of victualling Paris is due —informed the Parisians that the capital was provisioned with bread, meat, liquids, and alimentary substances of all kinds, amply sufficient for a population of two millions of souls for a couple of months, and on the day following (September 9th), with the view of adding to this stock, it judiciously enough decreed the suspension of the octroi and of customs duties on provisions of all descriptions. Unfortunately it was too late for this to prove of much effect. In the first place, the railways were completely blocked ; and then again, there was not sufficient time for the execution of orders on a large scale. With regard to cattle, it was useless importing them on private account unless the necessary forage for their keep was sent in at the same time. One good result, however, followed from the decree : considerable quantities of common wine were at once brought in to save the octroi, which would have amounted to nearly one-third of its value.

On September 11th, the Government gave notice that for the future the Minister of Agriculture and

<hr>

* Sarcey's " Siége de Paris," p. 39.

Commerce would fix the price at which butcher's meat was to be sold, and at the same time apprized the trade that a daily cattle market would be established at the Marché aux Chevaux—a somewhat ominous notification this—whence they could derive their supply. Subsequently, in pursuance of the foregoing decree, the price of meat, dating from the 16th of September, was fixed as under, and at this price, which was if anything below the average rate at which meat was then being sold, it remained until the stock became exhausted:—The prime parts of beef were priced at 3fr. the kilogramme, equal to 13*d.* the lb. avoirdupois; second rate parts at 2fr. 10c., equal to 9*d.* per lb.; intermediate parts, 1fr. 70c., equal to 7½*d.* per lb.; inferior parts, 1fr. 30c., equal to 5½*d.* per lb. With regard to mutton, the prime joints were—1fr. 80c. the kilogramme, or 8*d.* the lb.; second rate joints were 1fr. 30c. equal to 5½*d.* per lb.; and the inferior parts 1fr. 10c. or 5*d.* per lb. Fresh pork was priced at 2fr. 30c. the kilogramme, equal to 10½*d.* the lb.; and salt pork at 1fr. 80c., equal to 8*d.* the lb. The butchers were, moreover, required to indicate, by written labels placed on the meat itself, the particular category to which each part belonged, and to display the official decree fixing the price at which the different descriptions were to be sold, in some conspicuous part of their shops.

At first many of the butchers refused to sell their meat at the prices indicated, on the score that they were not sufficiently remunerative, and National Guards had to be constantly summoned to their shops to insure the regulation being observed by them. The *Journal Officiel* eventually notified that the shops of those butchers who refused to sell meat according to the terms of the decree, would be peremptorily

closed ; a threat which the authorities were saved the
trouble of enforcing by the butchers closing their
establishments themselves, at the same time that they
affixed placards outside announcing they would remain
closed during the war.    Eventually the authorities
and the butchers came to terms, and the latter kept
their shops open so long as a supply of meat was
assured them.    In some arrondissements, however,
"boucheries municipales," as they were styled, were
established by the mayors.    With reference to bread,
a fixed price for this was not decreed until four days
after Paris was invested, when it was appointed to be
sold at the ordinary rate of 45 centimes and 38 centimes the kilogramme, equivalent to about $2\frac{1}{4}d.$ and
$1\frac{3}{4}d.$ the lb. avoirdupois for the first and second qualities respectively.

One learnt from an official report published towards
the end of September that a day or two after the
Republic was proclaimed, one of the new adjoints of
the Mayor of Paris proceeded to inspect the numerous depôts where the provisions purchased by order
of the Imperial Government and confided to the care
of the municipality had been stored, when, although
certain of these depôts, more particularly that of the
Invalides, were found to be in an unsatisfactory condition, their general state was all that could be desired.
According to the same document, the stock of flour
belonging to the Government and in the hands of
the municipal authorities amounted on the 20th of
September, the day following the investment, to
upwards of 292,000 quintaux ; the stock in the hands
of the trade at the same period was set down at about
155,000 quintaux, giving a total of fully 447,000
quintaux, equal to about 44,000 tons.    Allowing for
an ordinary rate of consumption—namely, under

7000 quintaux per day—and adding the flour in sacks which was not included in the foregoing estimate, and was sufficient, it was said, for several days' supply, it might be calculated that there was ample flour to last for ten weeks, or to the end of November. In addition, between the public magazines and the dealers there was a stock of something like 100,000 quintaux of wheat, which, if the means could only be found for grinding it in Paris, would extend the supply of flour until the middle of December ; besides which the authorities had laid in a provision of rice, amounting to 150,000 quintaux, it was said, and the storehouses of the Intendance were known to be filled with provisions for the army, among which were considerable quantities of flour and rice. Taking therefore everything into consideration, it would appear that the quantity of farinaceous food within the walls of Paris at the period of the investment was very considerably in excess of the official estimate formed of it.

With reference to the stock of cattle at the same epoch, we have not the means of arriving at any very precise result. It was announced that on the 24th of September, five days after the capital was invested, there were in round numbers 150,000 sheep, 24,600 oxen, and 6000 pigs within the walls, which according to the report were then being well taken care of and picking up flesh. If to the foregoing figures five days' average consumption are added, the live stock at the moment of the investment would be increased to 175,000 sheep, 30,000 oxen, and 8800 pigs, which even including some 5937 milch cows, stalled within the walls and requisitioned by the Government during the siege for food, would have been little more than sufficient for a month's supply, providing Paris had gone on consum-

ing animal food in the same proportion as ordinarily—
that is, at the rate of 935 oxen, 4680 sheep, 570 pigs,
and 600 calves per day, especially if one takes into consideration the 46,000 head of poultry and game, nearly
50 tons of fish, besides 100,000 oysters, and 670,000
eggs which the city of bon vivants was daily in the
habit of devouring, and of which it would necessarily
be for the most part deprived when its communications were finally cut off.    In place of these a certain
quantity of salted and preserved provisions require to
be take into account, as no doubt at this epoch a considerable number of the pigs purchased by the
authorities had been already killed and salted down ;
a store of salt junk and dried codfish, the precise
quantity of which, however, never transpired, had we
know been laid in by the Government, together with
some millions of rations of preserved meat.    Moreover
orders had been given a few days before the investment, to kill all the game possible in the forests of
the State in the environs of Paris, and many thousand
head of game, including deer, hares, rabbits, partridges,
and pheasants brought down at this battu on a grand
scale, were consequently added to the Paris larder.

With reference to milk, assurances were given
that an ample number of milch cows were installed
within the walls to provide a sufficient supply of this
fluid for infants and invalids, but unfortunately during
the siege not more than a fraction of these objects of
administrative forethought succeeded in securing it,
through its sale not having been restricted in accordance with repeated suggestions made to the authorities.    Among the earliest evidences of the investment
were the notices affixed outside certain milk shops, intimating that they were closed through want of milk.

As regards grocery, Paris appears to have been

provided with at any rate a sufficient supply, and
it was not found necessary to fix the price of such
commodities as coffee, sugar, salt, &c., by decree.
The Government had charged itself with laying in a
considerable stock of salt, which the dealers nevertheless vended retail at the rate of 1½*d.* per lb.    There
was a profusion of chocolate, honey, jam, and sweet-
meats of all kinds for the sweet-toothed section of the
Parisian population; preserved vegetables too were
plentiful; anchovies also were in abundance.    It was
different, however, with such things as ham, bacon,
tongues, Australian meats, sardines, dried fish, cheese,
and concentrated milk.    Either only moderate quantities of these articles were in the hands of the trade
or else the stocks had been bought up for the purpose
of being held back, as the major part after attaining
rapidly increasing prices on the eve of the investment,
disappeared altogether from the shops during the
early days of the siege.    Satisfactory reasons were
given at the time for the stocks not being more considerable ; firstly, because owing to the stoppage of
credit cash had to be remitted with all orders ;
secondly, because traders hesitated to submit to the
considerable extra rate for carriage, arising from the
necessity which existed for having all goods expedited
by fast trains ; thirdly, on account of the risk to
which they were exposed of not receiving the goods
after remitting the money for them, owing to the confusion which prevailed on all the lines of railway
having their termini in Paris.

Paris could hardly hope long to enjoy the luxury
of fruit and fresh vegetables after the city was once
invested, nevertheless, owing principally to the grape
season being at its height, it was comparatively
speaking well supplied with fruit, and considerable

quantities of vegetables came in daily from the
environs—National Guards and Mobiles having been
told off for the especial duty of helping to gather
and bring them in—up to the period when the sharp
weather commenced. The supply, however, being far
from sufficient and more or less intermittent, prices
necessarily ruled high. The Government laid in a
large stock of potatoes, but the great bulk of them
appear to have rotted before the necessity of having
recourse to them arose.*

Whatever the chances might have been of the
Parisians having to endure the pangs of hunger,
there was little or no prospect of their suffering from
thirst. Of wine, which is more than meat to the
Paris workman and to the poorer classes generally,

---

* Remarkable laxity appears to have been observed with regard
to certain contracts. It transpired at the inquiry instituted by the
National Assembly into the proceedings of the Palikao and Trochu
Administrations, that under the Minister Duvernois a Mdlle.
Blanche Costar, whose vocation was that of a dressmaker, but who
had transformed herself into a dealer in potatoes, obtained a contract for the supply of those tubers. She came to an arrangement
with an American named Fréard, and stipulated for 3 per cent. for
herself, which, as the sum total of the goods to be supplied was
35 millions, would have given her upwards of a million of francs,
had the siege of Paris not interrupted the operation. Another
contract had been made with a person named Chavaune, who,
contributing nothing but the bargain agreed on by the minister,
had entered into a partnership with Fréard, who brought nothing
at all. The profits that were expected to be realized were nevertheless calculated at 1,227,700 francs. The relations of Fréard
with the Ministry of Commerce date from about the 17th of
August, when the minister accepting his offers, through the medium of a certain Vanderbrough, a bargain was made between
them for a sum of more than 20 millions of francs. After September 4th, Fréard appears to have found himself in London
with M. Duvernois, and there formed a company for supplying
France with all sorts of commodities, himself contributing nothing
but the treaty which he had made with the ex-minister.

Paris was known to be provided with more than its ordinary six months' stock, owing to the number of casks sent in when the octroi was abolished. In fact, so numerous were these that room could not be found for all in the cellars of the entrepôt, and they were stored on the quay in front, covered over with sand, some said to preserve their contents from the weather, others to protect them from the enemy's bombs. As for beer and spirits, these too were known to be abundant, consequently no kind of anxiety was felt on the score of the supply of stimulants running short.

With regard to the more insipid if more essential fluid, the Seine had to be depended upon for the principal supply. It was foreseen that the Germans would cut off the supply derived from the purer sources of the Dhuys and the Ourcq, and that the northern elevated districts would have to trust to the great reservoirs of Belleville and Menilmontant, while the lower districts would chiefly have to be supplied by means of the floating steam pumps installed in the Seine, which would keep the various fountains and reservoirs throughout the city constantly filled. In addition there was the artesian well at Passy, and another belonging to a large manufacturer, M. Léon Say, whose works were obliged to be suspended during the siege, with numerous ordinary wells, including many new ones which had been dug especially, and hundreds of old wells which had been cleaned out, so that Paris experienced no kind of inconvenience so far as its water supply was concerned.

Forage for the live stock and horses within the walls was an affair of quite as much moment as the general provisioning of the capital, of which indeed it was a part. Oats, hay, and straw, originally purchased for the horses of the cavalry and artillery, had been shipped abroad in considerable quantities, and were now directed upon Paris, which also derived large supplies from the provinces, and more especially from the environs.    To expedite the bringing in of the final harvests and the stocks of grain and forage amassed in the immediate neighbourhood of Paris, and avoid having to set fire to them, the Government at the last moment supplied the farmers with carts and vehicles of all descriptions, requisitioned in Paris for this especial purpose, and by this means rescued a large amount of agricultural produce.

As the inevitable moment drew near when the Germans might be expected, almost every one possessed of even the most moderate means laid in his private stock of provisions, that he might have something in reserve against those enforced fast days which it was feared the siege would exact the observance of far more frequently and rigidly than even the most stringent regulations of the Catholic Church.    Every day a class of people was encountered at the Halles who had never before been observed there, purchasing live fowls and pigeons with a stock of grass for feeding them, live rabbits, dried fish, bacon, cheese, eggs, dried vegetables of all descriptions, and even barrels of flour. The shops of the grocers and provision dealers were moreover laid siege to, and all such commodities as hams, tongues, brawn, cheese, sardines, preserved and potted meats, including Liebig's extract, macaroni, biscuits, and concentrated milk, commanded day by day gradually ascending prices.    The newspapers, too, did not think it beneath their dignity to give endless recipes for salting meat and preserving flour, eggs, vegetables, &c.

# V.

## THE INVESTMENT.

---

### I. THE LAST DAY OF LIBERTY.

SUNDAY, September 18th, was a splendid autumnal day, brilliant and balmy, as though it had been June. All Paris, abroad in the sunshine, is if anything elated rather than depressed at the novelty of the danger that menaces it, and the indefinite nature of which has a grim kind of fascination for a population that certainly lives more intensely than all the rest of the world. Everywhere a gay crowd is watching the fated city preparing its toilet of war. At the principal points of the enceinte a throng of sight-seers are inspecting the fortifications, to which thousands of hands are giving certain finishing touches— roofing in the stone casemates with earth, laying down platforms for cannon, placing gabions at the embrasures, posing sandbags on the parapet, drilling torpedo holes, pointing stakes for pièges-à-loups, fixing stockades, and planting earthworks, smooth and trim as flower-beds, with spikes, while the last stragglers of that long procession of vehicles, piled up with furniture or forage, and come to seek a refuge in Paris, await their turn to pass inside the city gates.* Some

---

* The owners of both showed their wisdom, for the ones saved their ormolu clocks, buhl cabinets, and Palissy platters from pillage, as the others saved their hay and oats from being requisitioned by the enemy—one of those distinctions without a difference to which a state of war gives rise.

groups finding the Bois de Boulogne closed to them, loiter round the various entrances and lament over the acres of trees which have already fallen beneath the woodcutter's axe ; others watch the National and Mobile Guards exercising in the Champs Elysées or the Cours la Reine, or stroll in and out the lines of low tents that crowd the Avenue de la Grande Armée, or the Champ de Mars, where the regulars are camped.  Some find consolation for privations in store in contemplating the numerous head of sheep and cattle stalled in the Jardin du Luxembourg and the Jardin des Plantes, whilst others are attracted to the quays to witness the first trial of the steam fire and pumping engines recently arrived from England—the ones in view of a possible bombardment, the others to fill the public reservoirs when the supply from the aqueducts is cut off.  In the Rue de Rivoli people are peering through the gilt railings of the Tuileries gardens, at the rows of cannons and caissons, and the artillery camp installed among the statues and the orange trees, or loitering in front of the Hôtel du Gouverneur de Paris to see General Trochu—the hero of the hour—and his staff ride forth.  But by far the largest crowd is collected on the Place de la Concorde, where mass is being sung at the foot of the Statue of the city of Strasbourg, which the Parisians, since the determined resistance offered by the capital of Alsace, have exalted into a veritable shrine.  The Place this morning is thronged with National and Mobile Guards, having green sprigs and autumn flowers in the muzzles of their rifles.  Among them, however, one sees none of Trochu's Bretons, for they have gone in procession with banners at their head, and priests by their side, to vow candles and other gifts to Nôtre Dame des Victoires, goddess of battles in the eyes of all good Catholics.

The prospect of Paris being taken by the traditional four uhlans riding across the drawbridge at the
top of the Rue d'Allemagne, and ordering breakfasts
for an unlimited number of their compatriots at the
Grand Hotel, had been a standing joke among the
English colony, who originally had no faith in the
seriousness of the defence, while the civil population
generally had made up their minds that the advent
of the enemy would be instantly signalled by the dull
roar of distant cannon. When, therefore, during the
morning several dull detonations on the western side
of the city were heard, if there was not the "whisper-
ing with white lips, The foe, they come! they come!"
it was yet confidently believed that the inevitable
moment had arrived, and that the enemy was endeavouring to force his way into Paris by a coup de
main, or coup de chien, as it is expressed in the
Parisian vernacular. The opinion, indeed, was wide-
spread that the Germans would at once begin to
bombard, and then sacrificing a certain number of
men, would press on between two of the detached
forts to the ramparts, and attempt to carry the city
by assault.* The reports which caused this temporary
alarm eventually proved to have resulted from the
explosion of a mine at the Château des Landes, and
some unsuccessful attempts by the French engineers
to blow up the bridges of Sèvres and St. Cloud.

Since the closing of the Bois de Boulogne, the military road in the vicinity of the ramparts had become
the favourite afternoon resort of the Parisians, and
certain points of it might very well be mistaken for a
fair in the neighbourhood of some garrison town.
Promenaders chat, laugh, and enjoy themselves seem-

---

* Sarcey's "Siége de Paris," p. 51.

ingly quite regardless of the quarter of a million
Germans, whose arrival they have been daily expecting, and whom they strongly suspect to be by this
time hiding in some of the neighbouring woods, else
why have so many come provided with opera-glasses,
through which they are, every now and then, peeping?
A certain quantity of cannon are by this time in
position on the ramparts, and naturally excite surprise
and admiration on the part of the fair sex.   The
larger naval guns are lying about on the green turf,
and little children kneeling down before them, peep
into their huge black muzzles, reminding one of the
lamb in Landseer's picture, and for the moment suggesting a certain affinity between peace and war.
Adults, who might venture to display a like curiosity,
would speedily find themselves arrested as spies by
one or other of the lynx-eyed guardians of the ramparts, whose military insignia appears to be confined
to their muskets and kepis, and who furtively scru-
tinize every one loitering for an instant near the
cannon, which they are proud of having committed to
their watchful charge, as though the fate of Paris
depended on their zeal in detecting so-called spies.
Even the prefect of police, who is found regarding the
fortifications with much too curious an eye, is arrested
to-day by one of these over-zealous citizen soldiers.

The omnibuses ran as usual to the pretty villages
in the immediate environs—by this time almost completely deserted—through some unpleasant scenes of
desolation, which, however, are as nothing to what
they will be when the siege has fairly commenced.
People stray, according to habit, in the open country
beyond the ramparts, enjoying themselves after their
own fashion, and certainly oppressed by no sort of
gloomy preoccupation.   In the neighbourhood of the

detached forts, crowds of men, women, and children, with soldiers and mobiles, are busy rooting up the vegetables neglected to be gathered in by their owners, and at several of the gates on the southern and north-eastern sides of the city, troops of these marauders arrive throughout the day, with their well-filled sacks, baskets, bags, and bundles. Thousands of people bent on obtaining a sight of the armour-plated floating batteries, and the gunboats, and of the works in progress for the defence of the Seine at Bercy, and Point du Jour, crowd the little river steamers, which run just the same as usual, while others make the tour of Paris by the Chemin de fer du Ceinture, to obtain such views of the detached forts and the environs generally, as its lofty embankments and the bright autumnal atmosphere will afford. The Place de Saint Pierre too, in face of the Butte Montmartre, swarms with people eagerly watching Nadar ascend in his huge captive balloon, the Neptune, to try and make out the whereabouts of the enemy.

Whilst Paris is thus amusing itself, a little scene is enacting in one of the bastions of the ramparts near the Ternes. The commander of the 5th section of the fortification—General Ambert, mayor of one of the aristocratic arrondissements under the recent Empire—is having an altercation with his men, pooh-poohing the Republic, and saying that a government must be ratified by universal suffrage, as the Empire was, before he can recognise it. This brings forward a hot-blooded captain, who in his turn refuses to recognise the general as his commander, and eventually the latter finds himself arrested by his own men, and marched off in custody, with a mob at his heels abusing him, and tearing at his epaulettes. On reaching the Ministry of the Interior he is given in

charge of the guard installed there, and subsequently
deprived of his command.  With discords such as
this in one of the principal elements of the defence, it may well be doubted whether the Parisians
will be united in presence of the enemy.

The Paris newspapers of the 18th, as if with a fore-
cast of this being the last occasion for some time to
come on which they would be able to supply their
readers with news from outside, published more than
an average quantity of foreign and provincial intelligence, including numerous translations from the
English and German papers.  Singularly enough they
contained a telegram from Neufchâteau—the last telegram from a distance Paris was destined to receive—
announcing that news had arrived from Metz by
means of a small balloon, in the car of which a packet
of some 5000 tiny notes had been found written by
soldiers of Bazaine's army to their relatives and
friends.   From these it appeared that the troops were
still blockaded under the walls of Metz, but were
suffering neither from hunger nor from sickness, and
were only in want of one thing—news—the very want
which Paris itself was then on the eve of realizing
in all its painful intensity.   A couple of telegrams
referring to the movements of the enemy in the
neighbourhood of Villeneuve-St.-Georges, supplied
all the information with which the Parisians were
favoured, respecting the advance of the German army,
and of the few official decrees published only one—
ordering mobiles billeted in private houses to keep
good hours, and be within doors by ten o'clock at
night—in any way interested the Parisians.   A new
proclamation of the German Governor of Lorraine,
reproduced in all the papers, aroused a momentary
indignation, soon forgotten  beside  a  racy  bit  of

scandal served up by the *Rappel*, which had secured copies of a couple of letters found among the seized Imperial correspondence, and written by a certain Mdlle. Marguerite Bellanger—the one to the highest judicial authority in France, and the other to the late chief of the State himself, whose relations with the ex-blanchisseuse were well-known, and who had had recourse to the good offices of the first President of the Court of Cassation to arrange a particular phase of the liaison. As may be supposed, Paris chuckled delightedly over this revelation, equally compromising for " Monsieur le Premier President," the " Ever Devoted but very Unhappy Marguerite," and her "Cher Seigneur," as she styled her blasé Imperial lover. Among the miscellaneous articles in the newspapers à propos of the "situation," was one on the "Treasures of Paris," the author of which—M. Paul de Saint Victor—intimated in somewhat grandiloquent terms that—

" The moment when implements of ravage and destruction were already rolling against the ramparts of Paris, appeared to be the proper one to remind the world on what kind of city the bombs of Germany were about to fall, and of the irreparable loss which civilization might thereby sustain. The sack of Corinth by Mummius, the pillage of Athens by Sylla, the capture of Rome by Genseric, suggest but a faint idea, since the patrimony of civilization, of which Paris contains within its walls by far the greater part, has largely increased in the course of nineteen centuries.

" Paris is not merely a centre of ideas, a workshop of progress, the salvation of peoples, the heart of Europe, and, as Montaigne remarked in his time, ' one of the noblest ornaments of the world.' It is also an immense museum, a mass of libraries, the receptacle of the chefs-d'œuvre of human thought and labour. Athens, it was said, counted as many statues as inhabitants. Paris counts more celebrated marbles, renowned paintings, unique manuscripts and artistic treasures than citizens. All the gold in the world would not purchase these objects of priceless value, and yet a single handful of iron might destroy them.

" Paris opened all her libraries and museums to the world with unbounded liberality. The hospitality of the mind was never practised more magnificently than by her. Does Germany wish to incur the terrible responsibility of their destruction? Each of her bombs may be a torch òf Omar flying through the air. It may set fire to a library, smash a statue, burn paintings, reducing to cinders one of the finest productions of human genius.

" All ruin of this kind would be irreparable, as our enemies know; for they are not deficient in artistic knowledge. None of the Prussian generals has the ignorance of Consul Mummius, who, at the pillage of Corinth, informed the ships' captains who were taking away the marbles of Praxiteles and the paintings of Zeuxis, that they would have to replace them if they lost them on the way. A destroyed Leonardo da Vinci, a consumed Raffaelle or Correggio, cannot be rendered back again. When a chef-d'œuvre is lost, a fruitful influence, an inexhaustible power of instruction perishes with it. The destruction of a single manuscript might render the library of humanity incomplete.

" Let one call to mind the sensation produced a couple of years ago by the loss of the Peter Martyr of Titian, burnt in a church at Venice. Cultivated Europe experienced a deep regret, a poignant grief. Every one felt that a void had been created in art, which no effort could fill up. Multiply infinitely this single catastrophe and you may realize the disaster which might result from a sacrilegious bomb thrown on the Louvre. The mere idea makes one shudder with horror. The smoke from the burning library of Alexandria threw on antiquity a less sinister and less blinding shadow than would be cast over the world by the bombs of Prussia setting fire to the library of Paris. A sudden eclipse would obscure civilization which centuries would be necessary completely to remove.

" Germany vaunts her moral grandeur, proclaims her spiritual sovereignty, and thinks the whole world ought to become the disciples of her philosophers and thinkers. This impious siege pushed to its last extremity would throw her back to Vandalism. Genseric would place himself at her head and thrust Goethe on one side. The destruction of Paris would oppress her with an eternal weight. From this ravage and this ruin she would issue barbarian. This idea consternates intelligence: one cannot understand the sons of Herder and Kant slaying science; nor the fellow countrymen of Winkelmann and Otfried Müller exterminating art."

The letters that had arrived over night at the Paris post-office from the provinces and abroad were duly delivered on the morning of Sunday, those to whom they were addressed scarcely suspecting at the moment that these were the last communications from the outside which Paris was destined to receive for nearly five months. The early morning train to Brittany running on the only line of rails that remained open, started from the station at Mont Parnasse as usual—travellers by it being, however, cautioned that they undertook the journey at their own risk and peril, since the presence of the enemy in the woods of Clamart, Bellevue, and Chaville had been already signalled by telegraph to the station-master. The semi-official *Electeur Libre,* apprized of this circumstance, energetically demanded " how long the lugubrious pleasantry was to continue. Who knows," it asked, " whether or no all the remaining woods in the neighbourhood of Paris are not swarming with Prussians at the present moment? Is surveillance impracticable ? or are we utterly incorrigible and determined not to profit by experience? Why are not gardes-forestiers, who know all the private paths through these woods, sent out in disguise to signalize the presence, number, and position of the enemy? Our forts could then dislodge these disagreeable neighbours with a storm of shells. If surveillance is impossible, why not shower petroleum bombs on the woods at hazard ?"

The boulevards were crowded as usual during the evening, and exciting topics of conversation were not lacking. The close proximity of the enemy was of course expatiated on, and the most extravagant rumours prevailed respecting engagements said to have taken place at one and the other point during the day, every one of which, moreover, largely redounded to the glory of French arms. Wörth, Weissenbourg, and Sedan had either failed to teach the Parisians that their troops were not altogether invincible, or else they sought to disguise the real truth from each other by parading these imaginary successes. Certain quidnuncs had. made the discovery that M. Jules Favre accompanied by a couple of secretaries had quitted Paris privately that morning, and they naturally concluded it was on a mission to the Prussian head-quarters, which could only refer to negotiations for peace, the desire of which was in almost all hearts if on but few lips. Two diplomatic documents had made their appearance—one in the *Journal Officiel* of that day—which might be regarded as the respective manifestoes of the negotiators. The first was a circular of Count Bismarck to the foreign representatives of the North German Confederation, the decided language of which was evidently designed to dispel any illusions which France, or Europe generally, might be under with reference to the terms upon which Germany would be disposed to conclude a peace. In this document the Count, after dwelling upon the fact that the French nation had urged on the war with Germany, pointed out that it would never forgive the defeat it had sustained, even if Germany were to evacuate France without requiring any cession of territory, pecuniary indemnity, or other advantage except martial glory ; the French nation, he maintained, would cherish hatred, and wait for a day of successful revenge. Under such circumstances the safety of Germany and the peace of Europe required, he said, material guarantees, and for this purpose Germany would seek to remove the frontier, and with it the point of French attack, further west, and would endeavour to possess French fortresses and convert them into defensive German strongholds.

Although the ostensible object of the circular

penned by M. Jules Favre was to explain the recently published decree expediting the elections to the Constituent Assembly, it had evidently been drawn up with a view to the negotiations in which he was about to engage, and which appear to have been brought about by the intervention of the British embassy at Paris. "We have not," he observed in this document, "the pretension to ask disinterestedness of Prussia. We take account of the feelings to which the greatness of her losses and the natural exaltation of victory have given rise in her. Still to impose unacceptable conditions upon France would only be forcibly continuing the war. It is objected that the Government is without regular power to be represented. It is for this reason that we immediately summon a freely elected Assembly. It is therefore immortal France uprising before Prussia, France divested of the shroud of the Empire, free, generous, and ready to immolate herself for right and liberty, disavowing all political conquest, all violent propaganda, having no other ambition than to remain mistress of herself and to develope her moral and material forces, and to work fraternally with her neighbours for the progress of civilization. Vainly those who set loose a terrible scourge try now to escape the crushing responsibility by falsely alleging that they yielded to the wish of the country. A majority emanating from personal power believed itself obliged to follow docilely, and voted trustingly. But there is not a sincere person in Europe who could affirm that France, freely consulted, made war against Prussia. I do not draw the conclusion from this that we are not responsible; we have been wrong, and are cruelly expiating our having tolerated a Government which led us to ruin. Now we admit the obligation to repair in a measure of justice the ill it has done. But if the power with which it has so seriously compromised us takes advantage of our misfortunes to overwhelm us, we shall oppose a desperate resistance, and it will be well understood that it is the nation, properly represented in a freely elected Assembly, that this power wishes to destroy."

The clubs were unusually energetic in their language on this particular Sunday evening. Citizen Blanqui at his own peculiar club, " La Patrie en Danger," vehemently condemned M. Thiers's mission to the foreign courts. " Why should we beg for peace from kings ?" demanded he ; " all monarchs are our natural enemies. Let us first vanquish them and then make peace on our own terms. The provinces, under the degrading influence of the creatures of the Empire, have been badly advised with regard to Paris, to counteract which the Government should send out energetic delegates to rouse them up to fight by our side." The Citizen Lermina, at the Folies-Bergère, protested against any kind of peace or armistice so long as the national soil was defiled by the presence of a single Prussian. " Let every one here present," exclaimed he, no doubt for the twentieth time, " swear with me to bury himself under the ruins of Paris rather than surrender." The suggestion, of course, brought down a round of cheers, and everybody appeared to feel that the patriotic sacrifice was already made, and that individually and collectively they " deserved well of their country." An orator at the Club du Maine demanded the peremptory closing of all shops except such as sold food or arms—the sole necessities at the present moment—the immediate arming of all the citizens, and the instant distribution of cartridges.

At another assemblage, Citizen Millière insisted that the grand work of national salvation was only to be accomplished by the appointment of a central committee, charged with watching the acts of their feeble and foolish Government. "Paris," complacently said he, "about to defend itself like Saragossa, or if need be, like Moscow, is at this moment giving a sublime example of patriotism and energy to the world." A speaker who came after indignantly complained that bankrupts were refused as volunteers. "My house," exclaimed he, "has been ruined by English competition. Because my bills have been protested, am I to be restrained from marching against the invader—because I cannot pay my debts, is that any reason why I should be debarred pouring out my life blood for the good of my country!"

At the Club des Miracles a Polish refugee maintained—on the nothing like leather principle—that the only way to save France was to resuscitate Poland, her ancient ally. He was followed by a speaker who demanded that all the inhabitants of Paris who had abandoned their homes at the hour of danger should be declared traitors to their country, be deprived of their civic rights and have their property confiscated. One ungallant citizen proposed that in the interests of the defence all the women should be at once sent out of Paris, a suggestion which brought at least a score of champions of the fair sex to their feet, urging with their habitual volubility that while the men were combating at the ramparts lovely woman could be succouring the wounded, encouraging the timid, or if need be making cartridges. A patriot of a scientific turn of mind came to the rescue, and pointed out another mode by which the fair sex could assist in the defence. "Here," said he, "is a hand-bomb of my own invention adapted for being thrown by women, and even children, from the upper storeys, should the Prussians succeed in entering the city;" and he urged the meeting to demand from the Government the immediate enrolment of a corps of female bombardiers. A prudent citizen next drew the attention of the assemblage to the enormous quantities of vegetables relinquished to the enemy in the environs, and called upon a hundred men of determined will to meet him on the morrow at the Place de la Concorde, to bring in these stores of too precipitately abandoned cabbages and cauliflowers.

Throughout the evening and far into the night telegrams kept continually arriving for the Governor of Paris from all points of the environs. First came one from Vincennes, announcing nothing more important than an exchange of shots between some francstireurs and a couple of hundred of the enemy's infantry on the opposite bank of the Marne. Another from Fort Rosny apprized General Trochu on the authority of a spy, that 20,000 Germans were massed in the valley of the Marne, and that some 6000 others were advancing in the direction of the fort, the francstireurs gallantly retiring before them. Mont Valérien despatched a missive saying the report caused by the blowing up of the Château des Landes that day had been mistaken for a cannonade; while as late as eleven o'clock at night Fort de l'Est signified that a lively fusillade was then going on between the outposts in the direction of Le Bourget. An earlier telegram from Poissy notified the presence on Sunday afternoon at Conflans, Andresy, Carrières, and Triel—all on the right bank of the Seine, north-west of Paris—of some 800 German soldiers, whose extreme youth, coupled with the heavy requisitions they imposed, and their promptitude in disarming the National Guards, seem

to have made a striking impression on the Mayor of
Poissy. These troops had already crossed the Oise,
and were preparing to cross the Seine, their artillery
being posted in readiness on the heights of Chanteloup
to protect their passage. It must have been some of
the cavalry scouts of this detachment who, about noon,
penetrated the yet leafy glades of the forest of Saint-
Germain, and, by aid of their admirable maps, making
for the point where the Western Railway intersects it,
cut the line of rails near Conflans, fourteen miles from
Paris—unmolested alike by francs-tireurs and gardes-
forestiers, thereby destroying the communication with
Dieppe and Havre, as well as the direct communication with Cherbourg and the rest of Normandy. At
almost the same moment others of the enemy's
éclaireurs had worked round on the south side of
Paris as far as Versailles, the mayor of which famous
town, which for weeks past had been most elaborately
barricaded, and had its National Guards armed to the
teeth, was startled on Sunday afternoon by the apparition of a death's head hussar in the courtyard of
the mairie itself, demanding to speak to the burgo-
master. A party of these black hussars had, it seems,
ridden up to the post at the Porte de Buc, and three
of them had been permitted to proceed to the mairie.
Finding there were none beyond the rank of non-
commissioned officers in the party, the mayor declined
to parley with them, whereupon they rode off, promising to renew their visit on the following day.

The principal telegram of all was from General
Ducrot, who, made prisoner at Sedan, had arrived in
Paris a few days previously, having, according to the
Prussian version, violated his parole, while according
to his own, he had escaped fairly enough from Pont-à-
Mousson disguised as a workman, after constituting

himself prisoner there, as he had agreed to do at
Sedan.   Making for the centre of France, by way of
Epinal, he reached Paris by the Orleans railway,
direct communication being at this time already interrupted.   It was commonly rumoured that on
reaching Paris, he found General Trochu—having
very little confidence in the undisciplined troops under
his command—had resolved to allow the Germans to
invest the city unopposed, preferring to await their
attack behind positions, which he hoped to render
impregnable.   General Ducrot is said to have persuaded the Governor of Paris to abandon this resolution, and proposed to him the daring plan of cutting
the investing army in two, throwing a portion of the
enemy's troops upon Versailles, and there destroying
them, and hurling the remainder back on the Orleans
railway, with the Seine in their rear.   Whether or no
General Ducrot suggested any such magnificent plan
is not positively known, but what is certain is, that
late on Sunday he proceeded to occupy the line of
heights extending from Villejuif to Meudon, with
four divisions of infantry, some cavalry, and a strong
force of artillery.

Some idea may as well be given here of the character of the ground where General Ducrot had posted
himself.   South of Paris between the Seine and the
Bièvre, and in advance of the fort of Bicêtre, is the
bare and barren plateau of Longboyau, or, in
military phraseology, the heights of Villejuif.   On the
west it slopes down to the valley of the Bièvre, in the
direction of Sceaux, where the ground rises again,
and a succession of sloping hillocks, studded with
handsome villas and pretty villages, extend north-west
in the direction of Chatillon, Clamart, Vanves, Issy,
Meudon, and Bellevue, where the road runs from Paris

to Versailles, dipping into a deep hollow at Sèvres, beyond which abruptly rise the woods of Ville d'Avray, or Bois de Fausses Reposes, and the picturesque heights of Saint Cloud.

From a cavalry reconnaissance made early in the evening,* General Ducrot concluded that one of the enemy's columns was marching upon Versailles by Bièvres, turning the woods of Verrières and Clamart-sous-Meudon,—the pretty village half hidden among trees on the Rive Gauche line of railway to Versailles, celebrated as the country retreat of the fabulist, La Fontaine—woods which, unluckily for the French, had on several occasions obstinately refused to burn. The general reported that a trifling engagement had ensued between some Zouaves posted in a farm in advance of an unfinished redoubt, on the heights of Chatillon, which formed part of his positions, and some Prussian infantry posted in a neighbouring farm, and whom he eventually drove off with a few cannon shots. After telegraphing this intelligence to the Governor of Paris, he proceeded to camp for the night on the positions he then occupied, intending to strike the blow, which was to save Paris, at daybreak the following morning.

### II. THE AFFAIR OF CHATILLON.

Paris woke up on the morning of the 19th of September to the booming of cannon, which resounded

---

* This reconnaissance would appear to have been the reverse of advantageous as, according to Dr. Russell—"The 5th German army corps bivouacked in the woods and villages near Bièvres, and on the heights above Palaiseau, were injudiciously alarmed by a night attack which ended in nothing and put them on the alert, at the same time that the Bavarians of Hartmann's army were warned that the enemy was at hand."

incessantly till noon, inducing the majority of non-combatants to believe that the battle which, according to the newspapers, was to decide " the fate of France and civilization," was raging under the walls, and that unless the most desperate resistance was made before the day was over, the enemy would be entering the city by a breach in the ramparts. As according to the official report no less than 25,000 cannon shots were fired off that morning on the French side alone, it will be understood that the struggle was a deafening, if not a sanguinary one, and some excuse can be found for the agitation which took possession of the Parisian mind. People flocked to all the favourite stand-points commanding views of the southern heights, and crowded the house tops in the neighbourhood of the ramparts; but for several hours they saw nothing beyond clouds of smoke rising above the horizon, and ammunition waggons mingling with long trains of ambulance carriages defiling slowly along the Routes de Chatillon and d'Orleans.

It seems, that as soon as day broke, General Ducrot made an offensive reconnaissance in advance of the positions where he had camped for the night, but the skirmishers he sent out were speedily driven back by the fire of the Prussian infantry. At seven o'clock, his artillery, numbering, it was said, 72 guns, took up its position, and opened a vigorous cannonade in the direction of the woods, no enemy, however, was to be seen, and for half an hour not the smallest movement on the part of the Germans was perceptible, but at the end of that time they commenced to reply from the fringe of the wood. Several French detachments then pushed forward, and entered the glades, especially on the French left, to carry Bagneux. The cuirassiers ventured too far, and coming suddenly upon a strong body of Germans concealed there, suffered heavy losses. At this moment some of the French advanced troops came upon a corps of Prussians at almost point blank range. The latter had their adversaries at a great advantage. They seemed to be quite at home in the woods ; each tree was a fortification, from which they took deliberate aim at their opponents, who would not turn their numbers to account, while they themselves presented deep lines to the enemy The firing was incessant and very fierce. Just at this time a battalion of Mobiles of the Seine came up and began firing into the wood where the 16th Regiment was stationed, threw it into disorder, and caused its precipitate retreat. The main body of the German forces had seized a height upon the French left, commanding the plateau on which their infantry was placed. Upon this height the Germans planted their artillery, and directed upon the French a perfect hailstorm of shot and shell. Their infantry regiments, composed in great part of reserves and young recruits, were drawn up in long columns on the plateau and suffered severely. This terrible cannonade shook them, and observing that some troops who had received orders, were moving off out of the wood, they also took part in the rearward movement. The Prussians then advanced, still keeping under cover, so that their shots rained on their adversaries, who could not so much as see the enemy, and knew not where to fire. At this juncture it is pretended orders were given to fall back, but whether or no the extreme right, composed, it was believed, of the best and steadiest troops, and to whom the duty of holding the heights of Meudon was confided, seem to have been seized with a panic, and influenced by the example set by a provisional regiment, formed out of the débris of the 1st and 2nd Zouaves, broke and precipitately took to flight, many of the men not halting until they found themselves safe inside the ramparts of Paris. The remainder of the right wing appear to have concentrated in good order round the recently constructed earthen redoubt on the plateau of Chatillon. The left wing feebly attacked, was able to hold its position on the heights of Villejuif. At this moment the Prussians suddenly opened a terrific fire, and General Ducrot was obliged to withdraw his troops under the protection of the forts. This movement he accomplished at four in the afternoon, after a struggle which had lasted the best part of the day with only a slight interruption at about ten in the morning. Having secured the retreat of the trains and waggons, he spiked the eight guns in the redoubt, under the eyes and fire of the Prussians, and withdrew under the fort of Vanves.* The Gardes Mobiles were said to have fought bravely, and with the steadiness of old troops, the battalion of Ille et Vilaine hold-

---

* "The Crown Prince of Prussia, who left Chaumes on the 18th for Corbeil, was on his march from Corbeil to Palaiseau when the attack began. He was separated by the Seine from his troops, and, misled by the sounds which seemed to come from two different directions, he and the greater part of his staff rode on to Villeneuve, and consequently could not get near the field, for the bridges were destroyed, and it was a long détour to make. The French had a fine opportunity, for in traversing the valley of Bièvres to gain the road from Choisy to Versailles their enemy's flank was quite exposed, and the result was that the rear brigade was very severely pressed indeed, the 47th Regiment suffering particularly; but the 6th Bavarian Brigade, debouching from the woods on the left flank of the French, came up in support, and the French retired, carrying off their guns and mitrailleuses indeed, but leaving, to their great discredit, the redoubt with its nine guns which were in position. The action extended from Villecoublay to Clamart, above Meudon itself, and as far as Petit Bicêtre, where the roads of Choisy-le-Roi and Chatillon intersect."—*Dr. Russell in " The Times."*

ing its ground to the last, firing slowly, and taking deliberate aim.

It was different, however, with the boasted Zouaves whom General Trochu felt constrained thus to gibbet in an order of the day:—

"An unjustifiable panic, which all the efforts of an excellent commander and his officers could not arrest, seized upon the Provisional Regiment of Zouaves, which held our right. From the commencement of the action the greater number of those soldiers fell back in disorder upon the city, and there spread the wildest alarm. To excuse their conduct the fugitives have declared that they were being led to certain destruction, while, in fact, their strength was undiminished, and they had no wounded; that cartridges were deficient, while they had not made use of those with which they were provided; that they had been betrayed by their leaders, &c. The truth is that these unworthy soldiers compromised from the very beginning an affair from which, notwithstanding their conduct, very important results were obtained. Some other soldiers of various regiments of infantry were similarly culpable. Already the misfortunes which we have experienced at the commencement of this war had thrown back into Paris undisciplined and demoralized soldiers, who caused there uneasiness and trouble, and who from the force of circumstances had escaped from the authority of their officers and from all punishment. I am firmly resolved to put an end to such serious disorders. I order the defenders of Paris to seize all soldiers and Gardes Mobiles who shall be found in the city in a state of drunkenness, or spreading abroad scandalous stories and dishonouring the uniform they wear."

Every one felt the reproaches of the Governor of Paris to be well merited, for throughout the afternoon, in the Chaussée du Maine, and other principal thoroughfares on that side of the city, isolated groups of disbanded soldiers, unaccompanied by a single officer, were encountered trooping into Paris. Here is the account furnished by one eye-witness of what fell under his own observation :—

"At the Champ de Mars, there was a frightful pell mell of horses without riders, carriages void of their guns, soldiers with neither arms nor knapsacks,

officers seeking for their companies. The soldiers
startled one by their downcast and positively idiotic
look. On interrogating them, one found it impossible
to draw a word from them. They seem paralysed,
thunder-struck. I hurried to the Porte de Montrouge.
Here one perceived the rout; soldiers of all classes
arrived disbanded, alone or in couples, some without
knapsacks, others still carrying their arms, but all
with the look of runaways. Artillery trains, ammunition waggons, ambulance carriages, strayed horses,
endeavoured to force a passage in inexpressible disorder.
On the pavement, on either side of the road, was a
great crowd of men, women, and children, who
anxiously questioned the last arrivals, or rated the
drunkards, for many of those coming in were drunk,
and could scarcely stand. Cries, songs, imprecations,
laughter, tears, the moans of the wounded, and the
oaths of the drivers; and, above all, the indistinct
murmur of the crowd, that suppressed rumbling
sound, like that of the ocean on a stormy day. I
went away overcome. In the meanwhile, the boulevards were excited almost to madness. People said
aloud that 20,000 of our soldiers had been crushed
by 100,000 Prussians, near Clamart; that the whole
army had thrown down its arms, declaring that it
would fight no longer, and that the victorious troops
were about to take the city by storm.

" All these rumours were exaggerated, nevertheless,
the truth, when it oozed out, was sufficiently inquiet-
ing. National Guards rendered perfectly furious,
arrested on all sides the disbanded soldiers, treating
them as cowards, and marching them off to the poste,
or to the Place Vendôme. The exasperated crowd
spat in the faces of these miserable wretches, who
dishonoured alike their uniform and their country

One learnt that the Mobiles, unlike the soi-disant veteran troops, had held their ground well, and people shouted : "Vive la Mobile !" "à bas les Zouaves !" "à bas la ligne !" Some demanded that the runaways should be shot, and others proposed to blow their brains out without any form of trial.

" In the evening, circulation had become impossible on the boulevards. An enormous crowd encumbered the foot-pavement and roadway, fighting for the evening papers, which, however, gave no news of the affair. One took refuge in the cafés, all brilliantly lighted up and crowded with officers of Mobiles, chatting and laughing as usual with the cocottes of the boulevards. There was an incessant exchange of gay propos, shakings of hands, shouts, laughter, ceaseless comings and goings arm-in-arm : a rather cynical spectacle, which ended by disgusting certain scandalized citizens."* The result was, that a crowd of some couple of hundred persons, including numerous National Guards, commenced to promenade the boulevards, shouting out, " All cafés ought to close at nine o'clock."

As they passed by Brebant's, at the corner of the Rue du Faubourg Montmartre, and at the moment some cannon shots from one of the forts boomed in the distance, hearing a piano playing some lively airs—which jarred terribly with the humour they were in—in one of the cabinets particulières, they compelled the preprietor forthwith to put out the gas and close his establishment. Other cafés were then cleared of their customers, and numerous cocottes were marched off to the post. Ere long such a scene of disorder ensued that at all the cafés chairs and tables were hastily removed inside, and these establishments closed that evening at an early hour.

---

* Sarcey's " Siége de Paris," p. 83.

But the agitation was not destined to end here. Some zealous citizens, walking with their noses in the air, professed to have observed lights of different colours, moving about in the windows of the upper storey of one of the houses on the boulevards. What could they be if not signals to the enemy? A crowd collects, every one is of this opinion. National Guards next arrive, who, after posting a detachment in front of the house, that no one might quit it, effect an entrance and search the apartments indicated, without however, discovering the slightest thing suspicious. The same incident is repeated at intervals on different points of the boulevards until midnight, and always with the same result.

A vigorous proclamation of Gambetta's was posted up the same evening, referring to the events of the day. " Citizens," said he—

" The cannon thunders! the supreme moment has arrived! Since the day of the Revolution Paris is upstanding, and in full vigour. All, without distinction of classes or of parties, display the most manly resolution. All of you have taken up arms to save both the Republic and France. You have within the last few days given the most manifest proof of your manly resolution. You have not allowed yourselves to be disturbed either by the cowardly or the lukewarm. You have given way to neither unreasonable excitement nor to despondency; you have coolly faced the multitude of your assailants. The first strokes of war will find you equally calm and intrepid, and if runaways should come, as to-day, to bring into the city disorder, panic, and falsehood, you will remain unmoved, feeling assured that the court-martial which has just been established for the trial of cowards and deserters will be able efficiently to protect the public safety and the national honour."

The military report of the affair slurred over the disgraceful conduct of the runaways by naïvely observing that " a part of the troops fell back with regrettable precipitation," a phrase that tickled the Parisians immensely, and was long employed by them whenever an occasion offered, in a jocular sense.

Such was the first real engagement before Paris, the

siege of which was now fairly inaugurated. Whatever may have been the amount of powder and shot expended at it, it attained no more than the proportions of an offensive reconnaissance, and yet it was for the moment dignified with the title of the battle of Chatillon, being named after a spot familiar to the majority of Parisians, with whom it was a favourite place of resort for pic-nic parties. The lofty plateau on which the redoubt abandoned by the French had been constructed lies between Forts Vanves and Montrouge, scarcely more than a mile in advance of either, and in front of the village, lying under the beautiful woods of Meudon, from which it takes its name.

All Paris, says M. Sarcey, slept unquietly on the night of the 19th. No one seriously closed his eyes, but lay anticipating every moment to hear the rappel beaten, for the impression was general that the enemy, pursuing his advantage, would attack about two o'clock in the morning.

### III. PARIS BLOCKADED.

At the commencement of the war scarcely a Frenchman dreamed of the possibility of Paris ever being besieged; to the national mind, which is all vanity, there was something too fantastical in the idea to admit of its being seriously entertained for a single instant. All the maps produced for the occasion were careful to include that broad tract of German territory stretching far across the Rhine even to Berlin, while it was thought sufficient on the other hand to take in Metz, or in any case to reach as far as Châlons. In Paris, too, every one provided himself with a stock of long pins having little tricolor flags at their heads, and destined to indicate on the map the advance of the French arms and to float now over Trèves, next over Coblentz, Mayence, and Cologne, and finally over

Magdeburg and Berlin. As to the fortifications of
Paris, the green turf of the ramparts suggested
nothing to the Parisians beyond a pleasant promenade
varied by an occasional déjeûner al fresco on a Sunday
or a fête day, while the fosse was regarded merely as
a convenient octroi boundary. Even when the siege
became imminent the newspaper strategists without
exception demonstrated the utter impossibility of investing Paris, pointing out that it would require at
least a million and a half of men to form the requisite
human girdle some fifty or sixty miles in circumference, and the best part of a month to shut the city
completely in, and yet on the second day of the arrival
of the German forces and on the same day that the
engagement at Chatillon was fought, the blockade of
the capital was consummated with scarcely a fifth of
that number. The couple of million of human beings
shut up within the walls of Paris first learnt of their
separation from the rest of the world by articles in
the newspapers all harping mournfully on one string.
"There are neither letters nor newspapers from the
provinces or abroad, the last railway lines are cut, the
last telegraphic wires have ceased to operate, the
isolation of Paris is complete." And as time wore on
each one's individual experience impressed this disagreeable fact more vividly on his mind.

Paris ere long discovered that not merely had the
railway trains ceased running, which was notified by
the various companies in the following dry fashion—
" Communications are suspended until further
orders," but that the omnibuses dared no longer
go beyond the enceinte. Well might the *Figaro*
exclaim, " Gracious goodness ! where are we now ? It
is only six weeks—no more—since we were told the
railway trains stopped short at St. Avold. Next it
was said they ran no further than Metz, then Frouard,

then Bar-le-Duc, Châlons, Epernay, Château-Thierry, Meaux, and so on. Well, what is the news to-day? The Paris omnibuses are obliged to cut short their journeys, and those of the Louvre-Courbevoie line go no further than the Porte Maillot."

And yet the authorities seem hardly to have realized the fact of the investment being really consummated, for that very day the postmaster-general "had the honour to inform the public that owing to the interruption of the railway communication the post-office would for the future take charge of ordinary letters only for the provinces and abroad, and not of registered ones." The reason was obvious enough ; the French post-office holds itself liable for the contents of registered letters up to a certain amount, and it simply proposed to guard against their abstraction from the mail bags should the couriers in charge of them chance to be intercepted by the enemy.

It was at one o'clock in the afternoon of the 19th that the telegraph wires to Versailles, the last which communicated with Paris fron the outside, were cut ; Versailles, spite of its barricades and its couple of thousand armed National and Mobile Guards having capitulated to the Germans only an hour or so previously, the uhlans consequently lost but little time in rendering the isolation of Paris complete. It seems that in accordance with the promise of the death's head hussar on the preceding day, some of the enemy's cavalry made their appearance early the following morning at the different gates leading into the town, all of which they found closed. Eventually an aide-de-camp, followed by a single cavalry soldier, was admitted and taken under an escort of National Guards to the mayor, when a long discussion ensued. It was then a quarter-past nine, and since daylight the cannon had been booming on the road from Versailles to Sceaux, in the plain of Velizy, about three miles from the town. The aide-de-camp required accommodation for the wounded, and also the keys of all forage stores. These points were warmly debated, and the officer departed to consult his general. Within less than an hour afterwards a captain of engineers, an aide-de-camp to the general commanding the 5th Corps, arrived alone. He was accompanied by two National Guards to the mairie, where the municipal authorities were sitting en permanence. Fighting was then going on at the farm of Villecoublay. General Ducrot was endeavouring to break this division of the enemy, or was defending the fortified position upon the heights of Meudon, commanding the left bank of the Seine and the forts of Vanves and Issy. The terms of capitulation were discussed until a quarter past eleven, when M. Raureau, the newly appointed mayor, taking his station at the Paris gate, read aloud to the assembled crowd the conditions that had been agreed to—namely, that property and person should be respected, as also public monuments and works of art; that the German forces should occupy the barracks, the inhabitants lodging the officers, and if necessary soldiers also, should the barracks afford insufficient accommodation; that the National Guard were to retain their arms, and be entrusted with the internal police of the town; the German troops to occupy at their discretion the barrier gates; that there should be no requisition, but the town was to supply at financial cash rates all that was required for passing or stationary troops. The last clause of the capitulation stipulated that on that day the Grille des Chantiers was to be opened to allow the 5th Army Corps to enter. Immediate steps were taken to carry out the terms of the capitulation, and the officer in command of the French troops in Versailles was conducted to the general commanding the German forces at Jouy, on his way traversing a part of the battle-field whence the wounded were being removed to the hospitals prepared in the palaces of Versailles and the two Trianons. At that moment the French guns were withdrawn, and the force which had maintained the fight fell back into the wood while the German columns commenced their march. Shortly before one o'clock they began to defile through the Rue des Chantiers, the procession, variously estimated at from 25,000 to 40,000 men, lasting until after five. The majority did not remain in the town, still a considerable force took up quarters there. The general installed himself in the Hôtel des Réservoirs, and the artillery bivouacked on the Place d'Armes and in the Avenue de St. Cloud. Two small incidents are deserving of mention. With the German troops there entered two small groups of Zouaves, who had been made prisoners in the affair at Villecoublay-Velizy. The crowd uncovered to them silently but respectfully, and a few cries of " Vive la France !" were heard. In the Rue des Chantiers, the first officer who came to negotiate for the capitulation was saluted by a cry of " Vive la France !" from a bystander. " My friend," said the officer, " it is Vive la Paix that you should cry." When the marching through of the troops had terminated, the requisitions commenced. Six and twenty oxen were delivered by the town, and ten casks of wine, together with the stores of forage, worth 300,000 francs, which the French military authorities wished to destroy, but which the town had purchased in anticipation of actual events. Subsequently, contrary to the terms of the capitulation, the National Guard were all disarmed.

Among the official decrees published on the day of the investment was one fixing the Paris municipal

elections for the 28th of the month, and another imposing fines according to an ascending scale on absentees.
A third notified that no depositer in the national
savings bank would be allowed to draw out a larger
sum than fifty francs from the amount of his investment—pleasant information this to needy though
frugal people on the very first day of a siege which
was certain to raise the price of provisions exor-
bitantly and would last no one could say for how long.

The five Academies which compose the French Institute launched a protest against the threatened bombardment, observing in the course of it :—

" No, we will not believe it.   It is repugnant to us to think that
a people amongst whom the sciences, letters, and arts are held in
honour, and who contribute to their brilliancy, should refuse to respect in war the treasures of science, art, and literature by which
civilization is to-day recognised.   And yet one has reason to fear
that the armies which at this moment surround the capital of France
are preparing to subject to the risks of a destructive bombardment
the monuments with which it is filled, the chefs-d'œuvre of all
kinds, products of the great minds of all ages and all countries—
Germany included — which this ancient and splendid metropolis
contains in its museums, libraries, palaces, and churches.

" It is repugnant to us once more to impute to the armies of
Germany, to the generals who lead them, to the Prince who marches
at their head, any such thought.   If, however, contrary to our expectation, this order has been conceived, and if it is to be realized,
we, members of the Institute of France, in the name of letters,
sciences, and arts, whose interests it is our duty to defend, we
denounce such a design to the civilized world as an outrage against
civilization itself; we signalize it to the justice of history, and we
bequeath it in advance to the avenging reprobation of posterity."

On reading the foregoing, Béranger's memorable
lines on a parallel occasion fifty-six years previously,
involuntarily recal themselves to mind :—

" Quoi ! ces monuments chéris,
Histoire
De notre gloire,
S'écrouleraient en débris !
Quoi ! les Prussiens à Paris !"

The last diplomatic courier came into Paris on the 19th. Captain Johnson, one of her Britannic Majesty's messengers, who after having been arrested by the Prussians en route had been permitted to pass their lines, and drove down the Faubourg Saint Honoré in an open caléche conducted by a postilion in the traditional jack-boots, scarlet facings, and hair à catogan. The general turn-out, no less than the semi-military uniform of the gallant officer himself, seemed to have aroused the suspicion of the mob, who, on the look out for spies, according to their habit, professed to see in the captain a spy employed by the English Government to supply information to the Prussians, and made attempts to arrest him, but some menacing broad-sword flourishes of his cane combined with the energetic attitude of the French concierge of the embassy—who so ably represented the British Government during the last half of the siege when the entire personnel had left—saved her majesty's representative from this indignity, and he succeeded in entering the court of the ambassadorial hotel in triumph. Here the mob dared not pursue him, for above the royal arms over the gateway hung a huge black board inscribed in letters upwards of a foot high, "Ambassade d'Angleterre," the union jack floating over all, and helping to form a most imposing display, no doubt considered highly necessary since the ambassador had taken his departure. Indeed in foreign climes the symbol too commonly counts for far more than the plenipotentiary does himself.

The Paris newspapers, although they had been proclaiming every day for the last fortnight that "the time for illusions had passed," seemed—many of them at least—quite as disposed as ever to continue the supply of comforting fictions to their readers. Here are samples of those published on the 19th. First the

*Gaulois* announced in large type a " victory by francs-
tireurs at Melun "—these valiant gentry, according
to this veracious print, having completely decimated
a regiment of Prussian dragoons. Another journal
described in mysterious language how that in the small
hours of the morning a regiment of the enemy marching
in silence to effect some important movement in the
plain of Vanves—in the environs of Paris—came
suddenly upon a mine which exploded under their
tread and at once killed 300 men. The opportune
unmasking and discharge of a couple of mitrailleuses
made, it seems, short work of the remainder in an
"admirable fashion." A third paper sought to cheer up
its readers by informing them that one of several over-
venturesome uhlans captured in the environs during
the last day or two had been dining with the officer
in command of the post at the Hôtel de Ville, and in a
moment of unreserve had confidentially confided to him
that the Germans were horribly disgusted at finding
Paris in such an admirable state of defence. These
were the kind of trivialities in which the Paris journals
having the largest circulation continued to indulge at
the moment the news of the complete investment of
Paris was signified to Berlin in an official telegram
couched in the following terms :—

" After the preparatory movements of the last few days all our
corps on the 19th advanced simultaneously, and completely surrounded Paris. The King on the same day reconnoitred the north-
east front of the fortifications of the French capital."

The precise nature of the investment which the
German forces had succeeded in effecting, as well as
the ulterior intentions of the commanders of the
besieging army, were indicated in some observations
made by the Chancellor of the North German Confederation to the special correspondent of the *Standard*

newspaper scarcely a fortnight previously. On being asked if he thought the French would defend Paris, Count Bismarck replied, " We shall not attack it." What would they do then? " We shall enter it without attacking it. We shall starve it out." But it would require 1,200,000 men to invest Paris. "True, but it would not be invested in that sense. We shall post our armies round it, according as is thought best; and we have 50,000 cavalry who will answer for the rest. They will perpetually sweep and scour the parts not actually occupied by our troops, and not a morsel of food will be able to enter Paris. Why should we attack, and undergo fresh sacrifices gratuitously? There are fighting persons in Paris, who might give us trouble the first, and possibly the second day, if we attacked. The third day, if we leave them alone, they will be more troublesome to Paris itself, food becoming scarce. We will begin with the third day."

As such scanty information as Paris obtained respecting the positions occupied by the investing forces was exclusively derived from reconnaissances extending over a period of several weeks, some notes, made by a correspondent of *The Times* shortly subsequent to this epoch, and which indicate the various points where the German troops were posted, are here reproduced. It should be premised that the tour made by the writer did not comprehend the immediate inside of the line of investment, which was considerably nigher to Paris than the road he appears to have taken.*

---

* The outer circle of investment was defined at the time with much distinctness by Mr. Conybeare, who also specified the positions of the particular corps. According to him the length of the outer circuit of investment, measured through the head-quarters of the various corps d'armée constituting the two armies investing Paris, was as follows:—The Crown Prince of Saxony's army fur-

"On starting to the south, from Versailles, where the Crown Prince's head-quarters are established," says the writer, " our road lies through Belle Epine and Choisy to Villeneuve-le-Roi, where are the head-quarters of the 6th Corps d'Armée. The splendid trees on either side of the Route Impériale are lying cut down and withered; the road, which had here and there been torn up, is now being replaced by regular cantonniers under Prussian orders. At intervals along the road are sentinels, who sometimes demand a pass, which the outposts always do. Between Versailles and Belle Epine to the north stands the redoubt of Chatillon, the pos-

---

nished the investment from Sartronville, situated on the right bank of the Seine, 4¾ miles north-east of St. Germain, to Chelles, a station on the Paris and Strasburg railway, five miles due east of Fort Rosny. From Sartronville, through Soisy-sous-Enghien, situated a mile west of Montmorency and the head-quarters of the 4th Army Corps, General Alversleben; then through Gonesse, five miles north-east of St. Denis, and head-quarters of the Garde Corps, General the Prince of Würtemberg; next through Le Vert Galant, 9½ miles east of St. Denis, and about a mile east of the Sevran station of the Soissons railway, the head-quarters of the 12th Royal Saxon Army Corps, General Prince George of Saxony, to Chelles, where the Crown Prince of Prussia's army takes up the running again, the distance was 24 miles.

The Crown Prince of Prussia's army completes the circuit of investment from Chelles, due east of Paris, round the south-east south, and west to Sartronville, 8½ miles due west of St. Denis. From Chelles through Boissy St. Leger, 2½ miles south of the eastern extremity of the St. Maur peninsula, through Villeneuve-le-Roi, thence in a straight line to Versailles (the Crown Prince's head-quarters, the King of Prussia's being at this moment at Ferrières), thence direct to St. Germain, thence along the left bank of the Seine to the Maisons-sur-Seine station of the Paris and Rouen railway, and thence across the Seine to Sartronville the distance is 42 miles, thus making the aggregate length of the outer circuit of investment, as measured along straight lines connecting the head-quarters of the various corps of the investing armies, at least 66 miles.

session of which has been stoutly contested. The Forts de Vanves and d'Issy, however, command this part of the country so well that the besiegers have to keep at a good distance. Although the forts on this side do not stand high, and are almost within reach of heavy pieces placed on the hills, still they effectually prevent at present the approach of an enemy.

" At Belle Epine a considerable body of troops—a large proportion being artillery—were stationed, prepared to meet any sorties. Orby, which is the next place come to, has been the regular place of reception for the wounded from skirmishes in the neighbourhood.

" Villeneuve-le-Roi is connected with Villeneuve-St.-Georges by a pontoon bridge over the Seine. The suspension bridge has been cut, and lies there impeding the navigation of the river. This town is busy only as a garrison town is always busy, with the daily occupation of the soldiers in cooking, repairing their clothes, and so on.

" Villeneuve-St.-Georges is not occupied permanently except by a pontoon train, but is a halting-place for thousands of passing troops—to-day for a regiment of Prussian infantry, while a Bavarian battalion is bivouacked in the fields outside. On account of this passage of troops—different ones every day—the town is in the worst condition of pillage and devastation of any that I have as yet seen. The place is literally smashed, the fittings of the shops and houses being all pulled down and broken, and in one café I saw horses stalled. Everything worth stealing has been taken ; the rest has been shattered, and the mattresses are only left in condition, I suppose out of fellow-feeling for those who shall sleep there the next day.

" Boissy St. Léger is approached by two roads. I take the southern one through Valenton, which town is strongly occupied. Between there and Boissy a most splendid view of Paris is obtained, the principal domes being distinctly visible, with the gilded roof of the Invalides glittering in the sun. Boissy St. Léger is now full of infantry, belonging to the 11th Corps, whose head-quarters are at the splendid château of Gros Bois, belonging to the Prince de Wagram. The stables and coachhouses here are generally crammed full of passing cavalry, the carriages, &c., being turned out into the yard. It may be thought that I am diverging very far south and east, but within about two miles of this place are the outposts, which are constantly exchanging shots with the francs-tireurs, and often lose a man or two. It must be remembered that from north to south the ground actually within the forts measures about eight miles, while that from west to east measures ten miles. The Prussian advance guards, would, I think, make a circle of about sixty miles, and the actual girdle of troops one of nearly 100 miles.

" From Boissy the army extends to Noiseau, where a fine view of Paris is again obtained, to Emerainville and Gournay-sur-Marne, all occupied by Würtembergers. Here the regular road is twice broken by blown up bridges, and Chelles is approached by a temporary wooden bridge, made, I suppose, to liberate the pontoon train for service elsewhere. This town is held by a large number of troops, principally infantry. Drilling has been going on all along our route, whereas the only drill I have seen the Prussians practise has been artillery, at which they are smartness itself.

" Chelles is utterly deserted, as were nearly all the villages en route. From what I have seen, the evil resulting from the desertion of towns and villages has been greater than has resulted from the inhabitants remaining. In the one case, everything is plundered and broken ; in the other the inhabitants are subjected to requisitions that almost ruin them. The handsome châteaux have suffered much through this desertion. The colonel in command at Chelles tells me that in one day's ride he saw at least 10,000*l.* worth of orange trees dead for want of water.

" At Clichy the Saxon lines are passed ; they occupy all this road through Livry to Sevran, the head-quarters of the Crown Prince of Saxony  At Sevran the staff, a band, and a good muster of troops are drawn up to receive the King of Prussia, who is there on an excursion through the armies on this side of Paris. Villepinte and Grand Tremblay are now the route. A large number of troops at the latter town form the north-east corner of the investing army. My course next lies west. Forts I have hardly mentioned, and shall only notice any that come in sight. Between Grand Tremblay and Roissy is a sad specimen of the devastation occasioned by the war. A very large pile of buildings, consisting of a farm, dwelling house, colza seed crushing mills, and an alcohol manufactory, evidently a month ago a very thriving establishment, now stands plundered and wantonly damaged, the furniture broken, books and papers scattered, looking-glasses pulled down and shivered, the steam pipes of the machinery broken, and so on. This destruction always occurs when the inhabitants have left, but I have not seen a worse example than this. The Prussians it seems had only been able to find one small wine cellar, and I left them at work dragging up the coachhouse floor in search of a second one.

" Through Roissy I come to Gonesse, which is a very

13—2

nest of typhoid and dysentery. The holding out of
Strasbourg and Toul has been the cause of a great
deal of this illness, through delaying so much the
supplies of food and clothing which would otherwise
have come from Germany. I am now so close to the
outposts (only a mile and a half) that a further advance to the river is made in following the circumference of the armed circle. This is to Sarcelles and
St. Brice.

"Near Gonesse railway station a long cavalcade
passed, and in the first carriage I recognised the old
King, looking fatigued and thoughtful. I have a fine
and distinct view of Paris by night. The gas has
evidently not yet been cut off, and a revolving electric
light illuminates a great area. This, I presume, is for
working by night at the fortifications and to prevent
a night surprise. From here I distinctly hear a
French march being drummed. A week or so ago
firing was heard in Paris, which may have been a
disturbance, but was probably the drilling of new
troops.

" I now approach what is at present the weak part of
the investment, but may possibly be the strong part
of the attack—viz., Montmorency and Enghien. From
these most lovely hills is obtained the finest view there
is of Paris. The Arc de Triomphe appears quite close,
although it must be many miles away. Below lies
St. Denis, its smoking factory chimneys being the
only sign of commercial industry that I have seen for
weeks, but these are probably manufacturing arms,
grinding flour, or doing something in aid of the defence.

" If I wanted to enter Paris, this is where I should
try—by night, of course, passing the Seine, and landing
under the very forts of St. Denis. A large force of

Prussian artillery is here collected. The road now
leads so very near to the strongest fort of Paris—viz.,
Mont Valérien—that very few soldiers are visible for
miles; two uhlans—who go about, as do all uhlans,
as if invulnerable—and a few sentinels hidden behind
houses, are the only troops on the road, which,
after passing Argenteuil, is not two miles distant from
the fort. At the foot of the mount is a French en-
campment, the only collection of tents I have seen, as
the Germans camp without them. In this respect
they are lucky in having Paris for their autumn work,
instead of Sedan, Wörth, &c., as they are well housed
everywhere in the deserted villages lying thickly round
Paris.

"The appearance of Mont Valérien is very imposing
and threatening—the bastions, topped by large barracks, make it more a citadel than a fortress. If only
100,000 good soldiers could operate under this fort,
they might soon make the Prussians tired of the business they have undertaken, but it is exactly these
100,000 trained soldiers which the besieged have not.
The very army they want is being starved in Metz.
It is much to be doubted, too, how far the Parisians
are supplied with field guns, and, even if they have
them, with artillerymen who can serve them.
Without these they will be sorely overmatched in their
sorties.

"Le Pecq is the next place to make for, where the
bridge across the Seine to St. Germain existed a week
or two ago; now it is destroyed, and its place is
supplied by a bridge of boats a mile further down the
river. The Seine here is about the width of the
Thames at Hammersmith, and should apparently have
been made use of to defend the town, but no resistance was made that I know of. A few days ago the

Prussians knocked down the railway bridge with
cannon, I suppose to prevent a sortie by train, or
perhaps it impeded the view from an observatory.
The French have cut down all the trees that might
prevent the troops in the forts from seeing Prussians
on the roads, and the Prussians have cut down and
are cutting down all the trees that impede the view
from their observatories, so that altogether an enormous quantity of timber has been felled for this
purpose, and still more has been sacrificed to impede
the advance of the invading army. The stumps will
be a monument of the war for some time to come.

"St. Germain does not appear to be fortified in any
way, although it stands on the slope of a hill which
commands the Seine for a great distance. On the
top of this hill is the terrace bounded by a white
stone wall and visible for a great distance. St.
Germain is only partly occupied by the inhabitants,
but the number of troops quartered here amply com-
pensates for any emigration. The pretty hamlet of
Marly, the village of Rocquencourt, and one other
village, all fully tenanted by soldiery, complete the
link to Versailles.

"The last time I was at Versailles I certainly never
dreamt of what I should see at the next visit. In
the rooms, the walls of which are covered by hundreds
of pictures, each representing a French victory, are
lying hundreds of wounded men, each representing a
French defeat. In the prefecture I had an interview
with the Crown Prince of Prussia. In the château
are the head-quarters of the Prussian commandant;
in the town are about 15,000 soldiers, making the
whole place look like Berlin improved. Going
along the streets, I constantly hear the familiar call of
the Prussian sentinel as a passing general has to be

saluted. Men in the streets are carrying their muskets to the mairie to be registered and kept till peace is declared. All day long the boom of cannon is heard, and the music of bands sounds through the town at intervals. People go to market as if nothing had happened. All these make such a mixture of peace and war, of content and misery, as it is impossible to imagine without witnessing."

### IV. THE MORROW OF THE INVESTMENT.

The Chatillon disaster, coupled with the irrefragable evidence of the investment, furnished the newspapers with abundant matter for desponding comment, and the military authorities were warmly blamed for neglecting to complete the redoubts at Chatillon and Montretout, and allowing positions of such importance, upon the fortification of which weeks of labour had been expended, to fall so readily into the hands of the enemy, who had now only to mount siege guns in them to be able to throw shells into the Champ de Mars and the Trocadero. "One endeavours in vain," said the *Temps*, with justice, "to comprehend how, in a city like Paris, means could not be found to finish these works, when at Sebastopol the Russians were able to throw up redoubtable fortifications in a single night."* The *Siècle* sought to mitigate the prevailing despondency. "For God's sake," it said, "let us

---

* In reply to the strictures of the newspapers, General Trochu subsequently issued a memorandum explaining that, " these various works, undertaken at a time when the siege of Paris seemed a very remote contingency, were to have had the character of permanent forts, destined to serve as points of support to an army outside of Paris, and were pushed forward for this purpose with the utmost celerity. But owing to military events being precipitated with the painful results which every one is acquainted with, those respon-

not permit a worse enemy than the Prussians penetrate our city, penetrate our hearts—let us not give
way to discouragement and alarm.  The enemy sur-
rounds Paris, and engagements are taking place on.
twenty points at once.  If our troops are obliged to
fall back on the forts, let us not give to a fact so easy
to be explained the character of a defeat.  France is
cruelly attacked, it is true, but she is not dead, and
she will not die."

---

sible for the defence of Paris had to change the character of the new
forts for that of field works, and with that object their completion
was pushed forward day and night.  But in the midst of the under-
taking, and several days before the enemy arrived in the neighbourhood of the capital, the system of labour was suddenly deranged
owing to the anxiety of the men for the safety of their families,
which for the most part had their homes in the banlieue, and the
difficulty they found in placing them in a state of security.  Nevertheless, at the date of the investment these works were good redoubts, having wide and deep ditches.  If they were not armed
with siege guns the reason was that it is not customary to put
pieces of this nature, which are difficult to remove, in mere earthen
redoubts, at a distance from the body of the place.  But all those
which could be occupied for external defence were so occupied.
The redoubt at Chatillon, for example, rendered a very efficacious
support on the 19th to the French troops during the obstinate conflict which raged about that point, and the redoubts of Hautes-
Bruyères and of the Saquet Mill were similarly of great use on the
same occasion."

  The General's explanation is a singularly lame one.  In asserting
that the Chatillon redoubt did good service on the 19th, he allows
it to be supposed that Ducrot's failure to impede the enemy's
advance might have been even more signal than it really was.  If
the redoubt rendered efficient support on that occasion, how came
it to be abandoned so readily when it was known that the position
not only dominated the neighbouring forts by some 250 feet, but
positively·commanded Paris, the possession of it, as the result
showed, enabling the besiegers to throw their first if not their only
shells in the city ?  With regard to the celerity pretended to have
been exercised in constructing these supplementary works of defence, we have the testimony of an independent witness which is in

Other journals, singularly enough, found grounds for hope in the fact that it was the seasoned soldiers who had taken to their heels. "This day of the 19th," said the *National*, "is the last blow dealt to our old military organization, and has furnished a proof that armies recruited like those of Prussia can only be successfully opposed by armies having, like hers, youth ; and, above all, the sentiment of nationality. Away then with the Zouaves and other fra-

---

direct contradiction with General Trochu's assertion. M. Simonin narrates, in the *Revue des Deux Mondes* (November, 1870), a visit which he made to the redoubt of Brimborion on the 18th of September, when he found not only Sèvres but Billancourt and Boulogne, although the latter were defended by Mont Valérien as well as by the Seine and the line of ramparts extending from Passy to Point du Jour, entirely deserted by their inhabitants :—"No one was to be seen excepting a few peasants in the fields gathering unripe vegetables ; all the houses had their shutters closed, not a single person was encountered standing at his door, everywhere was a deathlike silence. Mounting the height of Brimborion one observed a few workmen, with no officer present to direct their labours, leisurely turning over some earth, and a few woodcutters engaged in felling trees. There was scarcely any ditch, any tubes traced out, and almost another month or two seemed necessary to complete the work. Although every minute counted, the workmen lost their time in the cabarets, and thereby unconsciously betrayed the city. In the wood of Meudon some disbanded Zouaves had just killed a stag, and embarrassed with its antlers, made us an offer of them. These marauders were the worthy precursors of the runaways from Chatillon on the day following. A coachman who passed shouted to us not to go any farther, as he had just seen some uhlans, as he termed them, who had fired at him, and in proof of his assertion he pointed out a bullet imbedded in one of his wheels. Women and children, pale and terror-stricken, came flying from the neighbouring localities before the enemy. At daybreak the following morning the forts of Issy, Vanves, and Montrouge thundered ; we fought at Clamart and Chatillon without much honour for our arms, and the Prussians occupied the heights of Clamart, Meudon, Sèvres, and St. Cloud, and with them various unfinished redoubts, including the one of which we have spoken."

casses, the chevronnés, the grognards, the vieux lapins, the remplaçants, the substitutes, and other inventions of the same kind. Give place to the true children of France, to those who are animated solely by patriotism. Let us then be full of confidence, because to-day the fate of the country is in their hands, and because they are prepared to prove that old France is not dead." Of all the papers, the whilome sprightly *Figaro* was unquestionably the most lachrymose, moralizing as it did over the fate which had befallen Paris in the following fashion :—

"THE SILENCE OF DEATH."

" Since yesterday Paris is alone.

" Since yesterday all the railroads are cut, and letters no longer arrive.

" Let all those without families, and who were wont to repine at their lonesome condition, to-day bless it. They will never know the poignant grief and sad despair conveyed in these four icy words after the true official formula :

*The communications are interrupted.*

" This means that all you brave spirits who seized your rifles to defend Paris against the Prussian invasion, will receive no more tidings of those you love. You have begged them, on your knees perhaps, to fly from the danger that menaces us, from the danger you have disguised from them. They complied, weeping ; every day they have written to you, every day you have replied to them. Well, after to-day they will not receive your letters any more, and neither will you receive theirs."

The *Figaro*, however, could be grandiloquent as well as pathetic on such a theme as the investment of Paris. Witness the following :—

" Paris, the city of intelligence, where thought, liberty, and genius abide—the city which has passed through every phase, and remains the head and brain of the world. This immense ! this radiant city, is about to be besieged by the Germans ! She is about to give to the universe, whose centre she is, the unheard spectacle of a grandiose defence.

" She is invested. Messieurs the Germans dance round her. They will dance long who dance the last. We hated them, these Germans, who desired to rob us of the sea; to extinguish our commerce; to redo the work of nature and civilization, to the profit of Bismarck, William, and these princely squires who have gone into partnership under the style of North Germany and Company. We hated them because our interest no less than our instinct urged us to do so. To-day we must not merely hate them, but fight them ! not merely fight them, but conquer them! not merely conquer them, but crush them ! The environs of Paris—those fairy hills and valleys unknown to the poets of the Bible, when they sang of Paradise—must be their tomb. To-day we must have but one war-cry—' Conquer or die !' "

The rumours in circulation respecting M. Thiers's mission, and the visit of M. Jules Favre to the Prussian head-quarters, had given rise to plenty of angry comments at the clubs, and had aroused suspicions among the more bellicose of the population— sufficiently irritated at the deplorable result of the first engagement under the walls of the capital—that a dishonourable peace was about to be concluded. Numerous officers of National Guards, belonging chiefly to the fighting faubourgs, such as Belleville, Montmartre, La Villette, and the Faubourgs Saint Antoine and du Temple, thereupon determined to demand explanations from the Government on the subject, and accompanied by a considerable crowd, presented themselves early in the afternoon at the Hôtel de Ville for this purpose. The assurances they received were such as to satisfy them, but a deputation from the united clubs, which succeeded them, and came to lodge a series of complaints against the reactionnaires of the Hôtel de Ville, and were less easily talked over by M. Jules Ferry, the suave and fluent member of the Government of National Defence, whose mission seemed to be to control if he could not " wield at will the fierce democracy." To calm their minds, if not to revive the martial ardour of the patriots, later in the day the Government placarded Paris all over with a proclamation couched in these terms:—

" It has been rumoured that the Government of National Defence thinks of abandoning the policy for which it was placed at the post of honour and peril.

" This policy is that formulated in these terms:—

"NOT AN INCH OF OUR TERRITORY,
NOT A STONE OF OUR FORTRESSES.

" The Government will maintain it to the end."

It was on the walls of Paris that one read the latest war news, as well as the newest Government proclamations. Thus, to-day, we learnt from telegrams received during the night that early in the evening of the 19th, the enemy had proceeded to make himself quite at home on the eastern side of Paris, occupying alike the villages of Noisy and Bondy, together with the adjacent woods, posting batteries on the borders of the park of Raincy, and establishing an observatory in an isolated yellow house, in the corner of the park, positively within a mile of La Boisière redoubt, conveying the impression to Admiral Saisset that he was definitively posting himself with a view to the investment. Some cannon shots from Fort Noisy sent both infantry and cavalry scampering in all directions, and caused the yellow house to be abandoned for that night at any rate. Brie-sur-Marne was reported to be on fire, and the enemy had been detected endeavouring to pass the river under cover of the night, which caused some shells to be promptly launched in the direction of the bridge. The bridges of Sèvres, St. Cloud, and Billancourt were, it seems, effectively blown up about eight o'clock in the evening, after the first had been successfully defended all day long by the sharpshooters of the Seine and some National

Guards against repeated attacks on the part of the Bavarian chasseurs.

Telegrams received from time to time during the day notified first a fire of no moment at the fort of Vincennes, which had been readily subdued; next that Bondy was swarming with German soldiers, that they had again installed themselves in the yellow house, and had established advanced posts at nearly a couple of miles distance from the guns of Forts Nogent, Rosny, Romainville, and Aubervilliers; while at Chatillon they were to be seen masked in considerable numbers in a little copse under the church tower. Towards evening the enemy was signalled descending the quay at Sèvres, and information arrived that some Prussian dragoons had installed themselves in the château of Meudon. To-day the Mayor of Paris launched a decree interdicting the access of the public to the summits of all the more lofty public buildings and monuments, and the Bank of France held a meeting, at which, in view of pillage becoming the order of the day, either on the part of the Red Republicans or the Prussians, they decided all their notes should be collected in one huge pile, and at the moment of imminent danger, should be perforated in the centre so as to render them valueless as a circulating medium. During the afternoon some cavalry sabres were offered for sale on the boulevards by francs-tireurs, who professed to have taken them from uhlans, victims to the precision of their fire, and realized over twenty francs each.

One little incident of the moment, though insignificant in itself, spoke volumes in its way. The soi-disant Vicomtesse de Renneville, editor of the *Gazette Rose*, a well-known magazine of fashion, announced in the newspapers that " in presence of events in course

of accomplishment," as she delicately phrased it, she
felt constrained temporarily to suspend the publication of her *Journal des Modes.*  Imagine not Europe
merely, but America and Australia, and portions of
Asia and Africa also—two-thirds of the entire globe in
fact—deprived of their Paris fashions, and that "un-
bridled luxury of women," against which Churchmen
and publicists had been vainly protesting, exposed to
such an unexpected check.  The Parisian modistes,
knowing the all-powerful influence which the sex
exercise in the counsels of the world—in war as well
as politics—scarcely believed it would have been permitted to come to this, and through Count Bismarck
too, after whom and in whose honour new shades of
colour had been named ad infinitum—Bismarck riant,
Bismarck malade, Bismarck scintillant, Bismarck en
colère, Bismarck froide, Bismarck glacé, but who is
now only heard of as Bismarck menteur, Bismarck
renard, and Bismarck féroce.

The clubs were grand again this evening; the
burthen of their discourse being "the enemy is under
our walls, the cannon is thundering at our gates,
treason is in our midst—this was in allusion to the
Chatillon affair, insuccess, with the French, who regard
themselves as invincible, being invariably the result
of treason—the hour for talking is past, the moment
for action has arrived; let us arise as one man and
hasten to the ramparts, swearing victory or death."
At some of the clubs the number of oaths taken by
those who had made "a pact with death" and vowed
to die on the altar of the country, were so numerous
that this wholesale swearing seriously interfered with
the ordinary proceedings, and it was suggested to
dispense with the formality of oath-taking, and simply
to register these affirmations for publication in the

newspapers of the party, as an enduring testimony to their patriotic resolution. Of course, the moment a citizen had himself, in melodramatic fashion, called upon the assembly solemnly to witness that he had made his pact with death, he had played his part, the only one in which he took the smallest interest, and naturally enough felt bored at being constrained to listen to scores of his fellow-citizens making pacts with death in their turn. Eventually a compromise was effected, it being decided that on the morrow—the anniversary of the foundation of the first French Republic seventy-eight years ago—the oath should be sworn en masse, at the foot of the Statue of Strasburg. Certain patriots, not content with offering the sacrifice of their own lives, evinced great anxiety for the sacrifice of the lives of others, and proposed demanding of the Government the issue of a decree condemning every individual—who dared to speak in public of the possibility even of Paris surrendering—to death.

At the Folies-Bergère, one citizen scouted the idea of concluding peace with " this crowned corporal, this ambitious despot, intoxicated with blood and dishonourable success;" another responded that " France was prepared to combat to the bitter end, and crush its enemies beneath its own ruins, and"—according to the orator's ambiguous simile—"a despairing avalanche of hatred and anger against all tyrants, rather than its soil should be profaned by the presence of a single Prussian." Citizen Lermina maintained that " Paris having determined to defend herself would, if need arose, suffer unheard-of anguish and misery, and even die of hunger, for which she had sufficient heroism, but would never surrender, nor even treat for peace, so long as one of her enemies remained on French soil. With her it is a question of national dignity. Paris, the first city in the world, must maintain her rank and crush the senseless efforts of tyranny and ambition. Let her imitate Strasbourg, where ere long there will possibly not remain a single house or a single citizen; still, above the ruins, and the holocaust of corpses, there the French flag will float to represent the national honour. Paris can resist in the same fashion, and if doomed to fall, the survivors standing erect upon her ruins can appeal to France to avenge her cause, and crush the invaders ere they can regain their own country." Citizen Delescluze,* one of the chiefs of the ultra-democratic party, and president on this occasion, called upon those present "not to incline before a vile conqueror, and his cowardly menial, the cunning instrument of ignominy. An armistice may be spoken of to-morrow, but let us not succumb on that day, the anniversary of our great Revolution, which regenerated the entire world. Let us rather make a manifestation on the Place de la Concorde, there swearing to defend the country until death, and never to treat with the King of Prussia." This proposition having been received with acclama-

---

* He is a tall old man, with white hair and a fine physiognomy, whose words have an accent of conviction, which however seems oftener counterfeit than real. He has a vigorous though narrow mind, is a subtle logician, a clear and energetic writer, possessing an enormous influence over his own party, and respected by all other parties for the independence of his character, the loyalty of his life, and the many sacrifices he had made for his cause."— *Sarcey's " Siége de Paris."* A little of that general respect which, according to M. Sarcey, Citizen Delescluze commanded, must have been withdrawn from the member of the Committee of Public Safety, and the Delegate to War of the Commune of Paris before his death behind a barricade on the Boulevard Prince Eugène, on May 27, 1871.

tion, delegates were at once despatched to all the other clubs, inviting them to join in the proposed demonstration.

On rising next morning, the Parisians found the walls of the capital covered with a proclamation of Gambetta's, saying, in flowery French fashion—

" Citizens, to-day is the 21st of September.

" Seventy-eight years ago this very day our fathers founded the Republic, and swore, in presence of the foreigner who profaned the sacred soil of the country, to live free or die fighting.

" They kept their oath ; they conquered; and the Republic of 1792 has remained in the memory of mankind as a symbol of heroism and national grandeur.

" The Government, installed at the Hôtel de Ville, with enthusiastic shouts of 'Vive la République!' could not allow this glorious anniversary to pass without saluting it as a great example.

" May the mighty spirit which animated our predecessors instil our souls, and we shall conquer. Let us to-day honour our fathers, and to-morrow let us know, like them, how to secure victory by confronting death.

" Vive la France! Vive la République ! "

Towards noon some groups assembled in front of the statue of Strasburg, and shortly afterwards battalions of National Guards, having the barrels of their rifles decorated with green sprigs or flowers, proceeded to defile across the place and deposit wreaths of immortelles and bouquets of white flowers at the foot of the statue. Some orators having addressed the assemblage, urging " resistance to the bitter end," it was suggested to proceed in a body to the Hôtel de Ville. The proposition, however, was not very warmly received, being acted upon by only a few battalions, who marched thither with drums and trumpets sounding, to fête, as they said, the pretended anniversary of the first Republic, but really to demand the adjournment of the proposed elections, and the vigorous prosecution of the defence. Some delegates having been admitted to an audience with the members of the Government, the latter afterwards appeared at the windows of the Hôtel de Ville, when both the Mayor of Paris and Citizen Rochefort addressed the crowd, the President of the Barricade Commission assuring them that at the present supreme moment there could be no other question but " war to the death."

The clubs that evening decided that a new and more formidable demonstration should be made on the morrow, by the members of the Republican Committee, by National Guards, armed or unarmed—it was positively suggested " it did not matter which, although the manifestations without arms had always been ridiculous,"—and by the " people," meaning by the latter, of course, merely the members of the ultra-democratic party, which utterly ignored the presence in Paris of more than a million and a half of individuals opposed to its way of thinking. The object of this demonstration was to compel the Government of National Defence to accept the following programme :—

" 1. That no treaty be discussed with the Prussians* until they have been repulsed from the national soil.

" 2. That neither an inch of our territory, a stone of our fortresses, a vessel of our fleet, or a centime of our treasure be ceded to them.

" 3. That the elections be adjourned until after the war ; but that the Government being in need of material and moral assistance, Paris is to choose a Commune, certain members of which are to be despatched on extraordinary missions to stir up the departments.

" 4. That a *levée en masse* be decreed.

" 5. That the old police force be completely dissolved, all the members of it, of whatever grade, being at once drafted into the active army ; and all matters of police being confided to the vigilant care of the National Guard."

---

* In speaking of the invaders, the Parisians invariably styled them " Prussians," utterly ignoring the presence alike of Bavarians, Saxons, Würtembergers, Hessians, &c.

An orator at M. Blanqui's club, La Patrie en Danger, having pointed out that if these reasonable proposals were rejected, the manifestations conceived in a pacific spirit might possibly have another issue, a citizen sprung to his feet and recommended pitching the authorities out of window if they dared oppose the will of the "people," and replacing them by a Government essentially revolutionary. A citoyenne, numbers of whom were ordinarily present at these gatherings, was frantically cheered on declaring that she for one was prepared to shoulder the muskets which the seminarists refused to seize, and march with them against the enemy.

The manifestation was duly made, the Government were "interviewed" and apprised that, if the conditions were accepted, the citizen chefs de bataillon of National Guard would swear, one and all, to die for the Republic, and answer, moreover, for the men under their command pouring out their blood. M. Jules Favre haughtily responded, they were a Government of Defence, and not of Capitulation, while M. Henri Rochefort promised that Paris should commence its barricades that very night; whereupon the agitators, appearing satisfied, dispersed amidst shouts of "Live the Republic!" "Death to the Prussians!" In the evening there was a manifestation of a different character. Some hundreds of men and women, belonging principally to the working classes, promenaded the boulevards, preceded by a huge transparency lighted up by blazing torches, and representing an infuriated female flourishing a flaming brand in the one hand and a naked sword in the other—symbolical, some said, of France aroused and preparing to avenge herself; while others professed to recognize the figure as the

14—2

spectre of the Red Republic—that perpetual dread of the quiet bourgeoisie.

At the outset of the investment every one was impatient to see the military bulletins, believing that at least one pitched battle would have been fought outside the walls every day   No one dreamed that the Germans intended, or would have been permitted, to settle quietly down and make themselves comfortable for the winter in the abandoned villages and châteaux around Paris, acting only on the defensive.   For the first few days these bulletins simply indicated the positions of the enemy who closed in upon Paris with the precision of fate.   First we were told the besiegers had been throwing bridges over the Seine, between Vaux and Triel, on the north-west, then between Port Marly and Le Pecq, occupying the latter locality with St. Germain, Le Vesinet, and Chatou, together with other pleasant places in the environs; their scouts even appearing at St. Cloud, Rueil, and Nanterre. They could be discerned, we were informed, constructing works between La Courneuve and Le Bourget, on the Butte Pinson, in front of Montmorency, at Sèvres, and on the terrace at Meudon. Some occasional shells had been thrown from the forts whenever they daringly ventured too close in; reconnaissances too had been made in this and that direction, numerous skirmishes of no account had taken place, and the old admiral commanding at Fort Noisy, irritated at their persistently using the yellow house in the park of Raincy as an observatory, in spite of the shells he launched against it, had sent out a reconnoitring party to burn it down, compelling the besiegers to establish another in the rear of the Forest of Bondy.   Such was the military intelligence up to the morning of the 23rd, when there appeared M. Jules

Favre's narrative of his interviews with Count von Bismarck, of which it is necessary now to speak.*

### V. PEACE NEGOTIATIONS.

The war movement may have been impelled in Paris in the first instance by police agents, disguised in blouses, parading the boulevards, and singing the " Marseillaise ;" still, the Imperial Government found its most efficient auxiliaries in an unprincipled newspaper press, which had recourse to falsehood, vain boasting, and appeals to a fallacious patriotism, to inflame the public mind and rouse it to a necessary state of frenzy. With defeat came depression, but not calm sober sense. The overthrow of the Empire

---

* M. Jules Favre, the son of a Lyons merchant, and born March 21, 1809, had just completed his studies for the bar at the epoch of the revolution of 1830, in which he took part. Joining the Lyons bar, he associated himself with the insurrectionary proceedings in that city in 1831 and 1834, and the year following came to Paris to defend, before the Court of Peers, the accused of April, 1834. " I am a Republican," were the opening words of an address which brought him into prominent notice. Enrolled as a member of the Paris bar, he was in the capital during the revolution of 1848, and until elevated to the Constituent Assembly by the department of the Loire, acted as secretary to M. Ledru Rollin, at that time Minister of the Interior. For a brief period he became Under-Secretary of State for Foreign Affairs. He energetically demanded that proceedings should be taken against M. Louis Blanc for his participation in the troubles of the 15th of May, and upon the election of Louis Napoleon to the Presidency of the French Republic, became his consistent opponent, and assumed the lead of the democratic party after the flight of Ledru Rollin, in 1849. The coup d'état, however, threw him back into private life, and for the next half-dozen years he confined himself to the duties of his profession, defending Orsini, in a celebrated speech, in 1858. He was shortly afterwards elected Deputy for Paris to the Corps Législatif, and became from this time forward the recognized chief of the Opposition. The French Academy made him a member of their body in 1868. M. Favre died in 1880.

brought the illusion that France had rid itself of all responsibility with regard to the acts of the Government it had subverted ; that in proclaiming itself a Republic it had condoned the crime of declaring war against Prussia on the most miserable of pretexts ; and that Europe, lost in admiration of the retributive justice meted out to its ruler, solely because he had failed in his enterprise of seizing the Rhine, and giving credence to the assertion that the nation as a body had always been opposed to war, would interfere on its behalf, and compel Germany to grant such a peace as the vanquished might approve of. " Not an inch of our territory, not a stone of our fortresses," was in every one's mouth, as though France—ignoring the fact that twice within the century it had been compelled to cede territory, and had, moreover, twice surrendered Paris—expected on this occasion to enjoy comparative immunity after having been the promoter of the war. Count von Bismarck had, however, recently reminded Europe that within the last hundred years " France had invaded Germany no less than twenty times, and that Germany having been forced into the present war—which it had prevented during four years by care and by restraining those feelings of national self-respect so incessantly outraged by France—meant now for its future safety to demand the price of the mighty efforts it had been called upon to make."

In the exordium with which, in oratorical fashion, M. Jules Favre opened this narrative of his interviews with the German Chancellor, he observed, with some degree of inaccuracy, in reference to the Government of which he was a member, " We are before all men of peace and liberty. Up to the latest moment we opposed the war, which the Imperial Government

engaged in exclusively in a dynastic interest."* After
certain ambiguous allusions to negotiations in which
he had engaged with foreign powers, urged by him to
intervene with Prussia in favour of a peace, M. Favre
next intimated that one Power, meaning England,
from whom he had asked much more than he had
obtained, had particularly recommended the step he
had taken. He then detailed, for the benefit of Europe
in general, and of France in particular, all the circumstances of the two interviews which he had just had
with the German Chancellor—the first at the Château de
la Haute Maison and the second at that of Ferrières—
interviews the object of which M. Favre described as
follows :—

" Time was marching apace. Every hour brought the enemy
nearer. A prey to the most poignant emotions, I had promised
myself not to allow the siege of Paris to commence without making
a supreme attempt to stay the progress of the war, even if I were
alone in my effort. The reason does not require to be given.
Prussia remained silent, and none consented to question her. This
situation was unbearable; it allowed our, enemy to throw upon
us the responsibility of the continuation of the struggle; it condemned us to remain silent as to his intentions. It was necessary
to extricate oneself from this position."

After various delays in his quest after Count von
Bismarck, M. Jules Favre eventually secured an interview with him on the 19th of September, the place
of rendezvous being the Château de la Haute
Maison, belonging to Count de Rillac, and situated
near Montry, on the road from Meaux to Ferrières. M. Favre pledged himself as to the desire of
France for peace, and also as to her unshakeable
resolution not to accept any condition which would
convert that peace into a short and threatening truce.
Count von Bismarck replied that, were he convinced

---

* See page 30, *ante.*

that such a peace were possible, he would sign it at once. He acknowledged that the Opposition had ever condemned the war; but the tenure of power of the Opposition was more than precarious. In a few days, he observed, if Paris were not taken, the Government would be overthrown by the populace. Hereupon M. Favre interrupted the German Chancellor with vivacity, exclaiming that there was no "populace" in Paris,* but an intelligent and devoted population, which knew the intentions of the Government, and would not make itself the accomplice of the enemy by hampering the mission of defence. "As for our power," added M. Favre, "we are prepared to transmit it to the Assembly already convoked by us."

At this first interview Count von Bismarck claimed for Prussia—as the price of peace—the two departments of the Upper and Lower Rhine, and a portion of the department of the Moselle, with Metz, Château Salins and Soissons; whilst, on the morrow, at Ferrières, he communicated the conditions on which an armistice would be granted. They were the occupation of Strasburg, Toul and Phalsburg, by way of security, and in the event of a Constitutional Assembly meeting in Paris, a fort commanding the city—Mont Valérien for instance—would have to be given up to the Germans. To this stipulation M. Favre strenuously objected. "Why not ask for Paris at once?" said he. "How can you entertain the idea that a French Assembly would deliberate under your very guns? I have had the honour to tell you that I should faithfully transmit our conversation to my Government, but I really do not think I dare acquaint it with the fact of such a pro-

---

* The word " populace " has a contemptuous significance in France.

posal having been made to me." The Count having
replied, " Well, let us try and discover another combination," M. Favre proposed that the Chamber
should meet at Tours, keeping clear of all engagements respecting Paris. Count von Bismarck then
suggested that the King should be spoken to on the
subject, and reverting to the occupation of Strasburg,
he said, " The town is about to fall into our hands ;
it is a mere question of an engineer's calculation. I
therefore ask that the garrison should surrender as
prisoners of war."

"At these words," says M. Favre in his narrative
of the memorable interview, " I sprang from my seat
with pain (*j'ai bondi de douleur*) and exclaimed, ' You
forget you are speaking to a Frenchman, Monsieur le
Comte. To sacrifice an heroic garrison which commands
the admiration of the world as well as our own, would
be an act of cowardice, and I cannot promise even to
mention that you have put such a question to me.' "
The Count replied that it was not his intention to
hurt M. Favre's feelings ; that his proposal was in
conformity with the laws of war; moreover, if the King
consented, that clause might be modified. He then
left the room, and returned in a quarter of an hour.
The King accepted the Tours combination, but insisted
on the surrender of the garrison of Strasburg.

To these conditions the Government of National
Defence absolutely refused to subscribe, and M. Favre,
who was completely overcome with grief and wounded
pride, penned a letter to the German Chancellor
acquainting him with the decision. The French
Minister's eloquent narrative of his pilgrimage to
Ferrières produced an electrical effect on the vain and
impulsive population of Paris. It influenced all shades
of opinion, erased all differences, rallied to the Govern-

ment the most excited demagogues equally with the
soberest patriots, and united the city in a firm resolve
to prolong its resistance to the end.    For the moment
Paris attained to the heroic.

To avoid reverting on a subsequent occasion to these
negotiations for peace which so unhappily proved
abortive, it may be mentioned that Count von Bismarck
also issued a version of the interview between himself
and the French Minister for Foreign Affairs, in which
he professed to correct some inaccuracies in the narrative furnished by the latter; his main point being that
the real question under discussion was an armistice,
and not a treaty of peace.    To these observations
M. Jules Favre exercised his advocate's right of reply,
and concluded his comments upon Prussian rapacity
and ambition with the following words :—

"I ignore the destiny reserved to us by fortune, but I have firm
confidence that France will be victorious.    Were she conquered,
she would yet remain so great in her misfortune that she would be
an object of admiration and sympathy for the entire world.    There
is her real strength; there, perhaps, will be her vengeance.    The
European Cabinets,* who have confined themselves to sterile expressions of cordiality, will recognize it one day; but it will be too
late.    Instead of inaugurating the doctrine of high mediation,
counselled by justice and interest, they authorise by their inactivity
the continuation of a barbarous struggle which is a disaster for all,
and an outrage to civilization.    This bloody lesson will not be lost
for nations.    And who knows?    History teaches us that human
regeneration is by a mysterious law closely united to ineffable misfortunes.    France, perhaps, had need of a supreme trial; she will
issue from it transfigured, and her genius will only shine the
brighter from her having sustained and preserved it from succumb-
ing in face of a powerful and implacable foe."

---

* Notably Mr. Gladstone's Government.

## VI. ATTEMPTS TO PASS THE GERMAN LINES.

Of course, when Paris was invested, a considerable number of persons, Frenchmen as well as foreigners, who had no intention of seeing the siege through, but had either just missed the last train, or else delayed their departure a day too late, found themselves shut in; and a disagreeable practical lesson upon the consequences of procrastination was thus administrated to them. Frenchmen in this predicament had no alternative but to submit: with foreigners, however, the case was somewhat different, and the more impetuous, on finding themselves caught within the toils, made a bolt, and endeavoured to get through the German lines; whilst others, having great faith in the powers of diplomacy, followed the example of Mr. Micawber and waited patiently for something to turn up. Of the former only very few succeeded in their enterprise, the majority finding themselves reduced to turn back at the sight of needle guns relentlessly levelled at them whenever they attempted to pierce the line of investment, or even to parley with the German sentinels at the outposts. An account of some of these efforts to escape from Paris will give the best idea of the rigidness of the blockade which the besieging army had succeeded in establishing almost immediately after its arrival before the French capital.

A couple of bold Britons, who had laughed at the idea of the German army standing in the way of their reaching home without a considerable amount of preliminary manœuvring, and who had loitered unnecessarily over their preparations for departure, on finding all the railway trains irrevocably stopped, determined on a pedestrian trip a few miles out of Paris, fully expecting that at no very distant station

they would be able to secure a train to Le Havre.
They set forth, provided with passes from General
Trochu and the Prefect of Police, stating that the
bearers were British subjects journeying to England,
and their misfortunes began already at the Porte
Maillot—the gate by which they proposed to quit
Paris. At first they were informed there, that despite
their passes, they could not be allowed to leave; but
on the admiral commanding this section of the fortifications coming up, he permitted them to go their
way. though not without a few words of warning.
Accordingly they passed out over the drawbridge, and
presently found themselves in Neuilly. When they
reached the Seine fresh difficulties arose, for the
sentinel at the head of the bridge between Neuilly
and Courbevoie bade them wait until an officer passed
by. Happily one soon rode up, permission to pass
was granted, and the travellers went on their way; nor
was it until they had left Courbevoie behind them that
they were again stopped. This time the French outposts arrested their onward march, but on exhibiting
their passes, they were immediately allowed to proceed
afresh.

Hitherto they had been within the French lines,
and in perfect safety. Now, however, that they were
beyond them and between the advanced posts of the
combatants, their danger became considerable; they
were fair game for either party, and both sides might
have fired on them unexpectedly. In this dilemma
they put in practice a piece of advice given them in
Paris—pulled out their handkerchiefs, and never
ceased waving them as they followed the broad
road lined with trees and shrubs on either side and
leading towards Bézons, where they hoped to find a
passage across the second bend of the Seine. Here

they were, two peaceful Englishmen—one past the middle age, the other in the prime of life, dressed in unromantic civilian costume and chimney-pot hats, and one of them wearing barnacles—walking along a dismal country road, without a single being in sight, and liable at every step they took to be fired upon by some sharpshooter or Franc-tireur posted behind hedge or tree. And in fact they afterwards learnt that, stationed on one side of this avenue, which seemed interminable, were French Francs-tireurs, and on the other, sharpshooters of the German army; but they were blissfully ignorant of their danger at the time. Always waving their pocket-handkerchiefs to an invisible enemy, they at length reached the banks of the Seine opposite Bézons, where they found the bridge, by which they had hoped to cross the river, destroyed. Having hailed some persons on the opposite bank to come and row them over in a boat that lay moored there, they were intensely annoyed at receiving for answer that the Prussians had forbidden any such thing being done.

Near this place, however, in front of a small house, were a couple of little boys playing at see-saw on a plank, around which other planks were strewn. It occurred to the unfortunate pair that they might succeed in placing these boards across the water from one pile of the broken bridge to another, and thus effect a passage. Accordingly they resorted to this expedient; but in the first place the planks proved too short for the purpose; and in the next, the people on the opposite bank shouted menacingly across the river. Their ruminations over this unhappy posture of affairs were becoming exceedingly unpleasant, when one of the urchins at their side informed them that a little lower down the stream was a bridge still intact, and, moreover, volunteered to take them to it. Accom-

panied by this juvenile guide, they accordingly set
out, and ere long reached the bridge, where their con-
ductor left them. A minute later the younger of the
two Englishmen, having advanced somewhat ahead
of his companion, turned suddenly back, with a
startling cry of "The Prussians!" And there in truth
they were, or, rather, was one of their sentries, needle
gun in hand, who had popped up, like some Jack in
the Box, from behind a buttress, just as the foremost
of the strangers approached the middle of the bridge.
The wretched Englishmen instantly turned and bolted;
a ball whizzed past them ; but in a few moments they
had gained cover and were out of immediate danger.
Overtaking their juvenile guide, and learning from
him that a Prussian camp was close at hand, they
determined to repair to the enemy's quarters, exhibit
their papers, and request permission to pass. After
another half-hour's walk along a broad avenue they
suddenly came upon the Prussian sentries, to the
number of four, posted at a point where a by-road
intersected the avenue. Waving their handkerchiefs
and holding out their papers, the two bold Britons
advanced, but to their cries of " English ! Friends ! "
—uttered both in French and English—the
laconic though eloquent reply of a levelled rifle was
delivered. They found it utterly impossible to parley ;
to every attempt they made came the one answer,
" Be off ! " emphasized, moreover, by the action of
taking aim. At this moment some half-dozen rifle
bullets whizzed past their ears, and the four Germans
all fell wounded. Turning in alarm to see whence
the shots had come, our travellers perceived some half
score of Francs-tireurs bolting across a field in their
rear. At the same instant a trumpet sounded, and
a German detachment, attracted by the firing, was

seen coming up. The two Englishmen again took to their heels, rejoining their guide, who had left them a short way down the road. This little gentleman, nothing daunted, volunteered to conduct them to another Prussian outpost; and still bent on passing through the lines, if possible, they again accompanied him. A sharp walk along another avenue brought them upon some more German soldiers, including several brilliantly attired officers, whose presence inspired them with confidence. But it was in vain that they again endeavoured to parley, for they were not allowed to approach within a hundred yards of the sentries. The two unfortunates now gave up their enterprise in despair, and obeying the injunctions of the Germans to be gone, they retired disconsolately. Learning that Reuil was the nearest village, they next set off for that locality, and on arriving found themselves instantly surrounded. The people noting what bad French they spoke when replying to their inquiries, and hearing them converse together in their native vernacular, at once mistook them for Prussian spies. With an angry crowd of a couple of hundred persons, men, women and children, at their heels, they succeeded in reaching an hotel, and begged admission. This being refused, they were conducted by a crowd profuse in vituperation, and prodigal of insult, before the local Commissary of Police, to whom they exhibited their papers and explained the reason of their appearance at Reuil. Fortunately for them, the Commissary was satisfied with their story, and ordered the hotel-keeper to lodge them for the night. On the morrow he, moreover, gave them a certificate to assist them in returning to Paris, and appointed an ex-courier, who spoke German, to escort them back to the city. As their guide sympathized with them in their trouble, they eventually prevailed upon him to aid them in making a last attempt before finally retracing their steps; and with this view they presented themselves at various German outposts. It was in vain, however, that the ex-courier addressed the sentinels in the language of the Fatherland; they continued inexorable to his entreaties, and nothing remained to the downcast heroes but to take their melancholy way back to the prison from which they had fancied it would be so easy to escape.

Another curious adventure was that of the agent of a Birmingham small arm factory who, having delayed his departure from Paris in the hope of concluding a contract with the Government of National Defence, also found himself shut in. As his means did not allow him to adopt the costly mode of escape presented by balloon, he resolved to try and pass through the German lines on foot. He neglected to provide himself with a pass from the military authorities, but strapping his knapsack on his back sallied forth just as though we had been in piping time of peace, instead of with the blast of war blowing in our ears. He proposed to cross the Seine by the bridge of St. Cloud, which he had been told was not destroyed, and succeeded in making his way out of the city, and through the Bois de Boulogne, unchallenged. At the Rond Point, however, on the Paris side of the Seine, the sentry refused to allow him to pass, whereupon he turned back and tried to gain Suresnes by the bridge lower down. At this epoch only a moderate portion of the Bois de Boulogne had been destroyed, and as he was unacquainted with its many pathways and avenues it is not surprising that he speedily lost his way. Having foolishly started on his expedition at a late hour,, dusk speedily set in, considerably adding to his difficulties; and it was quite dark by the time he made the Porte d'Anteuil, to find the gate closed and the drawbridge up. Advancing as close as he could to the ramparts he shouted out in indifferent French that he wished to enter Paris; but voices on the other side at once warned him to be off. A second appeal to the sentries on duty brought him a similar response, together with a threat to fire upon him; and finally, on his persisting in his entreaties, he was answered with ˙a volley. The instant he heard the report he flung himself on to the ground, where he lay for the next half-hour, not daring to move. Believing the sentries would by this time think him dead, he crawled stealthily away till he had extricated himself from the pointed stumps of the trees cut down for military purposes, and then scampered off as fast as his legs could carry him.

Having eventually discovered one of the little huts erected to shelter the gardeners and workmen employed in the Bois, he remained here till daybreak, when sallying forth he advanced once more in the direction of the fortifications, this time flaunting a white pocket handkerchief at the end of his umbrella to indicate the pacific nature of his intentions. Finding the gate at which he arrived open, he was about to pass through when he was challenged by the National Guards on duty, who perceiving the muddy state of his garments asked where he had come from at this early hour. Our Englishman having stammered out a few words of broken French in an embarrassed manner, was instantly set down as a Prussian spy, and forthwith dragged off to the guard-room. After being searched, and having everything he possessed taken from him—including a small bottle which the sergeant on duty appeared to regard with considerable suspicion—he was placed under lock and key until the officer made his rounds. On the latter's arrival he was again questioned, and gave his own explanation of his presence outside the ramparts at that unseasonable hour, referring to his passport and other papers in proof of his being no spy. The officer replied that these proved nothing, as spies were invariably provided with papers placing them beyond all suspicion. "But," added he, "I am not without proof of your being a villain,"—an announcement which alarmed our hero, who fancied, from some address cards of the firm he represented having been taken from him, that he was about to be charged with supplying warlike materials to the enemy. His mind was relieved, however, when the officer produced the small bottle, taken from him, as the pièce de conviction. "I know very well," said this leader of citizen soldiery, "what you have been about with this bottle ; it contains some combustible fluid with which you have been trying to set fire to our chevaux-de-frise." Protestations were all in vain ; the officer refused to believe a word till the Englishman hit upon the expedient of proposing to drink what remained of the terrible liquid. The cork being with difficulty removed, the bottle was handed to him ; and while he gulped down a portion of its contents, the officer withdrew to a safe distance, as though he expected to see his prisoner spontaneously explode. Finding however that the distressed Briton merely smacked his lips, and was prepared to take a second draught, his curiosity became aroused, and he finally allowed himself to be persuaded to taste the liquid, when finding it to be some excellent Chartreuse Verte, he drained the bottle before returning it to its owner, and with many apologies for the mistake which had been made, had him instantly set at liberty.

A few days after the arrival of the German army before Paris, one of General Trochu's aides-de-camp, desirous of communicating with his family at St. Germain, instructed his English manservant to endeavour to proceed there. This was successfully accomplished ; but on the return journey the servant was stopped by a couple of German sentinels and marched before an officer in command of a small camp, where the men sat at breakfast around blazing fires, whilst near at hand were several large siege guns, each with as many as a dozen horses attached to it. Having explained that he was an Englishman, and that he was merely proceeding to one of the neighbouring villages, breakfast was ordered for him by the officer, who, after making a few inquiries respecting what was transpiring at St. Germain, also furnished him with a pass to enable him to continue his journey. On reaching Paris and informing his master of this incident, he was conducted before the Prefect of Police, whom he told that he had passed through the German lines on his way out, clad in peasant costume, and in the company of some neighbouring villagers. The Prefect at once gave orders for a half-dozen of his most intelligent *mouchards* to disguise themselves as peasants and set out on so many voyages of discovery, bidding them adopt much the same kind of tale as the officer's valet, if they chanced to find themselves stopped by the enemy's sentinels.

Three days after the investment of the city, a party of Englishmen, anxious to return home, ran the blockade in company in the boldest fashion—that is, in the conventional travelling carriage and pair. The

15—2

narrative* of one of the party describes that, on the 22nd of September, there was standing in the deserted quadrangle of the Grand Hôtel a single carriage, in which were stowed away five hand travelling bags and two huge hampers, containing what four Englishmen considered the necessaries of life for three days ; whilst tied to the roof above was the broad standard of England, and a vast white banner, which might yet come to do good service to the travellers. Around the vehicle were gathered all the remaining inmates of the Grand Hôtel, the half-dozen visitors who herded together on the first floor for the sake of society, and the six or eight servants left to wait on them. They were there to see four Englishmen start on the now perilous journey from Paris to London. The party, who were all men of business, "caught" in Paris when the last railway line was cut, were accompanied by an Italian friend, and had secured for charioteer an old English jockey, named Tommy Webb, who had gone over to France with Charles X., and now, in his declining years, had been reduced to driving Parisians about in a hack cab. After being stopped a first time at the French outposts just beyond Neuilly, for want of a *laisser-passer* signed by the Governor of Paris, the party were compelled to return into the city, and late in the day, baffled by red tape and routine, found themselves re-entering the courtyard of the Grand Hôtel. Mr. Wodehouse—Her Britannic Majesty's sole remaining representative in Paris—having with no little trouble obtained a special pass from General Trochu, the party renewed their attempt on the morrow. They soon got clear of the French lines, but in their

---

* Published in the *Times* newspaper.

efforts to penetrate those of the enemy they met with several melodramatic adventures. Continually stopped at the German outposts, at one moment they were only flying away from the fire of needle rifles to encounter the revolvers of Francs-tireurs; and when, after numerous vicissitudes, they succeeded in parleying with a German cavalry officer, nothing but a special permit from the Crown Prince of Prussia, to whom they addressed a written appeal, enabled them to proceed on their journey to Versailles. Thither they were conducted, all carefully blindfolded, by a troop of some twenty horsemen, and after being rigidly searched and interrogated by General von Blumenthal, they were eventually suffered to proceed on their journey to England by way of Rheims, Sedan, and Belgium.

Another successful attempt to pass the German lines was made by Captain Johnson, the same Queen's Messenger who, on his journey into Paris, had been taken, it will be remembered, for a Prussian spy. He left the capital in charge of a French naval officer, who led him some distance towards the outposts, where there was a strip of neutral ground to cross under very ticklish circumstances. At last a Bavarian sentinel was sighted, who sent for his officer, and Captain Johnson was placed under comfortable surveillance until the morning, when he was allowed to proceed, under escort, to Versailles. Here General von Blumenthal most courteously, but most firmly, informed Captain Johnson that, under no circumstances, could any Queen's Messenger be allowed in or out of Paris through the German lines again. After his Majesty of Prussia's pleasure had been taken, Captain Johnson received permission to continue his journey as a special and great national favour; but he also was obliged to return, it is said, by way of Meaux, &c., through Sedan, to the Belgian frontier, as the German authorities refused to send out with him any flag of truce, which might be supposed to recognize Francs-tireurs as legitimate soldiers.

The investment, which the Parisians had hitherto delighted to demonstrate to each other as being mathematically impossible, from this time forward may be said to have been complete; but the city was not entirely shut off from the world, as will presently be shown.

# VI.

## THE COMMUNICATIONS.

---

### I. THE FIRST COURIERS AND BALLOON ASCENTS.

FORTIFIED, armed, garrisoned, and provisioned, Paris, now that it was invested, had to solve the problem of keeping up communications with outside—if not precisely in the interests of retarded civilization, as certain of its journals with ludicrous self-sufficiency gravely suggested, now that the Germans had put the so-called "Capital of the Intellectual World" in quarantine—at any rate on its own particular account. If the blockade by a hostile army of a city of two millions of souls—a quarter of whom were under arms—was an event unprecedented in history, it was still more remarkable that the beleaguered capital should have succeeded in maintaining almost constant communications with the departments during the siege—a circumstance which was only rendered possible by the rapid advances made of late years in science. Apart from mere military considerations, the stubborn resistance which Paris offered to the enemy was due in no small measure to this facility of communication. Physical suffering of every description, when the mind is elevated by some noble sentiment, such as patriotism, is often endured by masses of people without a murmur; but the mental anxiety consequent upon the complete isolation of many thousands of human beings, influenced by strong

family ties, from all who are dearest to them, in unfit-
ting them for resolutely engaging in a struggle of
lengthened duration, is apt to defy alike the calcula-
tions of the statesman and the plans of the strategist.

It was, nevertheless, not so much for these reasons as
for purposes more immediately connected with the defence, that the Government exerted itself from the very
outset of the investment to secure some effectual
means of intercourse between the capital and the
departments.  On September 18 the last regular
despatch of letters from Paris was effected by the
train leaving the Montparnasse station of the Chemin
de fer de l'Ouest, at 5 P.M., the early mail train of the
following morning being forced to return ; and on the
20th the post-office authorities attempted to send out
the mails in three light covered vehicles drawn by
fleet horses, and by a couple of horse and five foot
carriers ; but save one of the last named, all were
driven back by the bullets of the German sentries.
The single courier (one Létoile by name) who succeeded in passing the enemy's lines, deposited his
letters at Evreux, and managed to get back into Paris
a week afterwards with some 150 letters which he
found lying at the post-office of the town he had
reached.  Henceforward, couriers travelling on foot
were exclusively employed, and on the 21st of September no fewer than eight-and-twenty of these
messengers were sent out in various directions, only
two of them, Brare and Gême, succeeding in
accomplishing their mission ; they reached St.
Germain, after various vicissitudes—being fired at by
German sentinels near Maisons Lafitte—with 3000
letters secure in their possession.  These were left in
charge of the St. Germain postal agents to be conveyed to Neauphle-le-Château, and the two couriers

set out on their return journey to Paris, which they reached early the same evening. All the remaining couriers despatched on this same occasion, with the exception of one named Poulain, of whom nothing more was heard, and who in all probability paid for his intrepidity with his life, returned to Paris with the letters they had taken out with them, having found it impracticable even to penetrate the enemy's lines, much less pass through them. Two of them, named Letrony and Delhôtel, who left the city by the Porte de Bagnolet, were arrested by some German sentinels on reaching Drancy, and · after being searched and compelled to strip, were eventually marched off to Prince Wittgenstein's headquarters at Roisy, a few miles eastward of Gonesse. The Prince contented himself with questioning them concerning the seriousness of the defence contemplated by the Parisians, and then ordered them to be conducted outside the German lines, with strict injunctions not to venture again within them.

Seven couriers sent out on the two following days met with corresponding failure, while of five who were despatched on the 24th, one alone—Gême, of whose success on a previous occasion we have already spoken —continued to run the blockade, and deposit his letters with the mayor of Triel, northwards of St. Germain. On the 27th, while four other couriers were obliged to renounce the enterprise confided to them, Gême and Brare engaged in a new and successful attempt, reaching Triel, and again returning in safety to Paris. On October 4th, Brare set forth once more, and was captured by the Germans, but succeeded in escaping and reaching Orleans. The day following two post-office couriers contrived to enter Paris, bringing in with them 714 letters, with which they had started from Triel five days previously. Of thirty-four other couriers despatched from Paris up to the end of October three were arrested, and after being imprisoned for several days, set at liberty, while the remainder returned to Paris without accomplishing their mission. The majority of these messengers, besides the ordinary letters which they carried with them, conveyed official despatches in cipher, which several did not hesitate to secrete beneath their skin, while others hid them either inside their coat buttons, or in hollow copper coins specially prepared, or else up key-pipes and pencil cases. Swallowing them would scarcely have answered, as after a time the Germans made a point of administering strong aperients to all strangers they had any suspicion of.

The Paris post-office authorities recommended their couriers invariably to describe themselves as fathers of families, on falling into the enemy's hands, thereby if possible, to ensure their being leniently treated. Couriers captured with only ordinary letters in their possession were commonly set at liberty after a brief imprisonment, and with a strict injunction not to venture within the lines again. Extracts from the confiscated epistles made their appearance from time to time in the German newspapers, and proved the hold which the habitual turgid language of the Parisian press had taken on the population generally. Such stereotyped expressions as "gronder le canon," "vomir la mort," "la sainte cause de la civilisation," "la liberté ou la mort," "malheur aux traitres," with which the writers hoped to astonish the trembling provincials, were of frequent occurrence. The ex-Emperor was roundly abused; was styled thief, traitor, deceiver, and wholesale murderer. Death and the most excruciating torments were invoked upon him, and the writers spoke of tearing him to pieces in effigy, as they could no longer get at him in person. Ladies and educated people expressed fears of civil war in Paris, but there was tolerably unanimous hatred of the enemy, and perfect confidence in the defensibility of the city. Some of the letters had apparently been written in the expectation of their falling into the enemy's hands. One indeed, after scolding the Germans unmercifully, naïvely added that if those wretched Prussians should chance to read it they would see in what kind of estimation they were held in Paris. A few of the letters breathed a more noble spirit—patriotic grief, self-sacrifice, and despair—whilst one writer, a wounded soldier, commented bitterly on the want of principle and veracity of the Paris press, as justifying the harsh judgment now passed on the French by foreigners.

Paris at this period was far from being exclusively dependent on the postal couriers referred to, otherwise its opportunities of communication would have been necessarily few and uncertain. After a time the land route became practically closed, and water communication being altogether impossible, one could only have recourse to the air. Naturally the idea of employing balloons to take out letters, early suggested itself to every one; but nobody believed there were sufficient aëronauts in Paris for anything like a continuous aërial service. On the 21st of September, M. Rampont, the General Director of the Paris Post-Office, issued a notice in which, after dwelling upon the difficulties attending the despatch of letters from the capital, he urged the public to make use of extremely thin paper, and to dispense with the customary envelope. This notice put every one on the tiptoe of expectation; and it soon tran-

spired that M. Rampont had already been nego-
tiating with Nadar, the well-known aëronaut, in
reference to the establishment of a regular balloon
service, but failing to arrive at a definite arrangement
had addressed himself, for present purposes, to the
proprietor of a balloon called the *Città di Firenze,*
which had been wont to ascend at different suburban
fêtes. It was, however, found to require extensive
repairs before an ascent could be risked; whereupon
M. Rampont purchased Nadar's captive balloon, somewhat inappropriately named the *Neptune,* and which,
installed at Montmartre for the purpose of watching the
enemy's movements, had been an object of attraction to
the Parisians for the past fortnight or three weeks. On
the 23rd of September, at a quarter to eight o'clock of
a bright autumnal morning, and with the wind due
east, the *Neptune,* restrained no longer by the powerful
tackle which had hitherto held it captive, made its
ascent from the Place St. Pierre, in charge of M.
Jules Duruof, a well-known aëronaut, in presence of a
crowd of functionaries, and amidst deafening shouts
of "Vive la Republique!" its freight comprising three
mail-bags, weighing about 2 cwt., and containing
some 25,000 letters. The instant the ascent became
known all Paris was watching the progress of the
balloon with the deepest anxiety, and every one re-
joiced at seeing it pursue a favourable course. Rising
to the height of a couple of thousand yards, it passed
over the west of Paris, in the environs of which the
aëronaut perceived the Prussians in clusters like bees
below him, and with a telescope could distinctly see
them pointing cannon at him. He saw the balls
ascending almost perpendicularly in the air, exhaust
their impetus, and then fall to the ground. Never
before was human being all alone in such a trying

position, defying the efforts of an entire army against his life. Some of the balls arrived sufficiently high, he said, to cause the balloon to vibrate perceptibly. Infantry also took cracks at him with their rifles all the way from Paris to Mantes, but he was entirely out of their range, and amused himself by showering down from time to time a quantity of Nadar's address cards upon their heads. After a voyage of about three-quarters of an hour, he alighted in the park of the Château of Craconville (near Evreux), belonging to Admiral La Roncière Le Noury, who commanded the sailors manning some of the forts of Paris. Such was the journey of the first balloon which left the beleaguered city during the German siege. M. Duruof proceeded to the Admiral's château, where the Prefect of the Eure speedily came to see him. The aëronaut had orders not to give the official despatches he had brought out with him to anybody but a General or a Prefect; but having had the good fortune to alight near a railway station in communication with Tours, instead of remitting them to the Prefect of the Eure, he proceeded to the then capital of provincial France, and handed them in person to the triumvirate which momentarily governed the uninvaded departments.

The departure of the next balloon, the *Città di Firenze*, which had been thoroughly repaired in view of its aërial voyage, took place at 11 A.M. on Sept. 25. With it went M. Mangin, the aëronaut, M. Luitz, a Government Commissioner, and 104 kilogrammes of letters, besides numerous copies of M. Jules Favre's narrative anent his interviews with Count von Bismarck, and also several carrier pigeons. Rising at once to a height of about 4500 mètres (some two miles and three-quarters), the balloon sought in vain for a

current of air to propel it onward; and passing over
Mont Valérien, remained becalmed for well nigh
forty minutes.    At length a light south-easterly
breeze carried it past Le Pecq, and eventually to
Carrière-sous-Bois, at an altitude of 1800 mètres.
Over the plain of Triel the balloon was again
becalmed for about three-quarters of an hour, and
it was only after ten bags of ballast, the seats of
the car, three bundles of letters, and a sack filled
with M. Favre's reports had been thrown out, that
the balloon, thus sensibly lightened, rose and crossed
the Seine.    The peasantry of the neighbourhood,
having perceived the falling sacks, collected them
together and brought them to the aëronaut on his
descent near Vernouillet.    Despatching the letters
to the nearest post-office, MM. Luitz and Mangin
then sent their carrier pigeons back to Paris, where
they arrived the same day with the happy news
of this second successful voyage amid the clouds.
From that day the transit of the Paris mails through
the air was an accomplished fact, and a decree appeared limiting the weight of all letters to four
grammes, or about one-eighth of an ounce.    At the
same time energetic steps were taken to accelerate the
construction of a considerable number of balloons for
postal purposes; the authorities, whilst awaiting the
delivery of a portion of this new aërial flotilla, having
to avail themselves of such balloons as already existed
in Paris at the epoch.

Thus, on September 29th, there ascended from the
railway-station at La Villette a triple balloon, the
*Etats Unis*—composed of two old balloons of unequal
dimensions coupled together, with their fastenings
sustained by a third and smaller balloon.    The
aëronaut was M. Louis Godard, who took out with

PREPARING FOR A BALLOON-ASCENT.

i. 238.

him M. Courtin, proprietor of one of the balloons in question, together with about 1 cwt. of letters. This voyage, undertaken in such a singular fashion, terminated more satisfactorily than had been anticipated, the *Etats Unis* alighting in perfect safety at Mantes. The *Céleste*, which ascended the next morning, in charge of M. Gaston Tissandier, and conveying some 2500 epistles directed to all parts of France, was less fortunate. The wind drove the balloon over the forest of Rambouillet, past Houdan, and towards Dreux; and it was only after it had been split literally from top to bottom by the high wind that the aëronaut succeeded in alighting. For several days subsequent to this voyage the wind proved unfavourable to balloon departures from Paris. Nevertheless, M. Ziper, an army contractor, who was charged with Government despatches for Tours, risked an ascent, the aëronaut suggesting that favourable upper currents might be met with. Instead of this, the voyagers were driven in a north-easterly direction, and only half an hour had elapsed, when, on a considerable quantity of gas escaping, the balloon rapidly fell into a large sheet of water. The travellers were within fifty paces of the Prussian sentinels posted in front of the farm of Chantourterelle, but five hundred yards from other German positions facing Dugny and Pierrefitte, and equally nigh to the redoubt of La Courneuve, occupied by the Francs-tireurs of the Press. From these points a fusillade was opened upon the unhappy aëronauts, who floated motionless on the water, pretending they were dead. In this situation they remained for the space of three hours. At half-past seven o'clock, when it was quite dark, M. Ziper and his companions navigated the car in the direction they believed some French troops to be posted, and on landing were met by a detachment of the Francs-tireurs of the Press and conducted to the fort of La Courneuve. The despatches they had with them were fortunately saved.

## II. BALLOON FACTORIES AND DOVECOTES.

The Government, with the view of always having at its disposal a certain number of balloons and aëronauts to replace those that might from time to time be sent out from Paris, arranged with M. Eugène Godard and his brothers, all well-known aëronauts, for them to organize at the Orleans railway-station a balloon factory and school of aëro-statics, at which sailors, selected of course from the nature of their calling, might be instructed in the art of conducting and managing balloons. About the same time, corresponding arrangements, so far as the construction of balloons was concerned, were made with an aërostatic association directed by MM. Nadar, Yon and Dartois. The convention stipulated that each balloon should be of the capacity of 2000 cubic mètres, that it should be manufactured of percaline, a particular kind of calico, and provided with a tarred hemp netting and a wickerwork car capable of holding four persons, together with all the necessary apparatus, such as valves, grapnels, bags of ballast, and so on. When filled with gas, and while sustaining a weight of 500 kilogrammes, or rather more than half a ton, it was to be capable of floating in the air for the space of ten hours. The dates of delivery were appointed at fixed epochs, and a fine of 2*l*. was to be imposed for each day's delay. Each balloon was to cost 160*l*., including the gas calculated at 12*l*., and the aëronaut's honorarium, estimated at no more than 8*l.* M. Godard contracted, moreover, to supply a number of small paper balloons about 18 ft. in diameter, provided with cars and netting, and capable of raising rather more than a cwt., their price being fixed at 6*l.* apiece, all expenses included. These "ballons libres," as they were styled —from their being abandoned to the mercies of the wind without any aëronaut on board—were designed to take out some newly authorized postcards, the contents of which were to be read by the postal authorities before being despatched, so as to make sure they contained no information likely to prove serviceable to the enemy, should the balloon fall into his possession. The cost of transmission was fixed at two sous, including postage between the town near which the balloon chanced to alight and the locality to which the card was addressed. A regular system of look-outs was to be organized in the departments to watch for these free balloons, which on their descent were to be taken to the mayor of the nearest locality, who was charged with delivering their cargo to the Post Office officials. Of course these ballons libres were only to be sent up when the wind was favourable, so that they might not run the risk of falling into the enemy's hands ; but, despite the precautions taken, several of them were captured by the Germans, and ere long they were altogether cast aside, it being found that the regular postal balloons sufficed to carry out all the correspondence of the capital when the accumulations of the past few weeks had been cleared off.

Very animated indeed at this epoch was the aspect of the balloon factory at the Gare d'Orléans. Under the vast iron and glass arched roof—on the long metal rafters of which sailors balanced themselves or sat

astride, engaged in suspending long strips of coloured
calico reaching almost to the ground, and to which,
moreover, already hung wickerwork cars, trailing
ropes and grappling irons—scores of women were
occupied, either in spreading out and ironing long
pieces of material, the better to search for flaws; or
else in soaking the calico to get rid of its stiff-
ness, or to reduce the mordant nature of the dyes.
Having been hung up to dry, the material was then cut
out to the various patterns, marked their full size upon
the ground, and after a preliminary varnishing a hundred or more work girls, seated at long tables and
superintended by Madame Godard, proceeded to sew
the seams with mathematical exactitude.    Then came
a second coat of varnish, both inside and out, adminis-
tered by douaniers and sailors, who next inflated the
balloon by means of a metal fan, which, besides
causing the varnish to dry the quicker, facilitated
the detection of any holes that might hitherto have
passed unperceived.  These, on being discovered, were
immediately sewn up.  The netting, dragging ropes,
and other tackle, together with the cars, were all made
by sailors, and the whole of the various operations
were performed beside each other under the same roof.*

---

* Annexed are some statistics respecting the balloons constructed
at this period for the Government, and which were supplied by
M. Godard to the *Journal Officiel.*

The balloons were 51 ft. 8 in. in diameter, 162 ft. 4 in. in circumference, with a total exterior surface of 8388 square feet, and
a capacity of 72,234 cubic feet.  Each balloon, which required twelve
days to manufacture, was composed of forty strips, formed of three
separate pieces, cut out of dried varnished percaline, and joined
together by a carefully sewn double seam.  The balloon having
been varnished, was then carefully fastened at the upper end to the
valve, a circular piece of oak, 2 ft. 7 in. in diameter, provided with
semicircular folding doors, opening inwardly by means of a cord

M. Nadar and his association originally established
their balloon factory—at which, although the sewing
was done by machinery, between one and two hundred
hands were nevertheless employed—in the ball-
room of the Elysée Montmartre, but subsequently

---

hanging into the car, when it was desired to let the gas escape, and
hermetically closing—a broad elastic band serving as a spring. The
lower end of the balloon was fastened to a strong wooden hoop,
2 ft. 7 in. in diameter, which was joined to a linen tube, 8 ft. 2 in.
in length, by means of which the balloon was placed in communication with the feeding gas-pipe. A strong tarred hemp netting,
fastened at the top round the circle of the valve, enveloped the
balloon down to the large suspended hoop, 6 ft. 6 in. in diameter,
placed two yards below the smaller one, and attached to it by
means of forty gabillots, which also supported the car.

The last named, constructed of solid wickerwork, was 4 ft. 7 in.
broad, and 3 ft. 7 in. deep, and had two seats. The ropes by
which it was suspended were platted into the wickerwork, and inside was a series of gabillots, designed to secure the bags of ballast,
despatches, &c. ; while outside there was a second series for the
pigeon cages, heavy packages, &c. From the lower hoop to the
bottom of the car the distance was 6 ft. 6 in., so that the total
height of the entire aërostatical apparatus was 68 ft. Inside the car
were placed a barometer, a thermometer, a mariner's compass, a miner's
lamp, several ropes, twenty strips of paper, each 65 ft. long, and
destined to try the direction of the wind, an oriflamme bearing the
balloon's name, a paper triangle like a kite, with which to make
observations on the currents and the speed, a parachute, between
300 and 400 bags of ballast, each containing 33 lbs. of fine sand, an
iron grapnel, 4 ft. high and 2 ft. 7 in. broad, a guide-rope, 656 ft.
long, half in mat-weed, half in hemp, two grappling ropes, &c.

The total weight of the balloon, independent of passengers and
cargo, was 1 ton 1 cwt. 73 lbs. ; the balloon itself weighing 4 cwts.
19 lbs., the netting 1 cwt. 11 lbs., the suspension hoop 24 lbs., the
grapnel 55 lbs., the grappling ropes 35 lbs., the guide-rope 99 lbs.,
the car 110 lbs. To test the balloon it was inflated with gas.
The ballast bags holding it to the ground were then removed ; the
car was filled with its complete load, allowance being made for the
weight of the three voyagers who were next expected to leave, and
when the balloon commenced to rise the three sailors manœuvring
it quickly let out the ropes, and the balloon was allowed to attain
an altitude of 655 ft.

16— 2

removed it to the Northern Railway Station, where the luggage department was transformed into cutting and sewing rooms, the arrival platform being devoted to the varnishing and inflating of the balloons, and other parts of the building to the manufacture and storing of the ropes, netting, cars, &c.

As regards the winged messengers employed during the siege of Paris, these were of two categories—namely, departure and arrival pigeons. The first, numbering upwards of 1100 of the most perfectly trained birds in all France, belonged to societies of Roubaix and Tourcoing, to MM. Hazebrouck and Lefèvre of these two towns, and also to M. Villefeu, and other inhabitants of Laval. Confided by their owners to the Mayor of Paris shortly before the investment, they were lodged at the Jardin des Plantes until required from time to time to carry out despatches to the north or west. Usually ten copies of each despatch were remitted to M. Casimir Derode, who had charge of the birds, and were fastened, under his superintendence, to one of the tail feathers of as many pigeons as there were messages to send out.

The arrival pigeons—those which were despatched with the balloons to bring back word of their safe descent, together with news from the provinces—were principally furnished by MM. Vanrosbeck and Deronard, of the Société de l'Espérance, and by MM. Cassier, Trichet, Noblécourt, Laurent, Goyet, and others. M. Cassier's dovecote, situated at Batignolles, in the centre of a somewhat carelessly ordered garden, was faced by a little pavilion, which the Post Office agent, charged to signalize the pigeons' return, used as his look-out station. On its arrival the pigeon entered its house by an opening in the roof, which, while allowing the bird to enter, did not permit its egress. A glance enabled the proprietor to detect the particular pigeon which had returned, as it was usually very fatigued, and would at once seek its habitual place in the dovecote it had quitted a few days previously. Not unfrequently the pigeon was found to have been wounded, either by some bird of prey or by shots from a German rifle. The season being, however, altogether unfavourable to these feathered travellers—as the autumnal mists obscured their sight, and the cold paralyzed their strength—far more lost their way on the road than fell victims to the enemy's projectiles.

The proprietor, taking the bird in his hand, after examining the stamp imprinted on one of its feathers,

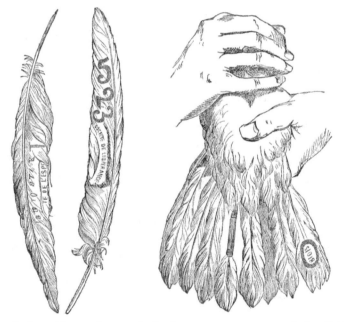

and denoting whence it had come, next ascertained if it had lost its despatch *en route.* On detecting this despatch, which was generally contained in a quill fastened to a tail feather that remained unmovable when the pigeon spread its tail to fly, the proprietor took the bird, either to the Director-General of the Post Office, or to the hotel of the Governor of Paris, where the despatch was removed and deciphered. The majority of the birds used as messengers during the siege were not carriers, but Antwerps, or crosses between Antwerps and English dragons, of moderate size, and having no pretension to beauty. They were principally young birds from five to eight months old, breeding pigeons not being found sure messengers. We may add that the speed of a good carrier has been estimated at from 1000 to 1200 yards per minute, but is greatly diminished by contrary winds. A southwest wind is understood to be most favourable to the bird's flight, as it is slightly charged with watery vapour, and the pigeon does not feel that excessive thirst which east and north winds cause it to endure.

### III. GOVERNMENT BY BALLOON.

The wind in the west quarter ordinarily means simply rain, but in Paris it came to signify no communication with the world outside. It was something to live for nearly a month in this " Centre of Civilization" (which, despite its title, was isolated from the rest of the world) and to feel that, in these days of rapid communication, one was shut up with a couple of million human beings without means of receiving a single letter or message from relative, friend, or stranger outside. Once or twice some old number of a newspaper penetrated through the living wall that encompassed us, and the Paris journals lived on it for days. The single piece of English intelligence received during the first few weeks of investment related to a monster meeting in Hyde Park in favour of France; and all the scraps of outside news at this epoch, if added together, would not have filled an ordinary newspaper column. But bad as this state of isolation was, it became almost intolerable when we could not commit our own thoughts, hopes, and fears to the winds of heaven, trusting—and too often idly trusting—that they might reach those for whom they were designed.

For fully a week at the commencement of October we had the wind in the west, and day after day balloons already inflated were restrained from taking flight. Hourly we watched the weathercocks, praying for that east wind which Canon Kingsley so much extolled. At daylight, every morning, pilot balloons were sent up, and invariably took a direction more or less easterly where the Prussians had spread themselves over the country for between two and three hundred miles. The Government—dissatisfied with the efforts of the Triumvirate of Tours, MM. Crémieux, Glais-Bizoin, and Fourichon, "*débile, sénile,* and *stérile,*" as they were nicknamed at the epoch—had decided that M. Gambetta should be conveyed beyond the Prussian lines in Nadar's balloon, the *Armand Barbès*, with the view of stirring up the departments to hasten to the relief of Paris, before famine reduced its chances of a successful defence. Accordingly, morning after morning, the Place St. Pierre, at Montmartre, was crowded to witness the ascent; but the wind, though it varied slightly, befriended the Prussians : so that the armies of succour of Lyons and of the Loire, of Normandy and of Brittany, were left to their own devices, and the tribune of the hour was retarded in his mission. At length, trusting himself to fate, and a temporary puff of south wind, "the young Gambetta"—as it was then the fashion to call this statesman of thirty-five—

clad in a long greatcoat and a round fur cap, which gave him very much the appearance of a Polish Jew, accompanied by his secretary, M. Spuller, and with a grandiloquent proclamation to the provinces, already prepared, in his pocket—ascended in the *Armand Barbès*, on Friday, October 7, amidst the acclamations of an immense crowd. Another balloon, the *Georges Sand*, in which were a couple of French functionaries and two Americans, charged, it was said, with a mission by the Provisional Government to purchase Remington rifles or Gatling guns, and other trifling contraband of war, made the ascent at the same time and at the same moment.

The balloons had to wait, on this occasion, till the morning mists dispelled and the precise direction of the wind could be ascertained. At length, M. Gambetta—who looked extremely pale—having listened to the pigeon fancier's final instructions as to the proper time for feeding the birds, and how to roll the despatches round one of the tail feathers, bade his friends adieu, and the travellers took their places in the cars. The aërial vessels, held down by a score or two of sailors, were swinging to and fro in the breeze with the oscillating movement of a pendulum. "Lâchez tout!" cried the pilot of the balloon which had the coming Dictator on board, and the moorings being cast off, the *Armand Barbès*, accompanied by the *Georges Sand*, rose to the height of several hundred feet, amidst loud shouts of "Vive la Republique! Vive Gambetta!" For the space of five minutes all seemed favourable, but the two balloons having cleared the heights of Montmartre, disappeared behind them, making, as the spectators thought, a rapid descent within the enemy's lines. It proved, however, to be a false alarm, and for some short time the balloons pursued a northerly course, and then diverged due east, which direction they continued to take until.lost to sight.

It was at this epoch that the *Débats* styled the rule under which France was then subsisting as " Government by Balloon ;" and the phrase was not an unhappy one, considering that not only all despatches, but the various official Commissioners and the most important Minister of the day, had to depend on the aërial mode of transit. M. Gambetta did not disguise his preference for railway travelling, and all Paris laughed over his expedition. Indeed, it furnished the text for a chanson de circonstance, to the air of " Batelier, dit Lisette, je voudrai passer l'eau," of which the following was the opening stanza :—

> " Gambetta, pale and gloomy,
>     Much wished to go to Tours ;
> But two hundred thousand Prussians
>     In his project bade him pause.
> To aid our youthful statesman
>     Came the aëronaut Nadar,
> And made mount the *Armand Barbès*,
>     With Gambetta in its car ! "

According to this same ditty, while passing over the German lines, Gambetta exclaimed to his companion :—

> " See how the plain is glistening
>     With bright helmets in a mass—
> Impalement would be dreadful
>     On those spikes of polished brass."

Naturally enough, the newspapers improved the occasion ; the versatile *Figaro*—which, for the time being, had become converted to Republicanism— maintaining that a nation whose principal Minister was capable of such an heroic feat, would ere long sign peace, not under the walls of Paris, but even at Berlin !

It was not until the fourth day after M. Gambetta's departure that any positive tidings were received of him.   One of the pigeons sent out with his balloon returned without a message; two of those taken with the *Georges Sand* likewise came back destitute of the slightest semblance of a despatch; and the Parisians were growing hourly more anxious, when, late on the evening of the 10th of October, a fourth pigeon arrived in the capital, bringing with it a communication in cipher from M. Gambetta to the Government.   This was dated from Montdidier, in the department of the Somme, and notified that the balloon had met with an accident in the forest of Epineuse, narrowly escaping the Prussian sharpshooters; that he (Gambetta) was about to start for Amiens, *en route* for Tours, and that the Government of National Defence was everywhere enthusiastically recognized.    The pigeon which brought this welcome intelligence—a male bird, of a bluish tinge, and of the Belgian breed—was at once christened " Gambetta."   On a subsequent journey back to Tours, it had the ill luck to be slain, so it was surmised, by a Prussian bullet.

It would appear that in passing over the enemy's lines M. Gambetta and his companions escaped death twenty times.   The Germans kept firing at them, and bullets constantly whistled past their ears.   A first attempt at a descent was relinquished when at an altitude of 200 yards some Prussian soldiers were perceived immediately underneath.   Their arms were piled, and while they rushed to seize them, ballast was thrown out, but the balloon did not mount sufficiently fast to prevent several balls from penetrating it, and one from grazing M. Gambetta's head.   At four in the afternoon, when the descent was renewed, near Roye in the Somme, the balloon caught on an oak tree, and at one moment the coming Dictator was holding on to the ropes of the car with his head hanging downwards. He escaped, however, this new danger with only a few slight scratches. The country people who ran up, at first threatened the travellers, whom they mistook for Prussians, with summary punishment; but when Gambetta displayed the national tricolour, and shouted " Vive la Republique!" and the aëronaut told them the name of the principal voyager, their enthusiasm became unbounded. The party were speedily extricated from their dangerous position, and conducted to the house of the mayor of the nearest village, which proved to be Tricot, near Montdidier. Just as they arrived there a man rushed up, breathless with running, to announce that the enemy were in search of the aëronauts. That same evening, however, M. Gambetta succeeded in reaching Amiens, and started next morning for Rouen, where, in reply to an address, he spoke of the resistance Paris was prepared to make, and called on the provinces to hasten to its assistance. "If we cannot make a compact with Victory," he exclaimed, "let us make a compact with Death!" His Norman friends applauded this self-sacrificing sentiment to the echo, and sanctified it in copious libations of cider, when shortly afterwards M. Gambetta was on his way to Tours.*

---

* M. Gambetta's aërial impressions were subsequently made public. According to these he was almost stunned with the over-powering idea of Nature's force and man's weakness. He felt, to his great astonishment, that he had no sense of the abyss beneath. The world seemed to recede from the balloon. Instead of being dazzled with the vast horizon which was opened to his gaze, he was stupefied at the total obliteration of the picturesque in the bound-less expanse beneath him. The earth had to him the appearance of a badly designed carpet, or rather of a carpet in which the dif-ferent coloured wools had been woven entirely by chance. Light

Subsequent to Gambetta's departure from Paris, the
Government decided on despatching other ardent Republicans through the clouds, to arouse the provinces
from their lethargy. Louis Blanc was asked to proceed
to England to awaken the sympathies of the British
nation in favour of France; Victor Hugo was also
offered a mission in the departments; but both of
these illustrious Democrats declined—the former on the
plea of a particular aversion to balloon travelling, and
the latter on the score that his mission was to consecrate
himself exclusively to the defence of the capital. Less
noted Republicans proved less mindful of their personal safety. Count de Kératry, who had advised the
suppression of the Prefecture of Police, and in support
of these views had resigned his post as Prefect, sailed
away—if one may so phrase it—in the *Godefroy
Cavaignac* balloon, on an important mission, it was said,
to Spain. M. Ranc, Mayor of the Ninth Arrondisse-
ment, and a political writer of some note, likewise
entrusted himself to the tender mercies of the wind in
company with a M. Ferrand, who, like himself, had
received an appointment as Government Commissioner.
These several journeys, although attended by melodramatic vicissitudes, ultimately resulted in safety.
Of all the balloons which left Paris at this epoch, by
far the most eventful voyage was that of the *Washington*,
which took out no fewer than upwards of 120,000
letters, besides conveying M. Lefaivre, a Post Office

---

and vastness were deprived of the value which shade and proportion
give them. Nature seen from a balloon was, in M. Gambetta's
estimation, nothing but " une vilaine chinoiserie."

It may be added that the voyagers by the *Georges Sand*—which
for some while continued within speaking distance of the *Armand
Barbès*—descended at Roye, not very far from the spot where M.
Gambetta alighted.

delegate, and M. Vanrosbeck, who had charge of thirty carrier pigeons. The aëronaut—a sailor, who had never been entrusted with the exclusive conduct of a balloon before—fell from the car in casting out his grappling iron; the Post Office delegate was subsequently pitched out by a shock against a tree, and when the Belgian pigeon fancier, left all alone, eventually succeeded in alighting, he was nearly being shot as a Prussian spy. The injuries sustained by the aëronaut and the delegate in falling from the car were fortunately only slight.

"This poor Republic!" remarked Charles Hugo at this critical epoch, " besieged and blockaded, reduced to despatch its commissioners to Lyons, Bordeaux, Lille, Marseilles, and other points of France through the air, and to apply to the defence of Paris the last desperate resource of Robert Macaire in 'L'Auberge des Adrets!'" He might have added that Paris was also dependent on balloons to learn the movements of the besieging army, which held it, as it were, in its grip. It is of these captive balloons, as it was the custom to style them, that we have now to speak.

### IV. MILITARY BALLOONS.

Military ballooning has always had an interest for theorists in the art of war; and previous to the commencement of the siege of Paris, General Trochu had requested M. Nadar—the initiator of the daring conception of the *Géant* balloon, that veritable castle in the air, which so completely failed to realize the sanguine dreams of its projector—to furnish a report upon the uses to which balloons might be applied towards assisting in the defence of the city. In this

report M. Nadar, with the approval of several of the
commandants of the forts, advocated the formation
of a corps of military aëronauts, and the establishment
of captive balloons at some half-dozen of the extreme
points of the line of defence. The idea was by no
means a novel one. The company of military aëronauts, created nearly eighty years previously by the
Committee of Public Safety, had rendered such signal
services to the armies of the First Republic, that
a school of military aërostatics was established at the
Château of Meudon, prior to the beginning of the
present century. This academy was dissolved by
Napoleon I., on the pretext that the professors incul-
cated Republican principles in the minds of their
pupils; and it was not until the Third Napoleon's
Italian campaign that military ballooning was again
heard of. At that epoch M. Eugène Godard signalled
from a balloon the offensive return of the Austrians
on the eve of the battle of Solferino, besides successfully taking a plan of one of the forts of Peschiera.
In America, too, during the War of Secession, military
aëronauts were frequently employed by the generals
on the Federal side.

At the commencement of the Franco-Prussian war,
however, the attempts made by French aëronauts to
induce the Ministry of War to consent to the establishment of a military corps, were unsuccessful; and
the Imperial Government did not even vouchsafe
a reply to the men who were willing to place their
lives and services at the disposal of the country.
M. Nadar was more fortunate with the Government
of National Defence, for, within a few days of its
installation, a balloon of his, called the *Neptune*,*

---

* Subsequently despatched from Paris, and replaced by a
smaller balloon called the *Strasbourg*. See *ante*, p. 236.

commenced making regular ascents at the Place St. Pierre, Montmartre, with the view of signalling the German advance upon the city. The extreme altitude attained was 1600 feet, and the balloon was provided with a series of reflectors, and no end of scientific appliances, enabling Nadar, on particular occasions, to take a glass negative every quarter of an hour, which he would send down in a little box gliding along a rope; and by means of which, combined with an optical chamber, the various military movements going on in the adjacent plain were depicted, with the object of enabling the defence to profit by them. Nevertheless, it appears that neither at the Place St. Pierre, Montmartre, nor at the Fort of Vanves, nor at the Place du Marché, at Auteuil—at all of which places so-called military captive balloons were successively employed during the siege—were results of any importance obtained.*

Whilst the ascents from the Place St. Pierre were matters of novelty, and attracted considerable crowds, the papers reported one morning that a Prussian spy had fired a revolver at the *Neptune,* hoping it would collapse and bring about the death of the intrepid aëronaut, who was just then the hero of the hour— for Paris must ever have its hero. Famous, Nadar had always been, but more for his eccentricity than anything else. His fantastic signature, which decorated his house on the boulevards in letters several feet in height, his temporary desertion of photography for ballooning, the immense losses he had sustained in endeavouring to solve the problem of aërial navigation, had all contributed to extend his reputation;

---

* *Révue des Deux Mondes.* "L'Aèrostation du Siége." Vol. xc. p. 623.

and soon adventures, rivalling those of the heroes
of antiquity, were ascribed to him.   A long account
of how he had engaged in mortal combat with a
hostile balloon went the round of the foreign newspapers, and was universally believed outside Paris,
for nothing too extraordinary could be related of the
man who, in one way at all events, was getting the
better of the Prussians; and who, while they were
anxiously guarding every outlet from the city, was
coolly despatching his messengers, through the air,
over their heads.   About this time it was that Albert
Millaud, who has since become known as one of the
most amusing of French satirists, published some
verses concerning Nadar, of which the following is a
translation :—

"What a strange fellow is Nadar!
　　Photographer and aëronaut;
He is as clever as Godard.
What a strange fellow is Nadar!
Although between ourselves, as far
　　As Art's concerned, he knoweth naught.
What a strange fellow is Nadar!
　　Philosopher and aëronaut.

" To guide the course of a balloon
　　His mind conceived the wondrous screw;
Some day he hopes unto the moon
To guide the course of a balloon.
Of 'airy navies' admiral, soon
　　We'll see him 'grappling in the blue;'
To guide the course of a balloon
　　His mind conceived the wondrous screw.

" Up in the kingdom of the air
　　He now the foremost rank may claim;
If poor Gambetta when up there,
Up in the kingdom of the air,
Does not find good cause to stare,
　　Why Nadar will not be to blame.
Up in the kingdom of the air,
　　He now the foremost rank may claim.

" At Ferrières, above the park,
  Behold him darting through the sky ;
Soaring to heaven like a lark,
At Ferrières, above the park,
Whilst William whispers to Bismarck—
  ' Silence, see Nadar there on high.'
At Ferrières, above the park,
  Behold him darting through the sky.

"Oh ! thou more hairy than King Clodion,
  Bearer on high of this report;
Thou, yellower than a pure Cambodian,
And far more daring than King Clodion,
We'll cast thy statue in collodion,
  And mount it on a gas retort.
Oh ! thou more hairy than King Clodion,
  Bearer on high of this report."


V. " ON ATTEND UNE REPONSE."

Westerly winds offered periodical impediments to the
system of aërial communication, which was, moreover,
attended by a far more serious drawback, as, while
balloons were leaving Paris almost daily, none could
hope to re-enter the city, for the problem of navigation
through the air was still unsolved. A commission,
composed of all the aëronauts who had quitted Paris,
was established at Tours to deal with this question;
and meanwhile the postal authorities tried to send
couriers into Paris, just as attempts had already been
made to send them out of it ; but of some eighty who
started only four succeeded in passing the German lines,
and these carried simply official despatches.

Paris was, if anything, more eager to receive letters
from the provinces than the provinces were to send
them, and amidst the uncertainty, not to say
despondency, which prevailed on the subject, the
*Figaro*, after its editor, M. de Villemessant, had
publicly announced that he would willingly allow one

of his veins to be opened in exchange for a letter from his absent wife, came out one fine morning with a notice headed, " A thousand francs to be gained per week." Herein it was stated that the editor believed he had discovered a means of communication, for which an intelligent man, who could furnish good references, was required. The prospect of 1000 francs a week, when 15*d.* a day was all that could be earned by shouldering a gun morning and night, brought a crowd round the offices of the *Figaro*, far greater than could be found at any butcher's; and it was only round butchers' shops, and at the Hôtel de Ville, when Major Flourens, at the head of the bellicose battalions of Belleville, threatened a demonstration, that Parisian crowds were to be seen at all in these times. But unfortunately not a single eligible individual presented himself. The *Figaro* thereupon announced that a retired poacher, accustomed to double when tracked by gardes champêtres and gardes forestiers; who was up to all manner of roundabout ways of arriving at an object straight before him; who could recognize the track of a Prussian as readily as that of a deer; and, above all, who could write, was the particular individual sought after. The right man seems to have been found at last, for the *Figaro* announced that anyone who sent a very light unsealed letter to the office, together with five francs, might count upon its delivery, and a reply in about a week or ten days after the courier's departure. The plan was to send him out with some two hundred tiny letters, which could be stowed away in a pocket, up his coat sleeve, in his hat, or, if necessary, in his boots. If he got through the German lines he was to post these letters, enclosing in each of them a slip of paper naming the town where he would await a reply by return of post; and on receiving the answers, he was to convey them to Paris. In view of his arrest by the enemy's sentinels, he was furnished with a large card, bearing on one side a statement in German, to the effect that he desired to be taken before an officer; and on the other, a touching appeal, also printed in the German language, and implying that his mission was but to carry a few words of consolation from the besieged to their sorrowing wives and children, or *vice versá.*

Rival newspapers denounced this scheme at once, and its originators in particular, insinuating that it would be a grand means of acquainting the Prussians with everything going on in Paris, and that Villemessant, who had received bribes from the Empire, must be a paid agent of Count von Bismarck. In consequence of these attacks the scheme was abandoned; and an architect named Itasse, who prepared to carry out the plan on his own responsibility, forgetting that in Paris—at that epoch at any rate—man proposed and the National Guard disposed, had his house invaded by a detachment of citizen soldiers, and was finally arrested and detained a prisoner, in company with a friend, until a commissary of police set both of them at liberty. The Post-office authorities subsequently intimated that they were not opposed to M. de Villemessant's plan, as, if carried through the lines, the letters would always have to be stamped and conveyed by post to their destinations, so that the revenue could be no loser. This declaration caused the scheme to be taken up in other quarters, and various associations were started to carry out letters from Paris and bring back replies; whilst, at the same time, several private balloon companies were established to convey passengers beyond the German lines. To prevent communications being made through this channel with the enemy, balloon ascents of every kind, unless specially authorized by the Government, were strictly interdicted; and no one was permitted to leave the city on an aërial journey without the joint authorization of the Minister of the Interior and the Governor of Paris, combined with the visa of the Minister of Finance, who received the whole of the £80 passage money paid by private individuals if the balloon were a Government one, and possibly part of the amount if it belonged to a private association. Private balloons were, moreover, prohibited from taking out printed matter of any kind to which the stamp of the Governor of Paris and of the Minister of the Interior was not affixed. This latter regulation was no doubt very generally violated, but the former one never.

The balloon advertisements which appeared at this epoch in the papers, were no doubt *bonâ fide*, but many of the letter agencies were established by ingenious swindlers, who, on demanding a certain sum for the carriage of a reply, engaged to return half the amount in the event of non-success. This half was always religiously refunded, the letters never being sent out at all, but destroyed after the postage stamps had been removed from them by the ingenious speculator, who cleared a handsome profit on the transaction. Of course there were some agencies which undoubtedly sent out couriers, and continued to do so until the inutility of the proceeding was shown. Among the private couriers who suffered for their temerity was an energetic woman, of Polish birth, imbued with the most intense hatred towards Prussia and Russia, and who had given several proofs of intrepidity during the Polish Insurrection of 1863. Quitting Paris on the west, she had arrived almost at the bridge of Argenteuil, when she was dangerously wounded while attempting to evade the enemy's sentinels, and had only just sufficient strength left to drag herself out of range, when she was perceived by some Gardes Mobiles and conveyed to a neighbouring ambulance.

## VI. NEWS FROM OUTSIDE.

Before Paris had been invested a fortnight, the Parisians, debarred even of such scraps of intelligence as chanced to be brought in by successful couriers— perhaps simply by reason of their unimportance— began literally to pine for news from outside; and ere long, whenever this was not forthcoming, there were not wanting those ready to invent it. The first rumour, however, which worked its way into general circulation proved, unfortunately, only too true. It referred to the fall of Strasburg, and was current on the boulevards on the evening of October 1st, being confirmed next morning by the Minister of the Interior, who, at the same time, had to announce the surrender of Toul. For the moment the shock was a severe one. Blank despair was on all countenances, and sadness in divers hearts. With the majority the feeling was not so much regret for the loss of these towns, as fear for the moral effect which their surrender was likely to have on the armed defenders of the capital. Countenances fell still lower when it was pointed out that the capture of Strasburg and Toul would, moreover, set free another army, and a considerable amount of siege artillery, to be employed against Paris; but the habitual confidence of the inhabitants soon returned, and some comfort was found in expatiating on the marvellous results to be achieved by a thousand new defence guns, carrying between four and five miles, and which, if not being actually cast, were for ever being talked about, and were most religiously believed in.

Every day, and almost every hour, for three weeks past, the statue of Strasburg, on the Place de la Concorde, had been the object of theatrical demonstrations. One day a party of Alsatians came to deposit a wreath of immortelles at the feet of the buxom-looking dame who personified the frontier city—armed with a short classic sword, and guarding the keys of France as though determined not to surrender them. Then, a band of Francs-tireurs would march to the spot, singing, "O! Strasbourg! O! Strasbourg! O! admirable ville!" and vow to vanquish the detested invader. All Paris hastened to follow the fashion of " manifesting " at the foot of the statue; and mobiles, national guards, free corps, and simple citizens, came with music at their head— playing the now wearisome strains of the whilom animating "Marseillaise"—and with bouquets, wreaths, and all the flowers of patriotic eloquence, to render homage to this new symbol of the national defence. The statue might in truth have been mistaken for one of the goddess Flora; for ere many days had elapsed, it was crowned with garlands, decked out with tricolor flags, smothered from head to foot beneath wreaths and bouquets of flowers, and lighted up at night with coloured Venetian lanterns; while its pedestal formed a sort of album, scrawled all over with patriotic effusions, and stuck round about with mock heroic stanzas, which, however much they may have done honour to the hearts of the writers, did none whatever to their heads.

Scrawls upon stone did not, however, suffice; and the next step was to open a register, richly emblazoned

with the arms of the Alsatian city, and having on its
first page a dedication from the Parisians "to their
brethren, defenders of Strasburg, and the brave General
Uhrich." Following, were the signatures of the members of the Government, who dared not withhold their
adhesion from the popular whim; and thousands came
daily to inscribe their names in the huge volume
which lay open upon a table facing the statue. On
one occasion a particularly patriotic citizen turned up
the sleeves of both coat and shirt, and deliberately
thrust the point of the pen into his flesh. When
sufficient blood had flowed, he affixed his signature
to the register, while the crowd, reverentially un-
covering, were lost in admiration at his Spartan act.

The National Guard were especially partial to
attitudinizing in front of this newly-devised shrine;
although one would have thought that with the
serious business which these citizen soldiers had in
hand, they would scarcely have wasted their time
over such frivolous displays. The Governor of Paris
appears to have been of this opinion, for he issued an
order of the day reminding them that, while the
enemy was constructing his batteries to attack the
forts, their place was upon the ramparts, rather than
in the midst of meaningless promenades and idle
manifestations. When, however, Strasburg at length
succumbed, the Government, seeking to ameliorate in
some degree the crushing effect of the news of its
surrender, by ministering to the popular feeling,
decreed that the souvenir of the frontier city's devo-
tion, and of the generous sentiments of the Parisians,
should be perpetuated by reproducing in bronze the
statue of the Place de la Concorde. This decree
remained, however, as it was no doubt intended it
should do—a dead letter.

At daybreak on the same morning that the fall of Strasburg and Toul became known, General Burnside, of the United States army, who achieved a certain renown during the War of Secession, arrived in Paris, from Ferrières, together with a fellow countryman, a Mr. Paul Forbes. They had been escorted through the French lines by order of General Ducrot; and after interviews with M. Jules Favre and General Trochu, the pair left Paris, on the following day, for Versailles. Returning to the besieged capital a few days afterwards, they had fresh interviews with the French Minister for Foreign Affairs and the Governor of Paris, and again departed for Versailles. Vague speculations were rife as to the object of these mysterious visits, which had reference, it was originally thought, to the contemplated departure of the American colony from Paris; but it soon became rumoured— the wish, of course, being father to the thought—that the Prussians, already discouraged at the prospects before them, had commissioned General Burnside to bear an olive branch to the Government of National Defence. Eventually, however, it was officially explained that, although the American general, yielding to some generous impulse, had endeavoured, without any authority, to effect a conciliatory arrangement between the hostile parties, yet his real mission was merely to bring a letter from Count von Bismarck to M. Jules Favre concerning the request made by the members of the Diplomatic Body, residing in Paris, to be allowed to communicate with their respective governments once a week.

Shut up within the ramparts of Paris, it should be remembered, were a score or so of highly important official personages, who would on no account entrust their mysterious correspondence, intricately tied up

though it might be with red tape, and sealed with
huge red seals, to the treacherous winds. These were
the Diplomatic Body—or, rather, its head and limbs
—the trunk having withdrawn before the investment of the city was accomplished. Through the
Papal Nuncio, their *doyen*, the remaining members
had requested the French Minister for Foreign Affairs
to ask Count Bismarck if notice would be given
them enabling them to leave before the bombardment
commenced, and also for permission for them to send
out a weekly courier until the German artillery was
prepared to open fire against the city. The German
Chancellor replied in a sarcastic strain, stating that he
regretted that military considerations forbad his
making any communication respecting the time and
manner of the bombardment, and also negativing the
application for a weekly diplomatic courier.

This mission of General Burnside's was of less
immediate interest to the Parisians than the store
of news from outside of which he was the bearer.
From some English papers brought in by him, the
Parisians first learnt that "Fritz's" army invested the
city from Versailles to Vincennes, and that the Germans had captured no fewer than 2500 prisoners and
seven cannons at the affair of Chatillon. A con-
solatory item of news was a reported Prussian defeat
near Monthéry. But little concern was manifested
in the now announced capture of Rome by the Italian
army; indeed, the fate of the Pope troubled the
Parisians far less than that of Garibaldi, who, it was
reported, was being forcibly detained at Caprera to
prevent his seconding the efforts of the French Republic. These scraps of more or less authentic
information were followed by items of utterly false
intelligence, mostly of a disheartening character, and

against which the Government thought fit to warn the citizens, publishing a hopeful but vaguely worded despatch from Tours, anent the expected armies of succour and the position of Marshal Bazaine. A copy of the *Journal de Rouen* managed, however, to find its way mysteriously into the city soon afterwards, and most of the hopes awakened by the Government announcement were shattered on learning that Orleans was lost to the French. They partially revived when it was also learnt that the delegation of Tours had decreed the oft-demanded *levée en masse*, summoning all unmarried Frenchmen, and widowers without children, between the ages of 21 and 40, under arms.

Fresh news from outside reached the beleaguered city when, on October 12, Paris was surprised by the arrival of a new visitor, Colonel Loyd Lindsay, who was permitted to pass both German and French lines, to place a sum of 20,000*l.*, raised in England, at the disposal of the authorities charged with ministering to the sick and wounded in the French capital. After two days' sojourn in Paris he returned to Versailles, being accompanied part of the way by Count de Flavigny, who had obtained an authorization from Count von Bismarck to proceed to Strasburg with 4000*l.*, subscribed in Paris, for the relief of the sufferers by the late bombardment of the Alsatian capital. M. de Flavigny was, however, turned back at Sèvres, his permit having been revoked.

After Colonel Lindsay's visit, rumours of ill-omen again crept into circulation, and one of the ephemeral journals of the hour—the *Vérité*—startled the Parisians one morning by categorically asking the Government if it did not possess a copy of the *Standard* for Oct. 5, in which it was stated that Lyons had revolted ; that Admiral Fourichon—one of the Tours trio—had resigned; that General Burnside had been planning an armistice; and that the enemy had driven back a southern army of succour. In addition, the *Vérité* inquired whether there had not been a very stormy discussion on the preceding day, concerning military matters, between the members of the Government. The authorities replied to these too pertinent inquiries by arresting the editor of the peccant journal, and arbitrarily consigning him for several days to the Conciergerie. Meanwhile, rumours flew about of the Orleans princes having joined an army of succour in Brittany; of Garibaldi having arrived at Tours; of Bazaine having made a new ineffectual sortie from Metz; of General Bourbaki having left that stronghold, either surreptitiously or with the enemy's connivance, and of having interviewed the ex-Empress Eugénie, in London. The Government maintained an obstinate silence concerning these reports; but soon afterwards it published a despatch from M. Gambetta, announcing M. Thiers's return from his mission to the European Courts, and General Bourbaki's arrival from Metz, with news that Bazaine's 90,000 men were keeping the enemy incessantly occupied. Lyons was stated to be quiet; and General Cambriels, commanding the southern army of succour, maintained, we were told, his positions from Belfort to Besançon. As usual, M. Gambetta spoke very hopefully, particularly alluding to a prospect of foreign mediation, and to the fact that the Germans were becoming worn out by the prolongation of the struggle.

**END OF VOL. I.**

For EU product safety concerns, contact us at Calle de José Abascal, 56–1°, 28003 Madrid, Spain or eugpsr@cambridge.org.